ELBERT HUBBARD'S
SELECTED WRITINGS

(V.5)

THE ELECT

Fra Elbert Hubbard

ISBN 0-7661-0387-0

ELBERT HUBBARD—*The Farmer*

THE ELECT

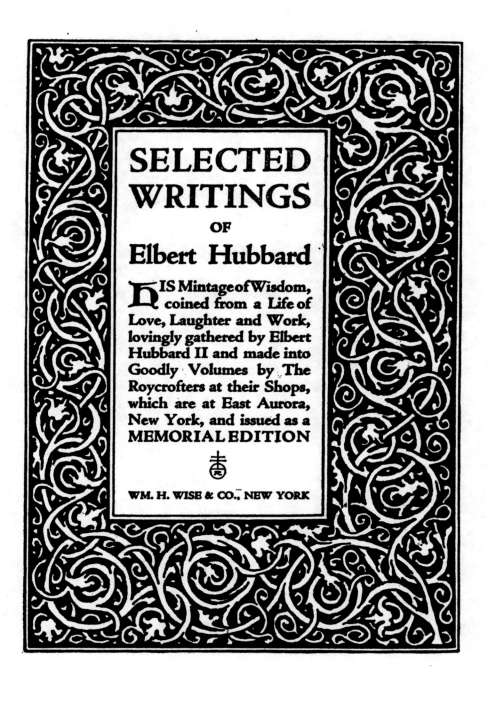

SELECTED WRITINGS

OF

Elbert Hubbard

HIS Mintage of Wisdom, coined from a Life of Love, Laughter and Work, lovingly gathered by Elbert Hubbard II and made into Goodly Volumes by The Roycrofters at their Shops, which are at East Aurora, New York, and issued as a MEMORIAL EDITION

WM. H. WISE & CO., NEW YORK

CONTENTS

Joaquin Miller 13

John Burroughs 35

Nancy Hanks 46

Tolstoy and Potter's Field 62

Carl Stoeckel 72

David Swing 78

Andrew Lang 90

Plutarch 94

John Alexander Dowie 101

Admiral Togo 112

Madame Montessori 115

Walt Mason 119

Golden Rule Jones 124

Ibsen 134

Stevie Crane 140

Thoreau 144

Jean Jacques Rousseau 151

Edgar Allen Poe 156

Emerson 160

Francisco Ferrer 167

Fra Junipero Serra 177

Talmage 181

Wu Ting Fang 189

Amiel 195

Sir Joshua Reynolds 199

Victor Hugo 202
Mutsuhito 210
Marilla Ricker 216
Marshall P. Wilder 235
Mangasarian 240
Socrates 255
Jean Paul 258
Robert Louis Stevenson 260
Horace Mann 266
Alfred Nobel 278
Ambassador Bryce 297
Max Stirner 300
Charles W. Eliot 308
Clara Barton 325
Diaz 373
Ben Greet 379
Brann 383
Wilbur Wright 386
White Hyacinths 391

JOAQUIN MILLER

Joaquin Miller

E wrote the greatest poem ever written by an American. He lives at Oakland, " on the Hights," and his name is Joaquin Miller.

We took the street car to the end of the line, and the conductor pointed to the road that led up to the hill. " Take that road and sail on," he said, and smiled in a way that indicated he had sprung the allusion before and was pleased with it.

We followed the road up the hillside. The day was one of God's own, done by hand, just to show what He could do. The sun was warm and bright; a gentle breeze, cool and refreshing, blew in with messages from the sea.

The road wound around the hill, and led upward by a gentle rise— back and forth, around and back, and soon we saw the roadway over which we had passed, a hundred feet below, with gardens between. Gardens everywhere! Gardens lined off with boxwood and fenced by nodding roses. Just above were orange and acacia trees, white with blossoms that showered their petals upon the passer-by ❧ ❧

And still we climbed. Up and up by that gentle ascent, up and up and up we went. The air was full of perfume and drowsy with the hum of bees. Birds twittered in the thick foliage, and at a bend in the winding road we saw a flock of quail running ahead of us and suddenly disappear among the masses of green.

Sandy was interested in finding out where the quail had gone; Ben mopped his forehead, and with coat on arm, talked of the Higher Criticism, the wonders of the universe, and how beauty was free for all—his preacher-habit still upon him.

Brudder and I turned and looked down upon the panorama spread out at our feet. Here was color—gorgeous, superb—the lilac of the wistaria winding in and out among the roses, while pale pink azaleas, delicate, esthetic and spiritual, trusted to our power of discernment to single them out from the more obtrusive masses of magnolia that everywhere sprang warm and voluptuous, heavy with perfume.

A little farther away the color was lost in masses of green that pushed off into a dark purple. Spires and steeples, and giant palms lifting their fronded forms in air told us the city was down there five miles away. And then there came a line of dark blue that wound in and out, and marked the bay, where little play ships stood in the offing—their prows all pointing one way. Submerged in the blue ether across the bay lay the city of San Francisco— her plots and her schemes, her ambitions and her hot desires, her tears of disappointment and her groans of griefs, all veiled and lost beneath the translucent purple blue coverlet of this lazy summer day.

Over to the left, clinging to the hillside, was Sausalito, replica in little of the villages that line the bay at Naples. There at Sausalito lives Bill Faville, Prince of Architects, making much monies, they say, over in the city, but hiding away here on the hillside in a cottage of three rooms, where Mrs. Bill escapes the servant-girl question and the jealousies of the smart set by living the life that is genuine. I will not say, " God bless Mr. and Mrs. Bill," because He has and will.

Just beyond Richardson's Bay, where phantom ships toss on the tide and wait for cargoes that never come, is San Raphael, and Dick Hotaling's ranch—fairest of playthings—three thousand acres—belonging to Dick and his friends, where plates are always placed for me and the Cublet, and chants from the GOOD STUFF are done in minor key as the sun goes down through the Golden Gate, with Dick's permission.

Beyond is Mt. Tamalpias, and still beyond this is Mt. Diablo where preacher Ben says I should go on pious errand bent.

Ben is a joker.

We trudge on up the hill, carrying coats and hats in hand. The air grows warmer, the flowers are even more plentiful.

We have been walking nearly two hours, and must have come five miles. The road skirts through a dense mass of dwarfed oak that covers the driveway as the elms arch Chapel Street in New Haven only more so.

" It is like this," said preacher Ben; and then he began to explain to me the Law of Paradox.

" The collection will now be taken," came a deep bass voice from out of the greeny gloom of the close growing oaks.

We started, looked, and there on a seat not twenty feet away sat the Poet. You could never mistake him—he looks like no other man on earth; personality surrounds him like an aura.

We stared.

" Come here and sit down, you rogues," called the voice.

The Poet did not rise—why should he? We had always known each other, though we had never met before. We shook hands and Ben and I took seats on the rustic bench beside him, Brudder lay on the grass at his feet, while Sandy renewed his interest in quail.

" Here I 've been waiting an hour," said the Poet, " I put on my Sunday clothes and came down to meet you, but I had about given you up. Ben said you were coming, but preachers are such damn liars—they promise Paradise and mansions in the skies and all kinds of things which they can never supply—I was afraid you were not coming! "

He arose. He is six feet high to an inch, and in spite of his sixty-two summers, straight as Sandy and just as strong.

He stood off and talked to us. He knew we were admiring him— how could he help it! His white beard fell to his waist, and his mustaches were curled up savagely after the manner of Emperor William, while his wide sombrero was cocked carelessly to the northwest. His long yellow hair fell to his shoulders. The suit he wore was of yellow corduroy that matched his hair, and his russet top boots, fringed at the side, matched the corduroys. The buttons on his coat were made of nuggets of Klondike gold; his belt was of buckskin with a big silver buckle between the bottom of his vest and the top of his trousers was a six inch interregnum of blue flannel shirt. A bright red necktie blew out from under the white beard; the trousers were caught over the ears of the dainty boots; one hand wore a gauntlet and its mate was carried in a small white hand, upon the middle finger of which was an immense diamond ring.

" You are looking at my ring—worth a thousand dollars or more, they say—given to me by a dear friend now in Purgatory, if Ben knows his business.

" I wear that ring in memory of a great friendship, and also because I love the diamond for its own sake—it symbols infinity, eternity. The diamond is pure carbon; at least, we can resolve it back into carbon, but this done we can not make it over into a diamond. It is like life, we can take it away, but we can not give it. The secret of the diamond is not ours—it took an eternity to produce it. I am as old as the diamond and I shall never die."

❡ We followed on up the hillside. The sun was sinking down into the Golden Gate in a burst of glory. " It 's all mine," said the Poet and waved his hand toward the western landscape.

We came to a queer old stile and followed along a grass-grown pathway. Soon a whole little village smiled upon us from a terraced outlook, that seemed surrounded and shut in by tall pines. The houses were about as large as dry goods cases—say eight by twelve. There were a dozen of them, owned by the Poet, and of all sorts of colors and shapes; all not worth so much as that diamond ring. Over every little house ran a regular riot of roses, red and white, in a mad race for supremacy. In one of the tiny cottages lived the Poet. We entered—there was only one room, a rag carpet rug in the center, a plain pine table, a bed in the corner. All around the room hung the Poet's clothes.

" I am an esthetic in everything but duds," explained the Poet, as he saw Brudder vulcanizing. " You see folks are always giving me things—there is an Esquimau suit of sealskin, then comes that leather hunting shirt and buckskin breeches. The next is my second best suit of corduroy, the next is a velvet coat given to me by the Woman's Club of Denver when I lectured for them. As you see, I have ten pairs of boots and six pairs of moccasins. That ministerial black suit I wear when I speak in Ben's pulpit." There was a Mexican saddle and bridle in the corner and bits of horse jewelry hung around on hooks.

" And your books? " I ventured.

" Books? " said the Poet, "Books? to hell with books! Books are for people who can not think."

It will be observed that the Poet's language is as picturesque as his raiment. His words fitted him like the feathers on a duck. Ben tried a swear word, but it was strangely out of place, and as for myself, I only cuss in print.

Joaquin Miller is the most charming poseur on this terrestrial ball, but he has posed so long and so well that his poses have now become natural, so he is no longer a poseur.

Up on the topmost crest of the hill he has built a monument, square, stern, rude, crude, and immensely strong, with frowning battlements and menacing turrets. The weather-worn rocks used in its construction give the building a Druidic look. It took three years to build this monument, the work being done mostly by the Poet's own hands. It is twelve feet square at the base, and about twenty-five feet high. What it was all for has been a question much discussed in the neighborhood.

The Poet is very proud of this monument—it really is a superb bit of handicraft for an amateur. I saw the craftsman's pride beaming out of the blue eyes, and so I worked the conversation around and lighted the fuse. And here is the story:

" I started to build that monument to the memory of Adam. I

thought that this spot must have been the Garden of Eden—and anyway, the Garden of Eden was no finer than this. And then I had caught glimpses of God walking around here in the cool of the day, and so my Chinese helpers and I began the monument. Then one day Preacher Ben came up here and told me what a bad man Adam was, and how Adam and his wife had made all the trouble that was in the world.

" Then I cast around to think who was the next best man. And I dropped on Moses.

" Moses was the greatest leader of men who ever lived. He led his people out of captivity—made them free, and there is nothing finer than to give freedom.

" So I said to my Chinese helpers, ' Here goes to Moses!'

" Moses was the son of Pharaoh's daughter, you know—a love-child—his father an Israelite. She hid him away in the bulrushes, and then went down and found him at the proper time, and flashed up one of the most touching little stories ever told—very beautiful and the most natural thing on earth. The child was brought up a prince, but his heart was with the Israelites, and you know how he finished up an Egyptian that he saw putting the thing on an Israelite. Oh, Moses had the quality—I expect to meet him in Elysium some day—he is our kind.

" How about the mistakes of Moses? Look you, my boy, Moses made no mistakes. Don't imagine that a man does not know just because he does not explain. Moses knew, but he gave out just what his people were ready for, and no more. He used to say, ' God told me this and God told me that,' which was all right. God tells me things every day—He whispers to me at night, and often I get up and go out under the stars and wait for His messages. All of the Mosaic Laws were for the good of the people, sanitary, sensible and right. Christianity is a graft on Judaism, and it all traces to Moses.

" Moses was what you might call an ornithological rara avis.

"When he died, God was the undertaker—no one knows where he was buried, but I am of the belief that he was buried right here —exactly under this monument, and so far my assumption has not been disproved.

"Now we will unlock the little iron door and take a look inside of the monument. You see these steel grate bars—looks like a furnace, does n't it? Well that is because it is—a crematory. My body is to be placed up on top, that steel cover is to be lifted so as to get a draft through, and twenty-five cords of good dry redwood will do the business. There is the wood corded right over there— we use a little now and then but we never let the pile get below twenty-five cords.

"I have invited all the preachers and priests, joss-house men and sky-pilots in Oakland, Alameda and San Francisco to attend my funeral. I have written the funeral address myself, and the preachers are to draw cuts to see who shall read it to the people

"Yes, the people are invited, too, and if the funeral takes place on a school day, I have arranged that the children shall all have a holiday. I love children and children love me—they come up here sometimes by the hundreds and I read to them. I never caused a child a tear. All the mean things I have been guilty of were directed towards grown-up men.

"No sir, no one shall wear mourning for me—death is only a change of condition. And Nature's changes are for the better. I want all denominations represented at my funeral, because I belong to every sect. I sympathize with all superstitions and creeds, because there is really but one religion—these seeming differences are only a matter of definitions evolved by certain temperaments. I worship Joss, Jehovah, Jove, Jesus, Mary the Blessed Mother, Ali Baba, and Mary Baker Eddy. All of the gods were once men, and these names all stand for certain things to certain people—each means all to you that you can put into it. A name is a sound, a puff of air, but behind the epiglottis, the eustachian tube, the palate, the tongue and the roof of the mouth, is a thought—I sympathize with that thought, even with error, because error is the pathway to truth, and so error is a phase of truth. I am Francis of Assisi, Novalis, Plato, Swedenborg, Porphyry and Buffalo Bill. I fill myself with aceticism, get drunk on abnegation, recite my own poems, and dance a two-step inspired by self-sacrifice. I am touched with madness, but sane enough to know it. I have a good time on nothing, and although I live 'way up here alone, yet I am in the company of good people—are n't you here? I am the Universal Man, and so are you, and everybody is, only they don't know it. What 's that Chinaman yelling about? Oh, he says breakfast is ready—I forgot."

When you visit Joaquin Miller, you are not shown to your room —you are given a house. The Poet puts his head out of the door and gives an "Allehoiah-ala-hoohoo-oo!" and out hops an Oriental, all dressed in white, and takes you to your cottage. You perform your ablutions (I trust I use the right word) at the spring, or the horse trough, and when you get back that heathen Chinee has opened your suit case, brushed your clothes, hung out your nightshirt, placed half a bushel of cut roses on the table and disappeared ৯ ৯

In ten minutes he comes back to tell you in pigeon English that supper is ready.

The dining room is in one of the cottages, set apart for a kitchen. The Chinee is a superb cook. Our table is set out under an arbor of roses, and we have vegetables to spare, and fruits galore, and nuts to crack, and a tin bucket of milk cooled in the running water of the spring, and loaves of brown bread which we break up in chunks; but there is no meat.

The Poet leaves us—he has work to do—but scarcely do we get back to the cottage, which we already call Home, before the Poet's bearded face looks in at the open window, and he asks, " Did you see that inscription on the Carnegie Library down at Oakland? Over the doorway are carved three words,

POETRY, LITERATURE, PROSE

" That is a personal biff—I told 'em so. I said, ' You fellows should have put it this way: Poetry, Prose, Rot, Tommyrot; and inside you should have carved these words: Oratory, Gab, Talk, Buzz, Harangue, Palaver, with the name of some good man who has a talent for each.' "

The nearest cottage to the one occupied by the Poet belongs to his mother, a Quaker-like old dame ninety years young, who fully realizes that she is part of the Exhibit.

There was a widespread conference between Mother and Son, and then the old lady asked, " Which one is it, did you say, that writes the LITTLE JOURNEYS? "

I saw I was being pointed out, and so I modestly scrutinized the landscape, while the old lady scrutinized me, walking around me twice. Then she sighed and remarked, " He does n't look so very smart to me," and went on solemnly with her knitting. Later, we became good friends—the old lady and I—although I was conscious that I was being compared furtively with the son of his mother—much to my disadvantage.

" He is greater than Shakespeare," said the old lady to me once confidentially—" only, do you know, he is such a fool that he tears up the best things he writes, and says he is going to write them over, but he never does."

And then she explained how this son went off to the Klondike two years ago, and was now planning to go again. " But I 've set down my foot! I found out about it and just put a stop to the whole business—the idea!" And the good mother sighed in a way that showed that she had troubles of her own.

We stood by the stile saying the final good-bye. The old lady had come down, too. " He tears up the best things he writes," said the old lady to me—" now tell him he has no sense!"

" And if you should," said the son, " she would be the first one to dispute it."

" Thank heaven, I have n't another son like you!" was the answer, and the boy of three-score dodged the old lady's cane, and answered, " Don't worry, sweetheart—you never will!"

We crossed the stile, and followed on down the winding pathway that ran through the grove of citron and orange trees. Looking up after five minutes' walk, we saw the Poet standing on a slightly jutting cliff just above, his arm around his mother. The old lady leaned over and called aloud to me in a voice touched with falsetto, " Don't go to Klondike—it is a fool idea!"

———

Joaquin Miller is dead. His body was burned on the funeral-pyre that he had made ready, and his ashes were scattered to the four winds. But the good in him abides. For him I had a great affection. For twenty-five years I wrote him every little while, anything that happened to be in my mind—foolish little nothings, stories about children, dogs, bears, cats—things I imagined, things that might have been so; and he in turn responded in kind.

Some of his letters I was able to read.

He sent me presents of books; bits for bridles; spurs; and if anybody gave him anything he did not want or had not the time to care for, he sent it to me by express collect. I joyed in the society of the man, perhaps for the reason that he was not on my hands, and that I did not have to endure his society for long.

When he came to East Aurora, everybody took a holiday, and we laughed and played and picnicked the livelong day.

Then we built a bonfire and told ghost-stories until midnight.

❡ Whenever I was in San Francisco, which has been about once a year for the last two decades, I made a pious pilgrimage to " The Hights." ❧ ❧

And usually I waited to see the sun go down and sink a golden
ball through the Golden Gate—with the permission of Joaquin.
His estate of several hundred acres at the top of the mountain was
purchased, about thirty years ago, out of the royalty received
on *The Danites*. The site overlooked the city of Oakland, San
Francisco, the Bay, and gave a panoramic view of the Golden
Gate and the blue Pacific beyond. He spelled it " Hights "
because a visitor once called it " The He-ights," and anyway
Joaquin did n't do anything as others did.

It was a tumbled mass of rocks, trees, vines, wild flowers, with
here and there a great giant redwood.

For agricultural purposes it would have bankrupted anybody
who owned it. Joaquin Miller bought the land for purposes
picturesque and poetic. No one else wanted it. To reach it you
had to climb up a winding road, a distance of about four miles
from the turnpike below, where eventually the street-car came
and stopped. Civilization has gradually moved that way, until
now the land has a tangible value, and if sold, it will certainly
clear off the debts of the dead poet and leave a snug little sum
for his heirs.

Miller got tired of the world at fifty. Perhaps the world was a
little tired of him. And here he fled for sanctuary. He had a little
money, a few hundred dollars; but he made raids down into the
lowlands, and gave lectures and readings for which he received
from fifty to a hundred dollars per evening.

Like Thoreau, he loved solitude—when he was able to escape it,
any time.

He occasionally got twenty-five dollars for a poem. And all the
money he made he invested in lumber, which was hauled up the
hill by a weary route. He constructed a dozen little houses about
as big as drygoods-boxes some with cupolas, curious little
verandahs, strange observatories.

Any visitor who came this way was given a house to live in, and told to remain as long as he wished and go away when he wanted to. There was one house used for a dining-room, and a Chinaman with a literary bias, clothed in spotless white, cooked for everybody present. The meals were set on a long table out of doors, if the weather was pleasant. Otherwise, you were crowded into the dining-room, and everybody helped himself; and after the meal you assisted John in doing the dishes.

Joaquin Miller was a friend of the Chinese. He worshiped Joss. He believed in all religions, but had absolute faith in none. Joss, Jesus, Jehovah, Confucius, Moses—these were his deities. All the gods of mythology were once men, and Joaquin had a great and profound regard for humanity. Humanity to him was essentially divine. He quarreled with no man's religion, always maintaining that religion was simply a point of view.

His conversation was entertaining, illuminating, surprising, witty, profound, contradictory. He had a way of abusing his friends when they called. Before you could formulate a word of greeting, he unlimbered his vocabulary. He told of your sins, your crimes, your misdemeanors, your faults, your foibles, your limitations. He knew where you had been, what you had done, and his frankness might have been positively shocking were it not for the fact that he carried it over the ridge until you laughed and everybody screamed for joy. I once went up " The Hights " with Clarence Darrow. Clarence Darrow was fresh from Boise City, where he had defended an alleged murderer and got him free.

Joaquin Miller called everybody by his first name. If he did n't know his name, he supplied one.

" Clarisso Darroisso," he said, " you are a murderer with false whiskers. You defended a murderer. You got him free. You took a part of the swag. You are partner with him. Neither you nor your client will be accepted by the devil in hell, and certainly God Almighty will not have you. What finally will become of you, I can not imagine !"

And so he continued to talk for about fifteen minutes, expressing his opinion of lawyers, as we sat down on the bench and laughed, until the eruption had spent itself.

On the gateway where you entered "The Hights" there was a sign: "No admittance; keep agoing. Better view higher up." This did not mean, however, that you were not welcome. Miller expressed things by contraries. His heart was friendly, tender, sympathetic. He was a poseur, but he posed so long that the pose was natural.

He wore long hair that fell to his shoulders. His beard came to his waist. His dress-trousers were buckskin, and he wore high-top boots with flapping ears. When he went down town he often wore jangling spurs. He wore a leather vest, with solid-gold nuggets for buttons, brought from the Klondike. His necktie was just plain red, the symbol of anarchy, and in it nestled a thousand-dollar diamond-pin ⚬ ⚬

Joaquin had no respect for law or for society—that is, if you believed his conversation. But the fact is that he was not a criminal in any sense. He only played in his mind at being a lawbreaker ⚬ ⚬

He got his name through his defense of an outlaw by the name of Joaquin. In merry jest his mining companions gave him the name of the man that he had so vigorously defended and whom they had helped to hang. And finally the name stuck. He accepted it as his own; and instead of Cincinnatus Heine Miller, he chose to be called plain Joaquin Miller. He was born in a moving-wagon, somewhere between Indiana and Oregon, in the year Eighteen Hundred Forty-one. He claimed Indiana as his birthplace, however, because that is where his parents started from.

He was the first, save the Hoosier Schoolmaster, to locate the Indiana "literary zone."

His name, Cincinnatus Heine, reveals the literary bias of his parents. Any one who loves Heinrich Heine and enjoys the wonderful lilt and lure of the Heine lines, and who knows the one fact about Cincinnatus, that he left his plow in the field and went to fight his own country's battles, is an educated person. Joaquin Miller would leave a plow in the field, any time, and he always maintained that Cincinnatus was only looking for an excuse to forsake the stump-lot.

Joaquin Miller was a poet by prenatal tendency. He was brought up among the Indians, and a deal of their poetic splendor and love of color splashed his soul. At times he was just as dignified, just as impassive, as any Sioux Chief.

When I met him in Washington, he wore his Indian leggings, deerskin coat, high-top yellow boots; and hatless, paraded Pennsylvania Avenue, followed by admiring and wondering crowds, and he beautifully oblivious to them.

Shortly after this he made a trip to England, and was received by Royalty as a specimen of the Sure Thing. And he was true to his togs, even when he visited the Queen, by her personal request, at Windsor Castle. He read his own poems to select throngs, and was paid the attention that nobility expects and demands. He was noble by Divine Right, and they by edict—at least this was his mental attitude. I think a little of this superfluous attention turned his head; and he came back home, expecting to walk through life and receive a similar adulation everywhere that England had bestowed upon him.

Alas and alack! Here in America there were many to say that he was an Egotist, a Poseur Plus; and, of course, he was. But his pose was as natural as the pose of a peacock, and his song much sweeter. He was at home everywhere and anywhere. Children loved him. Boys worshiped him. Women said, " Ah!" and " Oh!" when he entered the room. If a man thought he was sure-enough-easy, Joaquin could call him, just as Jack Crawford used to land on the beak of the party who got fresh on the subject of hair. Joaquin Miller loved his friends and hated his enemies. He had positive ideas, as long as he held them; and he could change them with lightning-like rapidity. He was writer, actor, speaker, editor, poet, gentleman. In him there was something specially childlike and innocent. Anything he had, he was willing to divide with any one who wanted it.

During the Nineties he had so many visitors, hoboes, tramps, criminals, poets, preachers, reformers, who called on him, that they nearly ate up his substance. But as long as he could get food for them, they were welcome. And he himself, at times, wrapped himself in a blanket and slept out of doors, in order that visitors might have his cottage.

He was Utopian, and was always picturing a society where friendship would be supreme, and where everything would belong to anybody who wanted it; where none would have too much, but everybody would have enough.

When we try to catalogue Joaquin Miller, we put him in with Buffalo Bill, Pawnee Bill, Buffalo Jones and Jack Crawford. But each of these individuals was different from the others. None had the wit, the scintillating brain, the eager imagination that Joaquin Miller possessed. The nearest approach to him would be Captain Jack, who has written some mighty good things and who can read them better.

Joaquin wrote several successful plays, notably, *The Danites,* in which McKee Rankin scored a big success.

His poem entitled *Columbus,* I have said is the best poem ever written by an American, and I am inclined to stick to the opinion, although I realize that poetry is largely a matter of time, tempo and temperament. Joaquin Miller began his literary career when twenty, by starting a newspaper in the placer-mining camp of Eugene City, Colorado. The editorials, however, were so personal the town held a mass-meeting and decided they would get along without a newspaper. And so they called on Joaquin en masse. They took all his type and dumped it into the creek, broke up his presses, and warned him that if he wrote or printed anything more, one of the redwoods would bear fruit.

One might have supposed that Joaquin would have felt slightly peeved over this lack of appreciation. Instead, however, he took it all as a good joke, remained right in town, and went to work as a placer-miner. He wore a red shirt, high-top boots, a wide hat. ❡ He let his whiskers and his hair grow, and when he had secured enough gold to make solid-gold buttons for his mountain-lion coat, he went down to San Francisco, and again took up literature. This time he was on the *Overland Monthly* and was a valuable find ﹏ ﹏

He proved himself pay-gravel: first as an advertising manager, next as a poet.

He had a way of carrying a pick on his shoulder as a badge of his occupation. Once he was standing in front of the famous Snake Drugstore, in San Francisco. Always around this window was a group gazing at the coiled snakes that slept in the sun. There they were, dozens of them, rattlers, blacksnakes, moccasins, water-snakes, stretching their sinuous lengths, moving anon uneasily in their sleep.

As Joaquin stood there, with pick over his shoulder, his companion said to him, " Bet you an ounce of gold dust you dassent smash your pick through the window and yank a few of the snakes out into the trail!"

" I take that bet!" said Joaquin; and crash went the pick through the glass into the coiling snakes, and out into the street the Poet of the Sierras yanked a full dozen rattlers. Then he started in to kill the snakes. The druggist ran out and called, " Hey, let them snakes be—they are mine!" " They were yours once, you mean," said Joaquin, and kept right on with the killing.

The fun cost Miller two hundred dollars, but was worth the money, to say nothing of the value of the advertisement for the *Overland*. ❡ Poetlike, Joaquin spent most of the money he made. It would have made no difference how much he made; he would have given it away. Yet he was never in want. There were always a few friends to whom he turned by divine right, and asked for his own; and he never asked for anything he did not need; and when he could, he paid it back. He was honest, sincere, affectionate, talented. Needless to say, he lacked synthesis. He added to the world's stock of harmless pleasure. He made smiles to grow where there was none before.

One man of this kind was enough. He died uncomplaining, and made every preparation, to the last detail, for his funeral.

For the past twenty years there was in readiness the big pile of well-seasoned redwood. The funeral-pyre was built by his own hands, with the assistance of his friends, the hoboes, the Chinese —and myself.

It was a work of love and joy.

Also, I assisted in building his famous monument to Moses that stood only a short distance away—a solid square mass of rocks. Moses was the great patron saint of Joaquin Miller. He was always quoting Moses, and telling of what Moses did. Some of the things that Moses forgot to say, Miller wrote out. I am not at all sure that Moses performed all of the wonderful feats that were attributed to him by Joaquin Miller. Joaquin said Moses was a great commonsense man. He always argued that all of the Mosaic laws were sanitary laws, provided for the well-being of people now and here. That the Mosaic laws should have been crystallized into a religious organization, to him was a great mistake, an unkind accident.

" The Lord spake unto Moses, saying." Over and over I heard Joaquin roll out the words, " The Lord spoke to Moses, and the Lord speaks to every man who thinks." This was his argument. I tried to show him once that his love for Moses was simply on account of the length of the Mosaic whiskers; and he said there was a good deal in this.

He had numerous pictures of Michelangelo's Moses that he would dig out of the artistic rubbish, heaped in his different cottages, from time to time.

One reason he liked Moses, he said, was because Moses had killed a man; and he believed there should be an open season for a certain type of individual.

Moses was the great liberator. He ran away from his own people when he was forty years of age. He lived in the desert for forty years; came back when he was eighty, and led the Children of Israel out of captivity. Moses was a hundred and twenty years old when he died; and went up on the mountainside and died alone with God.

This, to Joaquin Miller, was a beautiful passing, and he delighted in expatiating on it.

We do not mourn the passing of such a man. He did not fear death. Most certainly, he did not want any one to shed any tears for him. His faith in what he called " The Divine Economy " was supreme. He considered himself essentially divine, inasmuch as he was a part of the whole.

He was a beautiful Pantheist, a wit, a dreamer, an idealist, who had tasted life and found it good. He was as frank as Omar Khayyam, and as intellectually intrepid.

Following are a few selections from Joaquin Miller's writings, just to show the quality of his work.

COLUMBUS

Behind him lay the gray Azores,
Behind the Gates of Hercules;
Before him not the ghost of shores;
Before him only shoreless seas.
The good mate said: " Now must we pray,
For lo! the very stars are gone.
Brave Adm'r'l, speak; what shall I say?"
" Why, say: ' Sail on! and on!' "

" My men grow mutinous day by day;
My men grow ghastly wan and weak."
The stout mate thought of home; a spray
Of salt wave washed his swarthy cheek.
" What shall I say, brave Adm'r'l, say,
If we sight naught but seas at dawn?"
" Why, you shall say at break of day:
' Sail on! sail on! sail on! and on!' "

They sailed and sailed as winds might blow,
Until at last the blanched mate said:
" Why, now not even God would know
Should I and all my men fall dead.
These very winds forget their way,
For God from these dread seas is gone.
Now speak, brave Adm'r'l; speak and say—"
He said: " Sail on! sail on! and on!"

They sailed. They sailed. Then spake the mate:
" This mad sea shows his teeth tonight.
He curls his lip, he lies in wait,
With lifted teeth, as if to bite!

Brave Adm'r'l, say but one good word:
What shall we do when hope is gone?"
The words leapt like a leaping sword:
"Sail on! sail on! sail on! and on!"

Then, pale and worn, he kept his deck,
And peered through darkness. Ah, that night
Of all dark nights! And then a speck—
A light! A light! A light! A light!
It grew, a starlit flag unfurled!
It grew to be Time's burst of dawn.
He gained a world; he gave that world
Its grandest lesson: "On! sail on!"

ROOM TO TURN IN

Room! room to turn around in, to breathe and be free,
To grow to be giant, to sail as at sea
With the speed of the wind on a steed with his mane
To the wind, without pathway or route or a rein.
Room! room to be free where the white border'd sea
Blows a kiss to a brother as boundless as he;
Where the buffalo come like a cloud on the plain,
Pouring on like the tide of a storm-driven main,
And the lodge of the hunter to friend or to foe
Offers rest; and unquestion'd you come or you go.
My plains of America! Seas of wild lands!
From a land in the seas in a raiment of foam,
That has reached to a stranger the welcome of home,
I turn to you, lean to you, lift you my hands.

THE TALL ALCALDE

Shadows that shroud the tomorrow,
Glists from the life that 's within,
Traces of pain and of sorrow,
And maybe a trace of sin,
Reachings for God in the darkness,
And for—what should have been.

Stains from the gall and the wormwood,
Memories bitter like myrrh,
A sad brown face in a fir wood,
Blotches of heart's blood here,
But never the sound of a wailing,
Never the sign of a tear.

MY BRAVE WORLD-BUILDERS

My brave world-builders of the West,
Why, who doth know ye? Who shall know
But I, that on thy peaks of snow
Brake bread the first ? Who loves ye best ?
Who holds ye still, of more stern worth
Than all proud peoples of the earth ?

Yea, I, the rhymer of wild rhymes,
Indifferent of blame or praise,
Still sing of ye, as one who plays
The same sweet air in all strange climes—
The same wild, piercing highland air,
Because—because, his heart is there.

THE CALIFORNIA POPPY

The golden poppy is God's gold,
The gold that lifts, nor weighs us down,
The gold that knows no miser's hold,
The gold that banks not in the town,
But singing, laughing, freely spills
Its hoard far up the happy hills;
Far up, far down, at every turn—
What beggar has not gold to burn!

ADIOS

And here, sweet friend, I go my way
Alone, as I have lived, alone
A little way, a brief half-day,
And then, the restful, white milestone.
I know not surely where or when,
But surely know we meet again,
As surely know we love anew
In grander life the good and true;
Shall breathe together there as here
Some clearer, sweeter atmosphere,
Shall walk high, wider ways above.

Our petty selves, shall lean to lead
Man up and up in thought and deed . . . .
Dear soul, sweet friend, I love you, love
The love that led you patient through
This wilderness of words in quest
Of strange wild flowers from my West;
But here, dear heart, Adieu.

John Burroughs

IT is seven o'clock in the morning, I am writing this at Slab-Sides, and out through the climbing Morning Glories, upon which the dew yet sparkles, I see Old John Burroughs working intently in the garden. He is hatless and coatless, and his tumbled snow-white hair and beard, from this distance, seem like an aureole as he leans over at his work. The sun, peeping over the mountain top, seems to caress him. Its rays fall upon him like a benediction. He is the center of the picture; all around him is the green growing celery, and outside of this little valley, fenced in by nature's forest, rise the hills, emerald at the base, growing purple at the top—crowned by white mist—with here and there fierce jutting gray crags, as though to show by antithesis that this scene of sweet peace has not always been ✒ ✒

Old John Burroughs! Why do we call you "Old?" Not because you are sixty-six, come Michaelmas—bless me! no. Yours is the heart of youth. You never were so in love with life. Your ruddy face is bronzed by the kiss of the breeze; your eyes twinkle with merriment or fill with tender sympathy; you have the "flat back" that George Eliot tells about, in *Adam Bede* and your every attribute and gesture speak of expectant youth and God's great generous, free Out-of-Doors. The only sign of age I see upon you is your whitened hair. We call you " Old " as a mark of endearment —it is the tender diminutive. We remember Browning's lines:

> Grow old along with me,
> The best is yet to be,
> The last of life,
> For which the first was made.

And we are mindful, too, that the passing years have brought

you rich gifts—" Being old, I shall know!" And so when we speak
of you as "Old John," we do it with lowered voice, full of reverence,
mellow with love, and ripe with respect for a life well lived.

Old John has left me here to do the dishes and tidy up the cabin.
I saw he wanted to go to work in the garden, so I suggested a
division of labor. He protested a little—he always wants to do all
the unpleasant tasks himself—but finally consented, and went
away with a smile which said, "Go ahead, now we 'll see what kind
of a housekeeper you are!" And he will see. I am writing at his
table, with a pen made from an eagle's feather which we found
up on the mountain-side yesterday. This pad is his, too—and
mine, for he said everything here is mine; and it was no oriental-
ism, either.

What will he say when he comes in and finds the work not done?—
I promised to join him at the celery in an hour. I think I'll just
carry the dishes out and place them on the rocks in the little
stream; dish-washing is a waste of time. And as for disorder, what
could be worse than this table? But then Starr King had a great
lecture on the " Laws of Disorder." I really wonder if there can
be a law that regulates confusion! Montaigne said, " Nature is a
sloven:" still she seems to arrive. Perhaps what we call disorder
is really system, at the last. I have no doubt but Old John knows
every blessed thing on the table and where to put his hand on
everything in the cabin, even in the dark. Some girls came over
here from Vassar, once, Old John told me, and undertook the task
of cleaning up the place in the owner's absence. They put things
away so effectively that it was a month before he really began
to feel at home. I think I will just place the dishes in the stream,
and respect the Laws of Disorder—it would be a shame to make
a dear old man feel strange in his own house!

It is amazing what a lot of things are in this cabin—birds' nests,
birds' eggs, feathers, fungi, curious crooked sticks, and I believe
to goodness that all the books are meant for is to press flowers!

I wonder if Old John ever answers his correspondence! Here is a pile of letters unopened—surely they have been here a month or more. From these different pads of paper, partially filled it is evident that he has half a dozen subjects in hand currently; and when he writes he takes up the topic his mood prompts. This pile of notes under the flat stone must have been accumulating a long while—he is always making notes. The eagle's feather we found yesterday suggested a thought, and he said to me, " That eagle moulted the feather because he is growing a better one." He might have gone on and explained that life consists in moulting one's illusions; and that we form creeds only to throw them away tomorrow; and that the wise man is ready to relinquish everything and anything, confident that something better is in store—but he did n't explain or moralize. We walked four miles or more, " injun file," without a word. Then he turned to me and said, " I like you—we understand each other—we can be silent together."
❡ Clearly this habit of writing down his thoughts, as they come in the passing of the quiet hours, has long been a fixed one with John Burroughs. He makes memoranda on backs of envelopes, margins of newspapers, or on birch bark; and on the walls of Slab-Sides are various jottings in hieroglyph. Evidently it is all a good deal like the work of the magpie that hides things away and forgets where they are. But then John Burroughs doesn't care where they are, and I suppose the magpie does not either; only John has the thought hidden away in his brain-cells, and when the time is ripe it comes forth, just as a bee is born out of its sealed-up cell. I told John that old story about Emerson getting up in the night and groping for matches, knocking down the ˙family What-Not. "Are you ill, Waldo?" called his wife in piccolo accents. " No, my dear," answered the author of *Self Reliance*. " No, my dear, only an idea!" John laughed as if he had never eard the story before, and then explained in half apology that he himself makes notes of ideas only in the daytime—he values sleep (and What-

Nots) too much to think of writing at night. His face shows that—he sleeps like a boy, and eats like a hired man. His broad, brown hands are without a particle of tremor, and his strongly corded neck tells of manly abstinence and of passion that was never in the saddle.

Appetite has never got the better of this man, galloping him to the grave. He has not wooed the means of debility and disease, and put an enemy in his mouth to steal away his brains. For himself, John Burroughs has no use for tobacco or stimulants; and so you find him turning into the last lap of the three-score-and-ten with breath sweet as a baby's, muscles that do the bidding of his brain, and nerves that never go on a strike.

Yet he has been a man of strong passions and appetites. In stature he is rather small, but the way he carries the crown of his head and his chin, reveals the well-sexed man. He is a natural lover ✺ ✺

How do I know? Well, any man is a lover who writes well. Literature is a matter of passion. All Art is a secondary sexual manifestation, just as the song of the birds, their gay and gaudy plumage, the color and perfume of flowers. It is love writes all true poems, paints all pictures, sings all songs.

This man is a lover. Yet I know nothing of his private history, neither do I want to. He never told me " the sad story of his life"— only weaklings have the confessional habit—neither does he explain or apologize. His life is his own excuse for being. The man himself is explanation enough; every man is to a great degree the product of what has gone before—he is a sequence. More than that—man is a tablet upon which is written his every word, and thought, and deed. He is the Record of himself. The Record is the Man, and the Man is the Record. It will be easy to reckon accounts at the Last Great Day. The Judge will only have to unfold the heart and look—all is graven there—nothing was ever hidden nor can it be. God is not mocked.

This man will say to his maker, " See, thus was I—my claim is only this! " And the chief gem in his diadem shall be a great, sublime and all-enfolding love.

Why do I say this? I say it because the truth is this:—No man ever reached the spiritual heights that this man has attained save through the love of One. From this love of One, his love radiates to all—he becomes Universal.

Men who have not tasted the Divine Passion belong to a sect, a society, a city, a country. They work for their own little church, hurrah for their own society, canvass for their pee-wee party, fight for their own country. They can not love virtue without hating vice. If they regard America, they detest England. They are like Orange John of Harvard, whose loyalty to Cambridge found vent in the cry, " T' 'ell wi' Yale! "—a sentiment to which even yet most Harvard men inwardly respond.

John Burroughs is the most Universal man I can name at the present moment. He is a piece of Elemental Nature. He has no hate, no whim, no prejudice. He believes in the rich, the poor, the learned, the ignorant. He believes in the wrong-doer, the fallen, the sick, the weak and the defenceless. He loves children, animals, birds, insects, trees and flowers. He is one who is afraid of no man, and of whom no man is afraid. He puts you at your ease—you could not be abashed before him. In his presence there is no temptation to deceive, to overstate, to understate—to be anything different from what you are. You could confess to this man —reveal your soul and tell the worst; and his only answer would be " I know! I know! " and tears of sympathy and love would dim those heavenly blue eyes.

Yet when I alighted from a West Shore train, I got off alone, and he was the only man at the railroad station. No faces peered from the windows as he stood there leaning against the building; no one came out upon the platform to see him; the trainmen did not call out, " This is the home of John Burroughs! " Neither con-

ductor, brakeman, baggageman, nor mail agent glanced toward
the simple old farmer standing there, meditatively chewing a
straw. The fireman, however, knew him, for he dropped his
shovel and leaning out of the cab waved a salute which was
returned as comrade greets comrade.

John Burroughs was in no hurry to rush forward and greet me—
the only man that I ever knew who is never in a hurry about anything. He has all the time there is. We met as if we had parted
yesterday. I looked down along the long line of the train, and
hoped the fireman would swing off, too, and let the engineer take
his old train, alone, down the two streaks of rust to Weehawken;
but the fresh smoke was streaming forth from the stack, and I
knew the fireman was at his post. I was disappointed. He could
have washed his grimy face in the creek and we could have all had
dinner together — I quite liked the fellow! He might have gone
with us, and eaten a dinner cooked by the man who has made
one acre of waste ground produce, each year, a thousand dollars'
worth of celery, where there was no celery before.

I quite liked the fellow!

There! I've been sitting at this table an hour. Old John is standing up, looking this way—he thinks it is time his visitor should
materialize and do a little honest work. Now he is walking over
towards a stump where hangs his vest, with his watch in the
pocket, a watch of a Cap'n Cuttle pattern—he is going to see what
time it is. I think I'll just let the dishes go, and when Old John
comes in, I'll get him to talking about the times when he and Walt
Whitman lived together in Washington; and then we will have
dinner and he will not notice that the dishes are not washed. After
dinner I'll fix 'em up—it is really a waste of time to wash dishes!
Under my hand is a letter headed, " Emerson College of Oratory."
They are an ambitious lot—those E. C. O. girls! This one says
she recites, " Serene I fold my hands and wait!" She wants the
author to be so kind as to please write it out for her in MS. The

Poet has evidently started to comply, for here is the first stanza and two lines of the second. Evidently he could n't think of the rest and is waiting until he finds the book. That is a great poem, though!—the E. C. O. girl is right. It was written forty-three years ago—that's all—in Washington, when the author was twenty-three years old. He read it to Walt Whitman the morning after he wrote it, and Walt said it was pretty fair.

" Is it so, John? " I asked him the other day.

" Is what so? " he answered.

" Why, that mine own shall come to me? "

" Yes, if you hustle. Every truth is only a half truth—how about your own master-piece, ' Carrying the Lettuce to Gomez?'"

" That is all truth!" I answered, " I wrote it." " Is it truth though? Why, it is just about like that tramp you took when you walked the length of Ireland, and rode most of the way in a jaunting car."

I changed the subject, and began to talk about boys.

John Burroughs has written delightfully of boys and told how they live in a 'world of their own, oblivious absolutely of the interests of grown-ups. He is a good deal of a boy himself: he has the eager receptive mental attitude. He is full of hope and is ever expecting to see something beautiful—something curious. Each day for him is a New Day, and he goes out in the morning and looks up at the clouds and scans the distant hills; and as he walks he watches for new things, or old things that may appear in a new light. This habit of expectancy always marks the strong man. It is a form of attraction—our own comes to us because we desire it; we find what we expect to find, and we receive what we ask for. All life is a prayer—strong natures pray most—and every earnest, sincere prayer is answered. Old John Burroughs' life is a prayer for beauty. He looks for beauty and goodness, and lo! these things are added unto him.

John Burroughs and Walt Whitman were friends and comrades

in Washington during the war. Both were clerks in the Treasury Department; and when Walt lost his job because a certain man did n't appreciate " Leaves of Grass," John offered Walt a home and half of his pay until he should find another place.

John did not tell me this, but I know it is so.

Walt Whitman did n't waste his money—he was not dissipated—but he had a bad habit of giving dollar bills away to people whom he thought were less fortunate than he; so the natural result was he seldom had many dollar bills himself. Many people have criticised Whitman because he did not enlist and help fight his country's battles, instead of contenting himself with the rather womanish task of nursing the wounded. Whitman was a brave man, and he did not enlist simply because he had a supreme horror of war. That is, he loved the men on both sides and loved them equally well. This being true, his soul revolted at thought of levelling a gun at a brother, and then shooting when ordered to. Whitman did n't think it was necessary for men to kill other men; and he further thought that to abrogate your will and kill a man on another man's order, was quite as bad as to kill a man of your own volition. The proposition of transferring conscience to an intangible thing called Government, was quite as absurd to him as transferring your reasoning powers to something called Church—a man should be a Man. He did n't believe in a man abandoning his own free-will, as a soldier must. A soldier is a slave—he does what he is told to do—everything is provided for him—his head is a superfluity. He is only a stick used by men to strike other men; and he is often tossed to hell without a second thought.

The people soldiers kill are never any worse than they themselves—and very often are better. The Confederate soldiers were just as patriotic, just as sincere, just as brave, just as intelligent as were the Northern troops—everybody admits that now. For a Northern farmer who raised corn, to go down South and kill a farmer who raised cotton, was monstrous and absurd to Walt Whitman. And he thought that the man who killed another man was just as unfortunate as the man who got killed. There is no such thing as success in a bad business—killing men is a bad business. To kill another man means damnation for yourself—the man who kills another does kill himself. Walt Whitman looked upon every man as a part of himself, and the conviction of his life was that to injure another was to injure yourself—to help another is to help yourself ❧ ❧

Whitman had a profound regard for Lincoln, and one of his best and closest friends was Peter Doyle, the street car driver and Confederate soldier. Walt did n't blame Peter for going to war— Walt did n't blame anybody for anything. And he loved Lincoln for what he was and for the masterly way in which he did his work, and you will see by reading " Captain, My Captain," or that elegy unsurpassed, " When Lilacs last in the Dooryard Bloomed." Walt was quite willing to let every man go ahead and do the thing he wanted to do, until he got his fill of it and found it wrong—or right.

Now doubtless there be small men who pop up and ask in orotund, " What would a' become of this country in 1860 if everybody in it had been like Walt Whitman and John Burroughs?" And the answer is that if everybody in it had been like Walt Whitman and John Burroughs, there would have been no issue, and therefore no war. That old Silver-Top out there in the celery has done more than any other living man to inaugurate the love of Out-of-Doors that is now manifesting itself as a Nature Renaissance. Within twenty years a silent revolution has been worked out in favor of country life; and this new sympathy with our mute brothers, the animals, has come along as a natural result. A man down near Poughkeepsie said to me, " I believe John Burroughs has influenced everybody for twenty miles around here in favor of not killing birds and things."

And I answered, " Sir, John Burroughs has influenced the entire civilized world against killing things."

The seed which Thoreau planted, Burroughs has watered and tended. Yet as a writer he is just as virile—just as original—as Thoreau and, unlike Thoreau, he has no antagonisms. He has made the fragmentary philosophy of Whitman a practical working gospel, and prepared the way for Bolles, Seton-Thompson, Van Dyke, Skinner, and a hundred other strong writers; and all that army of boys and girls and men and women who now hunt the woods with camera instead of a gun; or my dear old father who prospects with a spade in search of ginseng, sarsaparilla, arrow heads and " relics."

Just a straw to show how the wind has veered: In 1889 a bill was introduced in the New York State Assembly to prohibit the hunting of deer with hounds. The bill met with a fierce opposition and was only passed, by a bare majority, after considerable delay and a determined fight. In the winter of 1900 another bill was gently and diplomatically presented, amending the first bill so as to make an exception in favor of one county. This county is in the Adirondack region, and is mostly owned by one man who uses the land as a game preserve for himself and friends. This man wanted the legal privilege of hunting deer with dogs—" for only a few days in the year," he explained half apologetically. Did the people of New York grant the gentleman's request?

Most certainly they did not. The bare mention in the newspapers that such a petition had been presented caused every Senator and Assemblyman to be swamped with letters of protest. The bill was hissed out of court. It was as if some one had asked the privilege of hunting men with dogs—we would have none of it. From what one Assemblyman in 1889 called "a mere freakish bit of maudlin sentimentalism of a few unknown cranks " to a fixed fact of public opinion in 1900—that is the way we have grown. And for this let credit be given John Burroughs, more

than to any other man. ❡ Well, well, it is nine o'clock—the sun
is getting clear above the hill-top. Old John will surely think
that all my talk about the " Tolstoy Act " is pure preachy-
preachment, and that I live my strenuous life by proxy. Oho!
I hear voices, women's voices—along the winding pathway.
Through the trees, three girls are approaching—Vassar girls,
for sure, on a pious pilgrimage. They are heading for the cabin—
I'll just tell them they can not see the Prophet until they wash
the dishes and make the shack all neat and tidy.

There! that lets me out.

Now for the celery!

Nancy Hanks

LINCOLN CITY, Indiana, is in Spencer County, forty miles Northeast of Evansville, and one hundred fifty miles from Louisville.

There was no town there in the days of Abraham Lincoln. The " city " sprang into existence with the coming of the railroad, only a few years ago. The word " city " was anticipatory.

The place is a hamlet of barely a dozen houses. There is a general store, a blacksmith-shop, the railroad-station, and a very good school to which the youth come from miles around.

The occasion of my visit was the annual meeting of the Indiana Editors' Association.

A special train had been provided us by the courtesy of the Southern Railway. There were about two hundred people in the party.

At Nancy Hanks Park we were met by several hundred farmers and their families, some of whom had come for twenty-five miles and more to attend the exercises.

As I sat on the platform and looked into the tanned, earnest faces of these people, I realized the truth of that remark of Thomas Jefferson, " The chosen people of God are those who till the soil."

These are the people who have ever fought freedom's fight. And the children of such as these are often the men who go up to the cities and take them captive.

In the cities the poor imitate the follies and foibles of the rich to the extent of their ability.

But here, far away from the big towns and cities, we get a type of men and women such as Lincoln knew. They had come with the children, brought their lunch in baskets, and were making a day of it.

We formed in line by twos and ascended the little hill where the mother of Lincoln sleeps. On the simple little granite column are the words:

NANCY HANKS LINCOLN
Mother of Abraham Lincoln
Died October 5th, 1818
Aged 35 years

Instinctively we uncovered.

Not a word was spoken.

An old woman, bowed, bronzed, with furrowed face, approached. She wore a blue sunbonnet, a calico dress, a check apron. The apron was full of flowers.

The old woman pushed through the little group and emptied her wild flowers on the grave.

No words of studied oratory could have been as eloquent.

A woman was paying tribute to the woman who gave to the world the mightiest man America has produced!

And this old woman might have been kin to the woman to whose resting-place we had journeyed.

A misty something came over my eyesight, and through my mind ran a vision of Nancy Hanks.

" Died aged 35," runs the inscription.

The family had come from Kentucky, only a half-day's journey distant as we count miles today by steam and trolley.

But in Eighteen Hundred Seventeen it took the little cavalcade a month to come from LaRue County, Kentucky, to Spencer County, Indiana, sixteen miles as the birds fly, North of the Ohio River.

Here land was to be had for the settling. For ten miles North from the Ohio the soil is black and fertile.

Then you reach the hills, or what the early settlers called " the barrens." The soil here is yellow, the land rolling.

It is picturesque beyond compare, beautiful as a poet's dream, but tickle it as you will with a hoe it will not laugh a harvest. At the best it will only grimly grin.

It is a country of timber and toil.

Valuable hardwoods abound—oak, walnut, ash, hickory.

Springs flowing from the hills are plentiful, wild flowers grow in profusion, the trees are vocal with song of birds, but the ground is stony and stubborn.

Here the family rested by the side of the cold sparkling stream. Across the valley to the West the hills arose, grand, somber, majestic *

Down below a stream went dancing its way to the sea.

And near by were rushes and little patches of grass, where the tired horses nibbled in gratitude.

And so they rested. There were Thomas Lincoln; Nancy Hanks Lincoln, his wife; Sarah Lincoln aged ten; and little Abe Lincoln, aged eight.

The family had four horses, old and lame. In the wagon were a few household goods, two sacks of cornmeal, a side of bacon. Instead of pushing on Westward the family decided to remain. They built a shack from logs, closed on three sides, open to the South *

The reason the South side was left open was because there was no chimney, and the fire they built was half in the home and half outside *

Here the family lived that first bleak, dreary Winter. To Abe and Sarah it was only fun. But to Nancy Hanks Lincoln, who was delicate, illy clothed, underfed, and who had known better things in her Kentucky home, it was hardship.

She was a woman of aspiration and purpose, a woman with romance and dreams in her heart. Now all had turned to ashes of roses. Children, those little bold explorers on life's stormy sea, accept everything just as a matter of course.

Abe wrote long years afterward: " My mother worked steadily and without complaining. She cooked, made clothing, planted a little garden. She coughed at times, and often would have to lie down for a little while. We did not know she was ill. She was worn, yellow and sad. One day when she was lying down she motioned me to come near. And when I stood by the bed she reached out one hand as if to embrace me, and pointing to my sister Sarah said in a whisper, ' Be good to her, Abe! ' " The tired woman closed her eyes and it was several hours before the children knew she was dead.

The next day Thomas Lincoln made a coffin of split boards. The body of the dead woman was placed in the rude coffin. And then four men carried the coffin up to the top of a little hill near by and it was lowered into a grave.

A mound of rocks was piled on top, according to the custom of the times, to protect the grave from wild animals.

Little Abe and Sarah went down the hill, dazed and undone, clinging to each other in their grief. But there was work to do, and Sarah was the " little other mother."

For a year she cooked, scrubbed, patched the clothing, and looked after the household.

Then one day Thomas Lincoln went away, and left the two children alone.

He was gone for a week, and when he came back he brought the children a stepmother—Sally Bush Johnston.

This widow who was now Mrs. Thomas Lincoln had three children of her own, but she possessed enough love for two more.

Her heart went out to little Abe, and his lonely heart responded. She brought provisions, dishes, cloth for clothing, needles to sew with, scissors to cut. She was a good cook. And best of all she had three books.

Up to this time Abe had never worn shoes or cap. She made him moccasins, and also a coonskin cap, with a dangling tail.

She taught Abe and Sarah to read, their own mother having taught them the alphabet. She told them stories—stories of George Washington and Thomas Jefferson. She told them of the great outside world of towns and cities where many people lived. She told them of the Capitol at Washington, and of the Government of the United States.

And they learned to repeat the names of these States, and write the names out with a burnt stick on a slab.

And little Abe Lincoln and his sister Sarah were very happy.

Their hearts were full of love and gratitude for their New Mother, and they sometimes wondered if anywhere in the wide world there were little boys and girls who had as much as they.

" All I am, and all I hope to be, I owe to my darling mother!" wrote Abraham Lincoln, years later.

And it is good to know that Sarah Bush Lincoln lived to see the boy evolve into the greatest man in America. She survived him four years.

Here Abe Lincoln lived until he was twenty-one, until he had attained his height of six feet four.

He had read every book in the neighborhood.

He had even tramped through the forest twenty miles, to come back with a borrowed volume, which he had read to his mother by the light of a pine-knot.

He had clerked in the store down at " The Forks," at Gentryville.

He had whipped the local bully—and asked his pardon for doing so.

He had spelled down the school and taken parts in debates.

He could split more rails than any other man in the neighborhood.

He had read the Bible, the Revised Statutes of Indiana, and could repeat Poor Richard's Almanac backward.

He was a natural leader—the strongest, sanest, kindest and truest young man in the neighborhood.

When Abe was twenty-one, the family decided to move West.

There were four ox-carts in all. One of these carts was driven by Abraham Lincoln. But before they started, Abe cut the initials N. H. L. on a slab and placed it securely at the head of the grave of his mother—the mother who had given him birth.

In Eighteen Hundred Seventy-six, James Studebaker, of South Bend, bought a marble headstone and placed it on the grave. Mr. Studebaker also built a picket-fence around the grave, and paid the owner of the property a yearly sum for seeing that the grave was protected, and that visitors were allowed free access to the spot.

In Nineteen Hundred Five certain citizens of Indiana bought the hilltop, a beautiful grove of thirty acres, and this property is now the possession of the State, forever.

A guardian lives there who keeps the property in good condition. A chapel, roofed, but open on all sides, has been built, the trees are trimmed, the under-brush removed. Winding walks and well-kept roadways are to be seen. The park is open to the public. Visitors come, some of them great and learned.

And now and again comes some old woman, tired, worn, knowing somewhat of the history of Nancy Hanks, and all she endured and suffered, and places on the mound a bouquet gathered down in the meadows. Abraham Lincoln can never die. He belongs to the ages. Memories of him will be passed on from generation to generation—the blessed heritage of all mankind.

And here alone on the hilltop sleeps the woman who went down into the shadow and gave him birth.

Biting poverty was her portion; deprivation and loneliness were her lot. But on her tomb are four words that express the highest praise that tongue can utter, or pen indite:

MOTHER OF ABRAHAM LINCOLN

At the Nancy Hanks Memorial, ex-Congressman Colonel Frank Posey spoke first.

Colonel Posey comes from the family that founded Posey County, famous for pleasantries, and famous, too, for the fact that it grows corn a hundred bushels to the acre, and wheat fifty bushels, and men and women in proportion.

New Harmony is in Posey County. There lived George Rapp, who founded the Rappites and paved the way for Robert Owen, who worked out a romantic scheme that sowed the seeds of Brook Farm ✍ ✍

In Posey County was formed the first Woman's Club in America, and the first Public Library as well. Restrain your smiles when Posey County is mentioned—you are on sacred soil.

Colonel Posey is an orator and a statesman. He is saturated with Lincoln memories, and radiates " the good old days." His speech was worth the journey, even if I had heard naught else.

Following Colonel Posey came Governor Willson of Kentucky, who reminded us in stirring phrase of what Kentucky has done for the Republic.

" He was born in old Kentucky," said the Governor—and the man who did not shout was n't present. The Governor was impressive and profound, and showed that he too was from the State that evolved Henry Clay. Next came ex-Vice-President Charles Warren Fairbanks.

We used to hear Fairbanks spoken of as " a human refrigerator-plant." Let the man who mentions cold storage with Fairbanks in mind be chilled by his own falsehoods.

Fairbanks is a warm, pulsing, manly man. He is nearly as tall as Lincoln was. Long of arm, long of leg, big in brain, with a voice vibrant and earnest, he played upon the heartstrings and memories of the audience as Paderewski toys the keys.

Fairbanks made a masterly address. He is close to the hearts of the common people—" the kind that God loves."

And these are the identical people with whom Lincoln spent his boyhood days. Here his character was formed.

He is the world's great Hoosier.

If it was n't the custom to work " the Lincoln type " business overtime, I would say that Fairbanks is essentially of the Lincoln model ❧ ❧

He has the sturdy commonsense, the directness and the simplicity of the rail-splitter. After the speechmaking the farmers closed in and shook hands with everybody, especially Fairbanks. He called many of them by name, and the way they listened to him and the way they greeted him gave the lie to all that cold-storage guff. I was with the man all day. His wit, his friendliness, his courtesy, were contagious.

I like Fairbanks as a man, and I admire him as a statesman. I also like his H_2O cocktails.

The man is delightfully sane. He has no fight with progress, nor does he have a lust to vivisect success and crucify enterprise. After Fairbanks came ex-Governor Durbin, a hundred-point man who had written out his thoughts and read them, like the good, simple businessman he is. There is nothing of the Colonel Yell of Yellville about Durbin. He is safe, sensible, sound. He gave us valuable facts spiced with a few poetic fancies, and he quit when he should—a rare, unique and strange thing for an orator to do. Honorable James E. Watson was present, but declined to speak. I think he wanted to give all of us who were in Class B a run for our legal tender.

But Jim's modesty went for naught. Or was his modesty " mere psychology? " In any event, there were wild, turbulent calls for " Watson—Watson—Watson! " And when some one sent up the cry of " Our Jim! " why, Jim came forward and in deep sonorous tones, spaced with graceful hesitation, such as Tom Corwin would have brought to bear, he paid each of the preceding speakers flowery meed of praise. And it surely listened good to all of us who had sawed the air and made the judicious grieve. But soon " Our Jim " was making a sure-enough speech, standing on his toes, a Jupiter of oratory sending the thunder of his wisdom and the lightning of his wit where'er he lists, splitting the oaks of ignorance and laying low the tall pines of prejudice.

James E. Watson of Rushville is a great personality.

At the Chicago convention he was the third favorite on the job. First was Elihu Root, next Herbert Spencer Hadley, next was " Our Jim."

Jim is young and full of political poetic prunes. He has no gray hairs, no bald spot—just a soft spot in his heart for chiffon and all other beautiful things.

He is always going to school, and will not be at his best for twenty years ᵴ ᵴ

As I listened to his rolling utterances, noted the dramatic pose of his athletic physique, and then looked out over his audience and saw how thoroughly he held them, I realized somewhat of the wonderful school in which Lincoln was taught.

Great oratory must be out of doors. It needs a setting, also it needs hearers of the earnest, honest, rustic, fighting breed.

Poverty and pioneer conditions breed statesmen—and statesmen are men who build a State.

James E. Watson has ancestors who kissed the Blarney Stone, but he himself feeds on the Honey of Hymettus.

And while Jim's diet may be Grecian, he himself symbols for us the little red schoolhouse, voices the opportunity of plains and prairies, stands for sanity, sanitation and safety, and knows naught of government by experiment and hysteria, much less of legislation by legerdemain.

But, say, Terese, come closer, so; what crops of genius those Hoosiers do produce! They surely have moved the literary zone from Massachusetts to their own fertile fields and valleys. Here Lincoln learned to write, and laid the foundation for a literary style matchless in its purity.

Edward Eggleston began the real trouble with his *Hoosier School Master.*

James Whitcomb Riley gave the world a new thrill, touched a million hearts, evolved a race of imitators, and put his fodder in the shock. He made more money than ever poet did before.
❦ Last week he gave the city of Indianapolis seventy-five thousand dollars for a fountain, thus showing his appreciation for a product for which poets of old had small use. Also, he gave his secretary a present of fifty thousand dollars. Was ever a poet so trusting before? As for George Ade, with his *Fables in Slang,* he did n't pollute the well of English undefiled. He just filled the old well up and put in a high-pressure system of his own. George owns a township, brought from the usufruct of his airy, fairy fables and his nonsensical, nebulous nuances that have helped us forget it.

General Lew Wallace built a block from the proceeds of his book, and has had a street-car line named in his honor.

John W. Kern, senior Senator, Spartan Superbus, perpetual candidate for the Presidency, Magnus, has written many good things, and now has an epic poem in press.

Booth Tarkington, the versatile and gently contumacious, has made much moneys and married more, and pounds the typewriter eight hours a day for the love of it, at so much per pound.

Meredith Nicholson has won all the success that is any man's due ❧ ❧

Albert J. Beveridge has written reams and reams of faultless, high-clutch, Silvertown-tire prose, and memorized most of it.

Charles Major, with his *When Knighthood was in Flower,* made us sit up nights and burn dollar gas. Maurice Thompson, Nature-lover, gave us gems in verse, rich and rare, besides his incoming parable *Alice of Old Vincennes.*

Albion Fellows Bacon, a mite of a woman with a mighty heart, has written splendidly and well; and also she taught her sister, Annie Fellows Johnston, how.

And surely we will not soon forget Gene Stratton Porter, who has made us love the birds, bees, butterflies and moths, and introduced us to the rainbow, the clouds and the sunrise.

Then down at Evansville, neighbor to Robert Dale Owen, was born and lived Adolph Melzer, protector of dumb animals, a voice for the voiceless, teaching the gentle doctrine of the divinity of all life.

Indiana is not the only home of the literary animalcule, but it is also the home of presidential timber and Vice-Presidents, potential and actual. Think of Hendricks, Fairbanks, O. P. Morton, Beveridge, Heminway, Kern and Marshall!

And of the diplomats not a few, with Denby and Foster carrying America to the Orient.

Colonel Denby not only has a proud place in history, but his picture is on the most popular brand of cigars manufactured since Sir Walter Raleigh taught Queen Elizabeth how to strike a match on the seat of her electric runabout.

Indiana comes nearer representing American democracy (with a small d) than any other State.

Political prophecies go wrong in Indiana. She may throw a Republican majority of thirty thousand, or a Democratic plurality of twenty, jumping on a Bull-Moose boomlet with both brogans ✒ ✒

In Indiana men are not herded and owned. Neither are the women—ask May Wright Sewell!

The fertile quality of the soil on the classic shores of the Wabash is mirrored in the famous Landis family.

Here were five Landis laddies—Charles, John, Fred, Kenesaw Mountain, and Walter.

All grew up to be men with health, animation, purpose, ambition, and marvelous hirsute effects.

Their habitat was the little village of Millville, in Butler County, Ohio, and in the Seventies they moved to Logansport, Indiana.

They carried newspapers, clerked in the post-office, taught

" deestrick skule," and one or two of them " went to college."
Two of them went to Congress at one time from adjoining
districts, and had seats on the floor next to each other.

It seems that at one time all of these five Landis boys were drawing salaries from the Government and when they used to meet
would join hands in a circle and sing, " Our Country, 't is of
Thee! " • •

There are two Landis girls, older than the boys, who have
remained at home and kept the lamp in the window burning for
their brothers, a pair of independent, self-reliant, evolving
women, instead of two depressed, whipped-out wives done for
by the marital steam-roller.

Strong and able as are the Landis boys, my opinion is that the
two girls intellectually have the Phi-Beta-Kappa key on them.
Their father was a surgeon in the War. He was at the Battle of
Kenesaw Mountain. And on the day the battle was fought,
Kenesaw Mountain Landis was born, and naturally they named
him Kenesaw Mountain and he has been Kenesaw Mountain
ever since. And always at war—with what he considers error.

❡ At present he is a United States judge in the Cook County
bailiwick. He is a very superior man, essentially an individualist,
full of the dramatic instinct, by nature an artist. People, who are
equally wise on every occasion, are not artists. In order to produce art you have to see things out of their natural relation. You
lift them up against the sky, and paint them with a broom.
Judge Landis would make ten times as much money practising
law, would have five times more fun, and would be a deal bigger
figure in private life than he is, cabined, cribbed, confined in a
judge's robe. A little experience on the bench is charming; also
it gives you a title that sticks to you the rest of your natural
days. But as a life career, it belongs to the class B man.

Whenever I see a Landis I feel like shouting to everybody in the
vicinity: " Make room! Make room for individuality! "

Then we must not forget Dan Voorhees, the tall sycamore of the Wabash, who pawed up the sawdust in the political arena for fifty years.

He was a graduate of De Pauw University and played a prominent part in the Hoosier Renaissance. His monument is the Congressional Library building in Washington, for he it was who supplied the initiative for this magnificent institution.

At Purdue University I was told by one of the professors that a John and George McCutcheon and George Ade graduated there in Eighteen Hundred Eighty-nine. For four years these three boys had prevented the police of Lafayette from getting their full quota of rest. These boys had also kept the entire college faculty from indulging in introspection.

How they ever got their degrees no one exactly knows, but the feeling is that they were graduated so as to get rid of them, on the theory that if you do not want a man in your employ you are perfectly willing to supply him a letter of recommendation to some one else.

Nevertheless, everything works together for good, whether you love the Lord or not. The McCutcheons have gotten along fairly well, and nobody claims that George Ade is on half-rations. George owns a township, and John McCutcheon is King of Cartoonists ๑ ๑

Here is a point that the historians have not touched upon, so far as I know.

Lincoln lived in Spencer County, sixteen miles from the Ohio River. He arrived there in Eighteen Hundred Seventeen, and remained there until Eighteen Hundred Thirty.

Forty-five miles to the West is the town of New Harmony, Indiana ๑ ๑

New Harmony was on the great highway to the West.

New Harmony is one of the most interesting historic spots in the United States.

A few things were done there in the line of civilization before they were done anywhere else in America.

New Harmony was the home of a communistic society known as the Rappites, or Harmonists, or Harmonyites.

George Rapp was driven out of Germany on account of his political socialism.

He had a plentiful lack of religious convictions and founded a religion of his own on an Utopian basis.

There were five hundred people in his community. These people represented the primal virtues of industry, economy, truthfulness, mutuality ᴣ• ᴣ•

They were a highly educated people—that is to say, there was no illiteracy among them, and this at a time when the outside world in that vicinity was densely ignorant.

The Rapp Colony was practically a college, and in fact the word college means a collection of people who are intent on cultivating their mental acreage.

The Rappites remained at New Harmony from Eighteen Hundred Fifteen until Eighteen Hundred Twenty-four, when they sold their estate of about three thousand acres to Robert Owen. Robert Owen is the world's first businessman.

He is the man who inaugurated the first factory betterments. He prophesied a day when every factory would be a school, and his factories at New Lanark, Scotland, were practically schools that attracted the attention of all Europe. Robert Owen was two hundred years ahead of his time.

He was accused in England of making war on established religion, and he found it convenient to move his ideal colony to the New World, and having got in touch with George Rapp of the Rappites he made a special journey to New Harmony, Indiana, and bought the community out with all of its belongings.

The Rappites moved to Economy, Pennsylvania, and built what is today the best-paying railroad property in America; that is to say, the Pittsburgh and Lake Erie Railroad, running from Pittsburgh to Youngstown. In addition to this, they had factories, stores, schools, churches, where equality prevailed.

The Rappites founded the first public library in America, possibly with the exception of the Free Public Library founded by Benjamin Franklin in Philadelphia.

These people had no paid priesthood. Every man and woman in the community who had anything to say said it in public.

The Rappites and the followers of Robert Owen were very much alike, representing the paradox of rounding the circle, for the Rappites are celibates.

The Owenites were practically free lovers, and celibates by way of variation, the opposites of things being alike, as every wise man knows. The simple point is that the center of advanced civilization practically was at New Harmony, Indiana, at the time when Abraham Lincoln lived in Indiana, only forty-five miles away, at a point which was well within the literary zone.

As far as New Thought and Free Thought are concerned, New Harmony had a well-defined expression in the Rappites and the Owenites long before the Massachusetts Transcendentalists had tuned their lyres. Transcendentalism in America had its rise in New Harmony, Indiana, and from the time that George Rapp reached New Harmony, Posey County, Indiana, in Eighteen Hundred Fifteen, up to the present time, New Harmony has been the center of new thought, free thought, earnest mental exercise, high endeavor, and all that makes for beauty, worth, excellence, truth, health and progress.

Orthodox theology and orthodox sociology apply the brakes to progress until the rubber smells, but New Harmony tried things on a practical working basis.

Now the question is: Was not Abraham Lincoln, in his Hoosier home, influenced by this storm-center of thought, only the distance of a horseback-ride away?

As far as we know, legend is silent, and certainly history is mute on this particular point.

The people at New Harmony are regarded with grave suspicion by the citizens round-about. Truth is always under suspicion, but it does not seem improbable that a little of the light which the Rappites and the Owenites produced by their little candle had thrown its beams clear to Gentryville, where Abraham Lincoln was splitting rails and where he lived until he was six feet four and weighed one hundred and seventy pounds.

Abraham Lincoln was a Hoosier.

From here he went forth to do the greatest work that mortal man was ever called upon to do. And today his name and fame are the precious legacy of mankind wherever flares freedom's torch.

Tolstoy and Potter's Field

THE last of the Titans has gone. Tolstoy is dead. The great line of seers and prophets that began with Isaiah and Ezekiel ended with the Great Moujik. In the shadow of that gigantic figure we are all small. Around the Colossus of Yasnaya Poliana we crawl and cringe and fret—little beings of a little day. His bare brown feet rested firmly on the earth. His majestic head was in the constellations. His heart covered and sanctified the race.

He was a man of sorrows—The Man of Sorrows of the century. Like Buddha and Christ, he believed he carried the burden of humanity. His mighty soul was gashed by the evils of the age. He saw that life and suffering were interchangeable terms; that man here below has been caught like a rat in a trap; that knavery, force and fraud ruled everywhere, especially in his own native land. He was a pessimist, if to see the truth and speak it is pessimism. He died facing a statue of the Buddha. He lived facing the rotten aristocracy of his country, the criminal Grand Dukes and that gigantic Graft called the Greek Church.

He was the one man that Russia feared. This is a stupendous fact, and Russia feared Tolstoy because she knew that a hand laid on him would have been the signal for an uprising of the whole human race, of which he was the Voice and the Heart.

No matter how large a man looms in the history of his time, he is always a part. No man can be an absolute law unto himself. The Past and the Present stand at his cradle. Each individual is related to an infinite number of things, dead and living. Tolstoy, like Hugo, Savonarola, Luther, was necessary to his time. Russia needed a Man, the World needed a Gospel—and Tolstoy rose and grasped the lightnings. For he was godlike in his majesty—a figure that awes and cows.

Tolstoy was the most significant figure of the century, because he came at the most significant period in the history of modern civilization. He was a reaction. He was the other half of the eternal law of action and reaction. The times produce the man, and the man reacts on his time. When the people need a liberator he appears. Secret forces are forever at work molding in mystery the man with the new message in religion, philosophy, morals, business ❧ ❧

At the time Tolstoy came the world had no soul—no insides. It had telegraphs and railroads, but no religion—in the spiritual sense of the word. Man can not live by machinery alone. All things exist in nature by the balancing of two forces: the centripetal and the centrifugal. A people who are impelled by the powerful attraction of external things and who have no counterbalancing center within are on the way to extinction.

Tolstoy said that there is something more than the body. Christ preached the same doctrine at a similar critical epoch in the world's history. Marcus Aurelius, an emperor, and Epictetus, a slave, had said the same. Man gropes today for something better. The old gods are dead; the old beliefs are rotten reeds. Pontifical pretense and theological sleight-of-hand no longer interest. The Church is useful matter in the wrong place.

When Tolstoy began to thunder in Russia, the Greek Church had still the old pride in her eye. Vain glory was emblazoned on her brow, and the lips of priests stank with the grease of the glutton. The Church was a braggart.

Today, thanks to Tolstoy, the Greek Church is being secretly investigated by every thinking brain in Russia. They have dragged the purple and laces off the old jade, and beneath they have discovered the Eternal Prostitute. And her paramour, the old autocracy, is making shift for its life. For every dart that Tolstoy hurled at that pair of immemorial bloodsuckers was poisoned and stuck in their dugs. ·

There was a stupendous rebellion in Tolstoy's soul: a revolt against the imbecility of merely living, like a rat, for the sake of breathing. A giant brooding sorrow stood in his eyes; an infinite compassion filled his soul.

Thinker? No, he was not that. He was greater than a thinker—he was a Seer, an Announcer, a Liberator, a spiritual John Brown. ❦ He chose the company of the peasant, of the lowly and the suffering, because he knew that they held the secret of existence. He sought out the erring, because he knew they were more sinned against than sinning. He was one with all men: the prostitute, the thief, were puppets. They need help, not Siberia.

And he spurned the complacent Phariseeism that swims in its own lard; he thundered against the smug phrase-makers, the professional optimists, the hypocrites on 'Change, the hypocrites on high.

He carried about him a transcendental nostaglia, a homesickness born of sweet memories, a " mansion in the skies," a divine despair, a somber to-hell-with-your-civilization!

He made his appeal directly to the heart of his listeners. That is the secret of his vast power. He went into the homes of the peasants, sitting with them at their meals, meeting them in the fields. He knew that the center of the universe was everywhere. So he preferred to look for it under rags rather than under imperial purple. Purple conceals so much that does n't exist. He believed all men were made of the same substance—that he, Tolstoy, was a potential drunkard and a possible murderer.

The Infinite was in this man. He who has universal sympathy possesses the Divine. He who understands mankind and loves mankind is God. And that is why we call Buddha, Christ, Emerson, Mary Baker Eddy and Tolstoy divine. This is the central conception that illumined the brain of Tolstoy, and this is the substratum of everything he ever wrote: Man is One.

He depersonalized himself. By a miracle he was the Race. There is no analogy to him in Modern Europe. To find his peers we must go to the Ganges and beneath the Himalayas. It is only there among those marvelous Hindus that dreams like Tolstoy's flourish and spread. It is only there that they understand that wonderful doctrine of Jesus: you shall lose yourself in order to gain yourself. Give all, if you would gain all. He who wants nothing possesses everything.

Mercy, charity, self-conquest, renunciation, and finally, through discipline, the extinction of the pain-absorbing and pain-begetting personality and union with God—that was the essence of Tolstoy's teaching. Among the forces that direct life, Tolstoy preferred Instinct to Knowledge. The Instinct of the animal is surer than that of man. Is it not that belief which he expounds to us in *Master and Servant*, when Vassili, having wandered in a sled in the night in a great snowstorm, abandons the reins to his servant Nikiti? The peasant and the horse find the lost road, then the village.

But they are lost again.

" What shall we do now? " asks the master.

" Let the horse go without guidance," replies the peasant. And the horse leads them both back home.

" The peasant and the animal have more wisdom than the educated man," says Tolstoy. God is in the heart, not in the head. Reasoning is an " ignis fatuus," a false light. Trust the Universal Soul, and you will " find the way."

What attracted and fascinated Tolstoy was that instinct is anterior to the modes of individual knowledge. Instinct is spirit. Knowledge is a vagary. Education is perversion of life. Abandon yourself and all your gorgeous gewgaws called position—and above all the gewgaw of Self.

This was his great doctrine of renunciation. He took direct issue with the Greeks, who taught the joy of life. He was the antithesis of Friedrich Nietzsche, who glorified even evil because it made existence majestic. How strange a doctrine to preach to the world today living its cat-and-dog existence! Give! Give! cried Tolstoy. Give! When you give you expand. Renounce that little thing that you hug in your bosom and you shall be lapped and laved in the Infinite ❧ ❧

Tolstoy may have been a sublime disease, but he was Sublime. And who among us is not diseased, let him cast the first stone at the great Russ.

In a world of mediocrities, fakers, make-believes, slick-fingers, gabby-jacks and pampered pharisees, Leo Tolstoy stands out gigantic, grand, menacing—a voice crying in the wilderness, maybe, but a Voice that reverberates to the stars and shakes the rotting dynasties of Europe to their foundations and sets a-tremble the dome of Saint Peter's.

In all Christendom, he was the only Christian. In Russia, he was an apparition of Justice.

Today, Leo Tolstoy is sitting with Buddha, Christ, Lucretius, Isaiah, Emerson, Goethe and all the other earth-gods who have passed into the Council-Chamber of the Everlasting.

Yet his religion was not mine, nor yours. The love of man and woman—the resultant love of beauty as manifest in art—was not for him.

But how vain to picture him by telling what he was not!

He was great on account of what he was. He asked for nothing, and so he was without fear. He loved humanity—not persons. He was a King by divine right, yet he loved the race too well to wish to rule.

The days will pass and Tolstoy will be to countless millions as the shadow of a great rock in a weary land.

Hail! Leo Tolstoy, hail! and farewell!

The early Christian churches, following the pagan practice of burying favored followers in the temple, were used for burial purposes.

When a member died he was buried in the church. So beneath the floor was a concourse of graves—coffins piled on coffins. Under these conditions the incense as a disinfectant had a practical use. But finally when the church could not hold any more, or there was great danger of infection from putrefying bodies, they began to bury the dead outside of the church, but near it.

Thus arose the custom of the burying-ground and church being practically one institution. The idea of depositing the dead in the church had its impulse in the doctrine of the Resurrection. In fact, it was so that the arisen spirits could be easily identified, and given their proper place in Paradise.

All of these burial-places in the church and surrounding the church were " consecrated ground." Infidels and so-called criminals were never buried there.

Very often there were bitter arguments as to the undesirability of allowing certain bodies to be buried in the church. And occasionally the bodies of so-called infidels were exhumed and removed. For instance, the body of Shakespeare was buried in the church at Stratford, and a threat as to what would happen to any one who tampered with the dead was placed over the grave, and still remains there, although there is doubt whether the body of Shakespeare, " the strolling play-actor," was not removed by the zealous churchmen.

Bodies of criminals executed by law were never buried in consecrated ground. Usually they were buried in the prison-yard. At Reading Gaol, in England, the custom still continues of burying the body of the criminal in the roadway, over which men and horses tramp—this as a kind of parting insult or post-mortem penalty ❧ ❧

The fear of being buried in unhallowed ground has darkened many a worthy life.

In the will of Leo Tolstoy, recently made public, is one line that will live.

No playwright ever had the imagination to put into the mouth of one of his mimes a sentence so thrilling:

" *Bury me in the potter's field !* "

In all the realm of wills, was there ever before a behest like this! The term, " potter's field," comes to us from the Bible. In the cities of the Orient it was the custom to bury the friendless, the outcast, the criminal, the unknown, in the potter's field. The potter's field was the dumping-ground for the refuse from the potteries—a mountain heap of garbage in the outskirts of the city, used by the potters as a place of deposit for the worthless, the unmentionable, and that which otherwise could not be disposed of.

It was the last synonym and symbol of the vile and forgotten. " Bury me in the potter's field! "

Most people strive for honors and clutch for recognition. But to seize is to lose. To demand is to invite refusal.

Often the only kind and loving words mentioned of those who hotly seek to annex and exploit are said at the funeral.

Then at the last the man is quiet, free from selfishness, hate, greed, jealousy, strife. He is at rest.

De mortuis nil nisi bonum. Speak no ill of the dead. And above the grave we erect a monument in memory of the departed, detailing his virtues, carving our compliments in cold granite. We speak well of the dead, because they have passed into the Land of Silence, and are powerless to injure or deprive us of that which we think is our own.

Jesus, dying as a felon, finds disgrace equalized by honor, and is laid to rest in the princely tomb of Joseph of Arimathæa, his body carefully wrapped in a perfumed winding-sheet, the stiffened limbs straightened by the tender, loving ministrations of the women who followed him afar. Dying among friends, the lowly who loved him, even though they did not understand him, Tolstoy did not ask even a " Christian burial."

His ambition and desire was to rest at last with the helpless, the friendless, the outcast, the unloved.

"Bury me in the potter's field!"

Only a man of commanding intellect, proudly secure in his claim on the gratitude of mankind, possessed of a serene, far-reaching world-vision, could have ever made such a request.

"What shall we do with you when you are dead?" asked the disciples of Socrates, just before the hemlock was passed to him. And the answer was, "Anything you wish, provided you can catch me!"

The body is not the man; it is only the husk of one.

The Crusaders—those fanatical myriads who went down through Europe to rescue the tomb of the Savior from the hands of the infidel would not have found the Savior, even though they had found the tomb where his outworn body was laid.

He is risen, he is not here.

He is risen, indeed!

What boots it where you lay my dissolving dust when it has played its part?

"Bury me in the potter's field!"

But if it is so done, the potter's field, where the body of Leo Tolstoy rests, will become a place of pilgrimage; and as the cross has become the symbol of redemption, and the scaffold was rendered glorious by Old John Brown, so will the potter's field be redeemed from the ignominy that has been its monopoly.

"Bury me in the potter's field!"

But the potter's field, by no possibility, can be the last resting-place of Leo Tolstoy.

It is easy to say that the economics of the man were absurd, and that, although he was a shoemaker, he never made a good pair of shoes. It is easy to declare that the peasantry did not need his help in plowing and scattering manure; but this does not dispose of the case. You can not lay his logic away in the dump and refuse of the potter's field, and thus dispose of the pulsing soul of a man made in the Image of his Maker.

Perhaps the methods of Tolstoy were mistaken, just as the methods of many reformers were wrong; but the heart of the man beat true to the tides of divinity that played through him.

To follow the literal example of the Man of Sorrows would never redeem the world. In order to bring us up to the line, he had to go beyond it.

" Bury me in the potter's field! "

The words are a rebuke, a chastening and a lashing with a whip of scorpions for every proud, arrogant, supercilious son of success who prides himself on his achievements. What are our railroads that girdle the continents with hoops of steel, our factories with their incense of commerce that obscures the sun, our buildings that scrape the sky, unless they be monuments to our humanity, our sympathy, our love!

What are our telegraph-lines that flash messages around the world in seconds, if the messages be not those of assurance and brotherhood! ❧ ❧

" Blessed are the feet of those who bring glad tidings." Even so. And business, which is the supplying of human wants, must be a consecrated thing, and not a selfish scramble for place, power and pelf ❧ ❧

Woe betide our railroads, if over them we do not transport the rarest, fairest jewels of human love, human sympathy, the mind that goes out to the mistaken, the erring, the foolish, the vicious, the absurd, the friendless. Can those who see the way clearly afford to scorn all those who have fallen and been mired in the mud, or gone down over the brink into hopeless darkness and night? ❧ ❧

" Whatsoever thy hand findeth to do, do it with thy might; for there is no work, nor device, nor knowledge, nor wisdom, in the grave whither thou goest."

At the last, the end of the race must be one. Death puts all on a parity. On Charon's toll there is no rebate. There are no palace-cars for the elect on their last little journey. Death plays no favorites. He can not be bribed, bought, coerced nor affrighted. His icy hand touches the strong, the purse-proud, the supercilious, and they are no more. In the tomb there is no high nor low, no rich nor poor, no learned, no illiterate, no virtuous, no vicious: we are all alike; we sleep the sleep of death together.

" Bury me in the potter's field! "

Leo Tolstoy is the greatest force for regeneration in the world today ❧ ❧

The brain of the man has ceased to vibrate, but his influence lives. He proclaimed, if any man ever did, the New·Time. He was never so much alive as he is now that he is dead.

He gave his life that Russia might live—Russia, the last, lingering, brain-bastile of the Western world.

Russia needed Tolstoy, this heroic figure, wearing peasant's garb, the garb of poverty, the garb of labor. Bare of head, bare of feet, he stands before our vision today, the proudest, strongest, sanest, most loving and loved man of modern times. Only pharisees fear him, only tyrants tremble at mention of his name.

It is not for us literally to imitate him, but it is our privilege to hearken to his appeal for the life that labors long and is kind; the life that gives much and demands little. For himself he asked not even the honor of a funeral over his lifeless dust, nor a word of appreciation, nor a song at twilight.

" Bury me in the potter's field! "

No man ever did, or could make such a request save one, whose memory lives enshrined in human hearts.

He has sent his soul into the Invisible, and being dead yet lives in minds made better.

" Bury me in the potter's field! "

Carl Stoeckel

ITCHFIELD COUNTY, Connecticut, is mostly made up of great green hills, that are speckled and freckled in the month of June with flowering laurel ﹌ ﹌

I think I never saw so much laurel, and such rollicking, happy, profuse, flaunting and unapologetic laurel as I saw dotting the hillsides as I rode from Torrington to Litchfield.

Laurel to me has been lacking; that is why I love it.

Some years ago The Roycrofters advertised laurel for poets, and then we also offered sage plants—and got many orders. But alas! we were short on sage and had no laurel, and so had to return the money ﹌ ﹌

But as I rode from Torrington to Litchfield, I was wondering why God had been so lavish with His laurel in this particular spot, when it came to me, all at once, that it was because Ol' John Brown was born at Torrington, and Litchfield was the birthplace of Henry Ward Beecher and Harriet Beecher Stowe.

⁋ John Brown walked out of Litchfield County a barefoot lad, slim and slender and serious, with a hook-nose, a protruding chin, and silent ways. It took him fifty years to arrive at Charlestown, West Virginia, and to reach the foot of the gallows. And on the coffin he saw resting there awaiting him, there were no wreaths of laurel. He climbed the steps with steady tread, his lips moved in prayer and then he said, " I am ready."

The noose was adjusted, the black cap was drawn down over his head and the sunlight shut out forever. The trap was sprung and the lean, bony body of Ol' John Brown swung and swirled between earth and sky.

Did that dispose of Ol' John Brown?

Oh, no, Terese, you can't dispose of a man with a mission that way. His soul goes marching on, even though his body lies mouldering, buried beneath a sour apple tree.

That is one of the things that the hemlock, cross, gibbet, gallows, guillotine, and fetters and fagots can not do—they can not stop great souls from marching on.

But curiously enough, the only souls that go marching on are those that throbbed with a yearning desire to make men free. There is only one thing worth living for, writing for, working for, dying for—and that is freedom.

On the way to the gallows, a mother held up her baby boy, and John Brown stopped long enough to kiss the cheek of the little black baby. John Brown could not take the baby in his arms, for his hands were tied behind his back. Happy l'il coon—Mammy's pet! kissed by Ol' John Brown on his way to launch his soul upon the River Styx. Did the black baby grow up and become a Sleeping-Car porter? If so, and I knew him, I would surprise him with a dollar the next time he pounds me on the back with the butt end of a whisk-broom.

To be kissed by a man who was on the way to the Ferry, going because he tried to make men free, is no small matter. It has been denied that John Brown kissed the black baby, but I guess, and I also reckon, that it was so, for I've seen that painting depicting the scene, by dear Tom Hovenden, who died rescuing a child from in front of a moving train.

John Brown was a fanatic, certainly, that is true. His methods were wrong—but the man himself was right, as every man is who lifts up his voice for freedom, and flings away his life that others may have liberty. The path of progress winds by the thorn-road, and all along one can trace it by the tracks of bleeding feet.

Through the generosity of Carl Stoeckel, the house where John Brown was born has been purchased and deeded to the people in perpetuity. It is a John Brown museum of many curious things, that once belonged to those Abolition Times. In this house is a bust of Brown, made by my St. Jerome, artist extraordinary, and Irish forever.

At Litchfield, set into a great granite boulder, is a medallion bas-relief showing the faces in profile of Henry Ward Beecher and his sister, Mrs. Stowe. Around the well-known faces are wreathed, in bronze, great clusters of laurel.

And when I saw the medallion, it was almost buried in living laurel, brought by myself and some more foolish pilgrims.

I wandered around the old village, knee-deep in its memories. I talked to the modest and scholarly man who is now pastor of the church where Lyman Beecher so long preached. " No, I do not call myself successor to Lyman Beecher," he said; " I am merely one of his followers." He showed me many books which once belonged to the Beechers and various manuscripts and notes for sermons. Also a big pewter gin-bottle which once stood behind the boxed-in pulpit and supplied inspiration for Lyman Beecher, " whose loins were wiser than his head," according to Carlos Martin ❧ ❧

It is through the influence of Carl Stoeckel more than any one else, that Litchfield County has awakened to the fact that there were giants in those days.

Not only that, but Stoeckel believes that there are giants and genii now, only we do not know how to play upon the reeds that will awaken them from their slumbers.

Stoeckel lives at Norfolk, a village not far from Torrington and Litchfield. If you are in an automobile you might go right through Norfolk, and never see it, it is that quiet, modest and unobtrusive. There is a fine old Colonial church there that lifts its steeple out of the mass of green. This church was built in Seventeen Hundred and Fifty, and I opine that Norfolk was about as big then as it is now. Norfolk is not a boom town, nor does Litchfield vie in enterprise with Wolfville and Red Dog. The old taverns of stage-coach times in Litchfield County have oats growing in the court-ways, and snag-toothed hostlers wait for coaches and outriders that never come. In some of these old road houses the smell o' hoss has been replaced with the odor of gasoline.

The village of Norfolk, to me, is a great place, because Mr. and Mrs. Stoeckel live there in a house built by Mrs. Stoeckel's grandfather in Seventeen Hundred and Eighty, four years after the Declaration was signed and John Hancock rode this way home to Boston, so to drink of the mineral spring waters and mitigate his gout.

Here hidden among the green hills, just for himself and his neighbors, Stoeckel has a choice little art gallery of paintings, all by American Artists.

Among these pictures is that famous one of John Brown on his way to be hanged, and several others by Tom Hovenden. Stoeckel did not tell me how much money he had put in pictures, but I know it is n't less than a hundred thousand dollars. His book-plate reads, " This book belongs to Carl Stoeckel and his friends." I asked him if he ever expected to make it read, " This book belongs to Carl Stoeckel, his friends and his enemies," and he said he might, only he did not care to recognize his enemies by assuming that they were such.

Oh, you say, if one is rich and owns a thousand acres, it is easy to be generous! In one sense this may be true, but how many rich people do you know who realize that wealth is a trust, and that to use it wisely and well for the benefit of society is both a privilege and a duty?

Mr. and Mrs. Stoeckel have organized a " Litchfield County Choral Society," and have set a thousand people in that one county singing. They hired a special teacher and sent this man from town to town getting people enthusiastic over vocal music. Clubs were organized, and then once a year there is a Sing-fest in the Music-Shed on the Stoeckel estate. If your salon is fine enough you may call it a " shed," just as you can call a skyscraper built of iron and marble, " The Rookery." This shed was designed by Rossiter the architect, who is a bird in his line. It seats two thousand people and is so compact and cozy that a conversational tone searches out every corner of it. Here come wending the pilgrims once a year to sing or listen, and then the whole town is taxed to give them food and shelter. Only two such singing centers do I know in America: one is Lindborg, Kansas, and the other is Bethlehem, Pennsylvania, where the good Pennsylvania Dutch love and honor the memory of Bach. ℂ Stoeckel traces to the same stock. His father was Gustave Stoeckel, the first Professor of Music at Yale. He was blown out of Germany by the social blizzard of Eighteen Hundred and Forty-nine, when for a like cause Richard Wagner was banished to exile, and the heart of Frederick Froebel was broken through the interdict that ignorance and tyranny placed upon the Kindergarten ❧ ❧

Carl Stoeckel has both his father's love of music and his love of liberty. John Brown did not care much for harmony as expressed in sweet sounds, and Lyman Beecher was too busy with the intricacies of theology, and bringing up his big family, to cultivate Bach and Buxtehude. But Carl Stoeckel sums up the virtues of all and each, and is redeeming at least one little corner of the world by the methods of Orpheus, Nordica, Schumann-Heink, Emma Eames, David Bispham, Walter Damrosch, Liza Lehmann, Horatio Parker, and many other great singers and players have gone there at the invitation and expense of Mr. Stoeckel and did good to the throngs who heard them.

And as if this were not enough, Mr. and Mrs. Stoeckel have made it possible for their friends and neighbors to hear speakers like Lyman Abbott, Rabbi Wise, Senator Lodge, Howard Griggs and dozens of other men of brains and phosphorus plus, who come here, give their message and go away full of delight and surprise that a man and woman should have the means, the inclination

and the generous heart o' them to bring the artistic and thinking
world to their door, just for the joy of doing good to their
neighbors ❧ ❧

And then the Stoeckels love birds as well as folks, for Stoeckel
up and buys a thousand volumes by my old friend Herbert K.
Job, the friend of the birds, and gives the beautiful books away
for missionary purposes.

No doubt but that Browning was partially right—" God's in His
Heaven," but fortunately, He does n't remain there all the time,
otherwise the sunsets would not lay golden robe upon the laurel
of Litchfield, and Mr. and Mrs. Stoeckel would " enjoy themselves" spending their money, instead of growing spiritually rich
by giving it away, filled with a passion for pictures, birds, music,
love, laurel and liberty.

David Swing

AVID SWING reached Chicago in Eighteen Hundred and Sixty-six. He had been receiving a salary of one thousand dollars a year as Professor of Philosophy at Miami College, Oxford, Ohio, and had been there for fifteen years. The college had two hundred and sixty students, and Professor Swing thought they needed him, but the College Board was not exactly of the same opinion. His management was not of the best, which in this case meant that he loved his pupils instead of disciplining them.

A former pupil in Chicago, knowing of this undertone of discontent, of which Professor Swing was beautifully innocent and delightfully ignorant, went to him and told him about the unkind things said of him.

Moreover, the facts were exaggerated, as the intent was to make it appear that the Professor was about to lose his place. Thus was he lured by a ruse to a new field, on a guarantee of at least as much as he was getting in the old.

Swing was always gullible. He was forever a countryman. " Long John" Wentworth once told Lyman Gage, a trustee of Swing's church, that the reason that the confidence men of Chicago did not take Swing in, being a stranger, was because they belonged to his church—an indelicate remark, but one containing enough of the saltness of time to save it.

Professor Swing was licensed to preach, just as most professors were who taught in Presbyterian colleges.

He was born in Cincinnati in Eighteen Hundred and Thirty, the son of a captain on an Ohio river stern-wheeler.

His father died during his childhood. In two years the mother married a worthy blacksmith in Clermont County, and here David was brought up, with all the stress and struggle that poverty and a short allowance of love lend. The experiences of youth, plus his temperament, wrote their lines upon his face, giving him that bold nose, the heavy jaw, the splendid teeth, the sad, dreamy eyes and the massive head that grew until he was sixty ✍ ✍

The mother who achieves does not often endow her children with the elements of success—she uses these in her own business. But the mother who is hungry to know, to do, to become, is apt to dower her sons with her unfulfilled desires, and they fight and succeed on the ruins of her failure.

We hear it said that virtue is not its own reward, and that innocence is no longer a sufficient shield.

David Swing, the blacksmith's helper, worked his way through Miami College, and then got stuck there, just because he was a star scholar. He was lured out into the cold and cruel world by good Chicago finesse and the love of a pupil, who with true Chicago insight saw that Professor Swing was getting pot-bound and must be rescued from himself.

So he came to Chicago, aged thirty-six, this beautiful, poetic soul, touched with divine mysticism. It was a noisy age and a noisy city, but beneath the noise and the dust, the bluster, brag and the brawl there was a current of deep, healthful, manly emotion ✍ ✍

For twenty-eight years Professor David Swing stood in the Cook County lime-light, reading his carefully written essays—one each Sunday—to throngs limited only by the size of the auditorium. The title of " Professor " followed him, kept alive by his former pupils, and finally developed from a term of endearment into a title ✍ ✍

Professor Swing became a Chicago asset, first criticized, doubted, assailed, then respected and beloved. He was always a curiosity, an attraction, and as people went to Brooklyn just to hear Beecher, so did they go to Chicago to hear David Swing.

Swing proves for us the power of personality. To set out with the intention of doing what he did would be fatal.

The man was bigger than his sermons—bigger than clothes, voice, gesture or spoken word. It is a wonderful thing to be a man, and I do not wonder that absolute honesty and simplicity have been confused with the Infinite, and worshiped as Deity incarnate. There is so little competition.

Swing's face was homely, his form angular, and his halting speech in any other man would have been unforgivable. He had a way of waiting for the right word—of packing a pause with feeling— which at first repelled and then attracted, because the auditor at last learned that always and forever the right word would come. It has been said that the heresy trial made Swing's fortune. The fact is that Swing had won before the Rev. Dr. Patton had made his fifty-seven accusations.

Let the minnows take heart—they are safe. Heresy-hunters are out for whales.

Patton, Editor of *The Interior*, paid Swing a great compliment when he opened up his siege-guns upon him.

The fire of Eighteen Hundred and Seventy-one had swept the home and church of Swing—all was in ashes.

One of the first good buildings erected after the fire was McVickar's Theater. This was secured for Professor Swing, and on each Sunday morning he stood on the stage and read in his own quiet, monotonous way his little essays to three thousand people, the exact seating capacity of the place.

I heard David Swing first in Eighteen Hundred and Seventy-two. I was sixteen years old and fresh from the farm. The theater building impressed me—its lavish magnificence, the glitter of glass, and the wonderful gas-jets, all ignited by electric sparks which jumped between little wires that ran over the burners! But the preacher did not measure up to the place. The surround-ings were so heavenly—this man was so homely. I was sure a mistake had been made, but my neighbor assured me it really was Professor Swing.

He had spoken for five minutes, and the absence of oratory had disappointed me. I was admiring the great chandelier and wishing they would turn the gas out and then relight it without the touch of human hands, when I heard the speaker drone, " I do not know where hell is—"

There was a pause, and then came this thunderbolt, tamed, quiet and subdued, " I do not know where heaven is. I do not know whether the devil is a person or an idea, but I think he is an idea, and not the idea of good men, either—" From that on I did not stray. I hung on every word. Down at Hudson there was a Baptist preacher who knew all about heaven, hell and the devil—at least he pretended that he did. But here was a man who convinced me that he was supremely great by the modest recital of a few things he did not know. The preacher who could afford to plead ignorance must have banked behind his ignorance a vast fund of knowledge. This was the way it impressed me. Swing won by his reserve— his battles were carried by the guns he never fired. His art was impressionistic, not realistic, and the accusation that his theology was the Holy Order of Divine Ambiguity had a certain point. When I sat that Sunday morning in the gaud and glitter of McVickar's Theater and heard this plain and simple man read his written essay, and so quietly turn the leaves, little did I realize that he was saying words for which men have paid the penalty of torch and fagot, and for which he, too, was to be tried on the same charges brought against Savonarola.

In fact, I had never then heard of Savonarola, otherwise I should have seen a resemblance in these men in both looks and mentality. The big nose, the thick lips, the indifference to praise or blame, the stubborn statement and restatement of facts obnoxious to the intrenched proud and popular—all in a voice exasperatingly gentle, courteous and suave!

Dr. Patton was the leading Presbyterian divine in Chicago. His paper, *The Interior,* expressed the policy of the denomination. As a speaker and a writer he was forceful, and if he did not always produce light he certainly generated caloric.

There is no doubt about the sincerity of Patton—had he been less sincere he would have been a safer, saner and more lovable character. He probably would have died for his faith, and also made others die for it.

But Patton was a man as well as a theologian, and so he never knew that his hatred of Swing arose from the fact that Swing had attained a popularity heretofore unknown to an American Presbyterian ♨ ♨

Patton pushed himself in the lime-light by persecuting Swing. That Swing should affiliate with the theater was also a cause of offense, for in the Seventies church-members eschewed the theater as a place of reproach and went to the play only when visiting in another town.

Patton argued that Swing was making this palace of sin popular; that people who went to hear Swing on Sunday, would find it easy to go on Monday to the same place and see John McCullough, Lawrence Barrett, or Charlotte Cushman.

Second, Patton contended that this popularity attained by Swing was not on account of his preaching Christianity, but because he assailed it and was supplying the enemies of true religion their ammunition ♨ ♨

In April, Eighteen Hundred and Seventy-four, formal written charges were laid before the Chicago Presbytery by Dr. Patton, and the fight was on.

Among the long list of accusations was the statement that Swing had denied the existence of a personal devil; that he had spoken well of John Stuart Mill; and that he had lectured for a Unitarian Church and donated his services, the money being used to paint said Unitarian Church.

The trial came in September, and continued for a month. Patton was on hand, bitter, obstinate, jealous, zealous, severe. He opened the proceedings each day with prayer. Swing was once invited to pray, but declined, which was argued into proof of his guilt. Swing was calm, smiling, gentle and patient. All Chicago was with Swing, save some of the Presbyterian faithful.

The evidence appears to us at this day and date as simply silly. Days were spent trying to show that Swing used the words Sin, Regeneration, Salvation, Communion, Redemption, Heaven, Hell, Devil and Faith in poetic ways not justified by one who believed in the Confession of Faith.

The verdict of the jury was " Not Proven." This meant on polling the jury that they believed the man guilty. With good Scotch persistency this jury, made up of course by Presbyterians, refused to reconsider and make it either " Guilty " or " Not Guilty." Patton asked them to make it " Guilty, with an appeal for clemency," but Swing's counsel refused to accept such a verdict. Patton then intimated that if Swing did not resign from the Presbyterian denomination, that he would strengthen the evidence and renew the charges.

Swing was tired of the fight, and resigned.

His own church, the Fourth Presbyterian, refused to give him up and proposed going out of the Presbytery in a body. Swing would not allow this to be done, as he declared his desire was not to break down or injure the denomination.

He proposed to quit preaching and go back to School-teaching. And then fifty leading business men, with good Chicago enterprise subscribed one thousand dollars each to a fund to keep David Swing in Chicago.

And there he remained for twenty years, a beacon light of poetic commonsense, sending his rays over the whole great city—over the whole West—an educator, and an inspirer: gentle, lovable, homely, beautiful, kindly, cultured David Swing!

Some men succeed by what they know; some by what they do; and a few by what they are. Swing prevailed because he was what he was—because his soul was mortised and tenoned in granite. When speaking or when silent, he supplied an atmosphere—and he who gets an atmosphere has won.

Swing was a great man—great in his freedom from whim, jealousy and pettiness; great in his charity, sympathy, patience, poise, unresentfulness, devotion and good will; great in his love and truth and beauty; great in his abiding faith in humanity and his unfaltering hope for the race. These things dowered him with that luminous serenity—that celestial sanity, that divine calm which made courage continual and culture a habit.

As a case of Swing's quality the following is typical:

" Literature is a gallery of spiritual ideals. There we meet Antigone and Hypatia and Evangeline; there we meet all the dream faces that ever stood before the soul of genius; there we meet Christ himself. It is that sacred mountain-top upon which humanity becomes transfigured and passes a few hours in shining garments for the body and in rapture for the soul. Man should expand these hours into days.

" All literature is one and the same thing—the utterance of the human heart. Let its name be Greek or German or English, it abounds in religion, pathos, sympathy, loving kindness. It has always been the portrait of man's inmost feelings. It is the beauty and wisdom of God attempting to reappear in the life of man ⚬

" The strings of the harp called 'letters' are attached to the heart. Touch literature anywhere and the human face flushes. At the mention of the word human life in sadness or joy comes before us. Helen of Troy poses in gracefulness; Andromache and her child part from Hector; the plumed Achilles hurries along in his chariot; the woods whisper; the nightingale sings; Dante and Beatrice appear; Hamlet acts; Ophelia dies; Paul and Virginia make of Mauritius a paradise and a grave; ' Little Dorrit ' is the beautiful dove of the prison; Fantine sleeps in a hillock which soft rain levels and flowers conceal. Literature is not learning. It is man's holiest passion.

" The Greek language is still almost an unsurpassed tongue. Eighteen hundred years have added only a small area to the scope of that vast speech. There is scarcely a question of the present day that was not reviewed by the Greek thinkers and stowed away in their manuscripts. Their essays on education, on health, on art, on amusements, on war, read almost as though they were written yesterday. Even that question which seems our own, the creation and property of this generation: whether women shall vote and follow many pursuits, is fully discussed in Plato's *Ideal Republic* ✒ ✒

" Literature is running in advance of the pulpit. There are three reasons for this leadership. The literary mind has all the world to draw from. If you will read Carlyle or Hugo or Motley and then read a volume of sermons you will note the great difference between the breadth of the two forms of reflection and speech. Literary men are released from the authority that dominates the fields of theology. Their style and subject-matter are as flexible as silk. Their harp not only plays many tunes but it is permitted to learn all the new pieces of music. High literature speaks for mankind, not for a sect or a party. What was the gospel of Browning? What that of Tennyson? What that of Emerson or Whittier? All are soldiers of Christ indeed, but of Christ incarnate in human character and human deeds.

" Education is the awakening of the heart, it is life, vitality, the arousing of the spirit. It is not the amassing of truth, like pouring water into a cistern; it is opening a spring. Education must not ruin itself by making the heart so sensitive that it faints at the sight of a criminal or a fool, or sit down and sulks, refusing to march any longer to the optimistic music. Christ-like is the culture which, seeing the griefs of the world, runs toward them

with healing in its heart, not away from them as Goethe did ♪•
" One of the most attractive passages of Virgil is where, at the
prayers of Juno, Æolus smote the hollow mountain with his spear
and let loose the winds, that they might sweep over the deep.
With a shout they leave the mountain and soon they are rolling
along before them great waves and are tossing the ships at sea.
Darkness and thunder hasten to mingle in the tumult. Not in
such terror but in such beauty are to be seen great intellectual
forces rushing forth from the mountain of learning. Influences
cross and recross our world wider and deeper and more powerful
than the winds of Æolus. The Classics tell of a lake called Avernus.
Avernus means birdless. Located in the crater of an extinct
volcano, a poisonous air, issuing from the infernal depths, hung
over the dark water and stupefied the sense of any bird that tried
to pass from shore to shore. Suddenly the wing became powerless
and the eagle with his pride and the nightingale with its song fell
into the waters of death. There is a lake of pleasure, of folly, of
sin, lying near the homes of the young. A deadly air hangs over
it. Forgetful or ignorant of its fatal vapors, the young spread their
wings upon its hither shore—those wings that were made in
heaven and good enough for angels. But at last their flight is
checked and they fall into the dark flood. The vast marble
quarries near old Athens were useless until Greek culture came,
Mount Pentelicus was composed wholly of white marble, the best
on our globe. Happy world when Greek genius touched it, spirit-
ualizing it, and made it tell the story of beauty and piety and
progress! Emblem, this, of our new mountain of marble—not
Pentelicus, but America—our liberty, our religion; a rich quarry,
but waiting for the touch of a new genius. What a land were this,
could it only be spiritualized!
" Washington came up from Virginia, Lincoln down from Illinois;
both came in one spotless honor, in one self-denial, in one patience
and labor, in one love of man; both came in the name of one

simple Christianity; both came breathing daily prayers to God, as though to picture a time when Virginia and Illinois, all the South and all the North, would be alike in love, in works, in religion, and in national fame. ' The flag is still there '—more glorious over the schoolhouse, the church, the home, and the farm, than over a red field of war.

" Let us learn to be content with what we have. Let us get rid of false estimates, set up all the higher ideals—a quiet home; vines of our own planting; a few books full of the inspiration of genius; a few friends worthy of being loved, and able to love us in return; a hundred innocent pleasures that bring no pain or remorse; a devotion to the right that will never swerve; a simple religion empty of all bigotry, full of trust and hope and love—and to such a philosophy this world will give up all the joy it has."

Epigrams from the sermons of David Swing:

It is easy to be either of two things when neither of the things can be understood.

He who travels much will soon have nothing to carry.

Men must be kind to young ideas; each truth is the presence of God ❧ ❧

Wealth is valuable only when it is a partner of the soul. Only the soul can be rich.

The baneful power of superstition lies in the fact that man is religious ❧ ❧

There is no competition in culture. The fine arts travel in a group. No art can endure isolation.

The wooden plow has not grown any more rapidly than the wooden god.

Each great false dogma acting a long time makes the kind of heart it needs.

The newspaper hauls the rough marble out of which the historian builds an eternal temple.

Of a deep and difficult problem we must, all things being equal, take the richer, sweeter side. It is always to believe the best. Many repetitions and much time do not confer truthfulness upon a remark ✒ ✒

If there is anything sweeter than honey it is the study of the bee. Egotism is the nomination and election and coronation of self. In ignorance minds may unite, but as they think they move towards variety. Thought opens like a fan; it never closes again ✒

Much is said about thought transference, but the more important question is the quality of the thought to be exchanged.

Truth, once uttered, strikes a vast sounding-board, and echoes forever ✒ ✒

There is a poverty which makes great men, hence the proverb, " The rot of riches and the push of poverty." But there is also a poverty out of whose sunless bog not even genius can climb. Great fortunes are like the clouds which the sun lifts from the sea to be poured out in rain and sent back to the sea. Wealth finally becomes commonwealth by a law of gravitation.

Extremists are valuable, because they render a truth conspicuous. They are the guides of the race.

Permanency is joined to change; antiquity seems a full partner of youth!

One can not see much until he has behind his eyes a cultured mind ✒ ✒

Capital is the storehouse of seeds, but labor is their field, their rain, and their summer-time.

The flag of union labor is too sacred to be carried by a fanatic, a criminal or a fool.

As Kidd was not a merchant, but a pirate, so much of our industry is not labor—it is martyrdom.

It is often necessary to endure evil in public affairs but it is disastrous to pretend that it is good.

The more an age seeks the one aim of amusement the less happy it will become.

Curious world—if a man does not work for pay he will starve; if he does his profession will starve.

Deer run, birds fly, and serpents crawl, but man talks himself forward ꙮ ꙮ

It is better to express ten ideas in one language than to utter one idea in ten languages.

The highest ideals are best reached from the humble home. To be too near any one thing—that is fanaticism.

The radicalism of a man is more often the eccentricity of doing a thing instead of talking about it.

A materialist is a soul domesticated out of its immortality.

Zululand is full of conservatives.

Andrew Lang

NDREW LANG is dead; but his spirit abides, and that gaiety, in which there was no bitterness, is his priceless legacy to us. Few men think sharply and crystallinely. This man did. His verse always fetches up. He tells us something because it is too good to keep.

The name of Andrew Lang adds another to the long list of Scotchmen who have dowered the world with ideas. Lang was born at Selkirk, in Eighteen Hundred Forty-four, and was therefore sixty-eight when he died—an age at which most men are just beginning to rest on their oars and take things easy after " life's fitful fever."

Old Ursa Major, it will be remembered, nursed a time-honored and utterly inexplicable grudge against the Scotch.

Yet, had it not been for one Scotchman, James Boswell, it is fairly certain that the name and fame of Doctor Johnson would have suffered partial, if not total, eclipse. For, as Macaulay aptly observed, most authors are known and read because of what they have written, whereas Johnson's personality is familiar to us even when, as is the case, his sonorous productions have been dumped into the capacious ragbag of old Father Kronos, and lost in the shuffle ✺ ✺

Boswell's famous *Life* is a brilliant portraiture of Johnson that can never fade.

As a boy, Andrew Lang attended school at the Edinburgh Academy ✺ ✺

Later he studied at Saint Andrew's University, and Balliol College, Oxford.

He was a classical scholar of profound erudition, and the wealth of literary and historical allusions in his writings reminds us of nothing so much as a page from Macaulay, who wrote things which, as he lightly averred, " every schoolboy " would recognize at once. And probably not since Macaulay have we had the unusual example of a man whose literary interests were so unlimited and all-inclusive.

Lang could not rest content with one widening vista, one horizon, one narrow sphere of activity; his vision must be bounded only by the universal horizon—he must touch life at all points and understand all its aspects.

Andrew Lang had drunk deep from the Pierian spring. His was true culture, if there is such a thing, and we believe there is. By some he has been accused of arrant dilettanteism, a charge implying what Lamb was pleased to call " superficial omniscience."

To others Lang represented a " syndicate," and the implication is a genuine compliment to the man's versatility.

Andrew Lang was thoroughly at home in a wide multiplicity of literary fields.

As an all-round litterateur he had, perhaps, no peer among modern writers.

He was a poet of marked ability, a first-class critic and book-reviewer, a graceful essayist, a faithful and charming translator, and an enthusiastic Classicist.

Not essentially and primarily a stylist, in the sense in which Walter Pater and Edgar Saltus, for instance, are stylists, he yet possessed an easy, fluent style which radiates through all his works and renders them eminently readable and entertaining. He commanded the Midas literary touch, and transmuted into purest gold whatever he committed to paper.

Despite the fact that he was a prodigally prolific penman, his works were endued with unfailing freshness and novelty of treatment, and were never tinctured with the odor of midnight oil ِ◌ ◌

I once attended a banquet in London where Andrew Lang had

been announced as the principal speaker. The chairman had introduced him. He arose, but before he could loosen up his oratorical batteries, the band started to play *Auld Lang Syne*. It was a " bromide," but Lang laughed with the rest of us, as if it were all new.

For years Lang contributed to the London *Daily News* signed reviews and editorials, quite equal in their way to the essays with which Addison and Steele popularized *The Spectator* in Queen Anne's time.

As a translator, Lang did notable work. His prose version of the *Iliad,* done in collaboration with Walter Leaf and E. Myers, and of the *Odyssey,* with Professor Butcher, are among the very finest translations with which Homer has been honored; and it was Matthew Arnold who declared that in the last analysis Homer was really untranslatable. Lang also translated the Idyllic Poets—Theocritus, Bion and Moschus—preserving the spirit of the originals most admirably. Likewise, his rendering of the old folk-yarn, *Aucassin and Nicolette,* is a classic.

His *Letters to Dead Authors* remind one somewhat of Walter Savage Landor's *Imaginary Conversations,* although they are free from the gross anachronisms that of necessity characterized the *Imaginary Conversations.*

Andrew Lang was always interested in anthropology and folk lore. He compiled a series of fairy-story books for children, named after the primary colors; as, the *Blue Fairy-Tale Book,* the *Red Fairy-Tale Book,* the *Green Fairy-Tale Book, Olive Fairy Book,* the *Red Book of Animals,* and so on.

In this work of compilation and editing he was ably assisted by his wife. It really takes two to do anything. Lang's work in this fascinating field, however, was not all in the nature of research. He wrote first-rate fairy-stories himself, such as *Prince Prigio, Prince Ricardo of Pantouflia,* and *Gold of Fairnilee.*

Andrew Lang was an ardent admirer of Joan of Arc, and he

defended her reputation with might and main in his famous controversy with Anatole France.

Merry Andrew was an able controversialist. He loved a goodly war of words as well as a Bull Moose—almost.

On any righteous occasion his hat was in the ring, but it was n't a sombrero—and it never needed reblocking at the conclusion of a bout of verbal fisticuffs.

Doctor Johnson could never brook rhetorical opposition. His friend Goldsmith used to say that Johnson was sure to get the better of an argument, even if he had to resort to a knotted bludgeon to do it.

Lang was scarcely that kind of a controversialist. His particular delight lay in vanquishing an adversary with the adversary's own favorite weapons—roasting him on his own gridiron, so to speak. Throughout his life Lang retained the Scotchman's fondness for outdoor life and the healthful habits of recreation. He was devoted to cricket, golf and fishing.

His classic introduction to *The Compleat Angler* would have delighted the heart of good old Izaak himself.

" For my part," he writes, " had I a river, I would gladly let all honest anglers that use the fly cast in it."

Some idea of the extent and variety of Lang's published works, can be had by running through the following list of titles, which, by the way, does not begin to exhaust the number of books bearing the impress of his genius: *Ballads and Verses Vain; Rhymes a la Mode; Books and Bookmen; Letters to Dead Authors; The Politics of Aristotle; Myth, Ritual and Religion; Letters on Literature; Lost Leaders; Life, Letters and Diaries of Sir Stafford Northcote; Angling Sketches; Essays in Little; Homer and the Epic; Cock Lane and Common Sense; The World's Desire; With H. Rider Haggard; The Homeric Hymns; A History of Scotland from the Roman Occupation; Magic and Religion; Alfred Tennyson; The Mystery of Mary Stuart; The Valet's Tragedy; John*

Knox and the Reformation; Homer and His Age; The Book of Dreams and Ghosts; Ballads and Lyrics of Old France; A Defense of Sir Walter Scott; The Border Minstrelsy; The Companions of Pickle; and many others, an enumeration of which would, in the language of an old chronicle, be " too tedious to mention."

Plutarch

F all the writers that lived in Rome in that wonderful time which we call the Age of Augustus, none now is so widely read as Plutarch. Plutarch was a farmer, a lecturer, and a Priest of Apollo. On investigation, I find that the office of Priest of Apollo corresponded about with that of an American Justice of the Peace.

Between pasture and palaver, Plutarch became rich, and owned an estate on the Isle of Malta. And there he lived when Paul was shipwrecked on his way to Rome.

Plutarch never mentions Paul, and Paul never quotes Plutarch. What a pity they did not meet!

Plutarch wrote the lives of twenty-three Romans, and compared each with some noted Greek, usually to the slight advantage of the Greek; for although Plutarch lived under the rule of Rome he was born in a province of Greece, and his heart was true to his own

It is quite probable that no sure-enough literary man—who knew he was one, and acknowledged it—would mention all of the many trifles which Plutarch brings to bear, shedding light on the subject

Whether Plutarch gathered some of these airy, fairy, pleasing tales of persiflage from his imagination or from the populace, is a question that is not worth while discussing. Practically all we know of the great men of Greece and Rome is what Plutarch tells us.

It is Plutarch's men who live and tread the boardwalk with us. the rest are dead ones, all.

The only men who endure are those whose lives are well launched on the inky wave. Heave ho!

Such trifles as Cæsar's remark that he was deaf in one ear; that

Pericles had a head like an onion; that Cleopatra employed a diver to attach a salt codfish to the hook and line of Mark Antony; that Socrates made pastoral calls on Aspasia; that Aspasia was very well acquainted with Cyrus, King of Persia, and from him gained her knowledge of statecraft—these are the things that endear Plutarch to us.

The things that should n't be told are the ones we want to hear. And these Plutarch discreetly gives us.

Shakespeare evidently knew Plutarch by heart; and it was the only book he knew. He was inspired more by Plutarch than by any other man who put pen to paper. It was the one book in which he dived and swam, in the days of his budding and impressionable youth; and most of his plots are those of Plutarch. Lives of great men all remind us—of a great many things that we would do if we were able.

Biography broadens the vision and allows us to live a thousand lives in one; for when we read the life of a great man we unconsciously put ourselves in his place, and we ourselves live his life over again.

We get the profit without the risk, the experience without the danger ﺱ ﺱ

It is Plutarch himself who says that tragedy is always pleasing to the onlooker, for the reason that he is inwardly congratulating himself that he is out of reach of danger.

Mark Twain said there are only six original stories, and four of these were unfit for ladies' ears, and that all six of these stories trace back to Rameses the Second, who had the felicity to live ninety-six years.

This remark of Mark Twain traces a direct pedigree to Plutarch, who said the Egyptians lived life in its every phase; and anything that could happen to any man or woman happened in Egypt, therefore all stories of misunderstandings, tragedies, comedies and such can be traced to Egypt.

Herbert Spencer was once beaten at billiards by a smart young man. Spencer proved his humanity by making a testy remark to this effect: " Young man, to play billiards well is an accomplishment, but to play billiards too well is proof of a misspent youth." In Plutarch's life of Pericles he has King Philip say to Alexander, " Are you not ashamed to sing so well ? "

And Antisthenes, when he was told that Ismenias played excellently upon the flute, answered, " Well he is good for nothing else; otherwise he would not have played so well."

The simple, plain commonsense of Plutarch is revealed in almost every page in such phrases as this: " Superstition causes nervous fear and much trembling of the limbs, and mental agitation. From signs and wonders seen in the skies, and the thunders and lightnings and eclipses and certain movements of the heavenly bodies, fear follows, but when understood these are found to be the harmonious workings of Nature. Therefore, the cure for fear and superstition is a love of all natural objects."

Could we now express the matter better?

Plutarch's writings have passed into the current coin of language. His works are literary legal tender, wherever thinkers meet. Whoever writes, and writes well, is debtor to Plutarch for much wit, wisdom and gentle philosophy.

Academic writing dies and is forgotten. Information about men, women and events, and that which relates to practical life, lives on and on.

Nine-tenths of all personal stories of the Greeks and Romans trace to Plutarch. For instance, when the mother of Themistocles was taunted with being an alien, she replied, " True, I am an alien, but my son is Themistocles."

When Themistocles was asked what he could do, he answered, " I can take an insignificant village and make of it a great city." This sounds like the remark of Augustus, " I found your city mud, and I left it marble."

The words of a man do not necessarily live; but the words put into his mouth by a ready writer often do:

The breezy, epigrammatic, friendly style of Plutarch appeals to people of every grade of intellect.

Note the following quotations from Plutarch, and see how this man has ingrained his words into all literature.

It was the saying of Bion that, though the boys throw stones at frogs in sport, yet the frogs do not die in sport, but in earnest. For to err in opinion, though it be not the part of wise men, is at least human.

Simonides calls painting silent poetry, and poetry speaking painting. These Macedonians are a rude and clownish people, that call a spade a spade.

Pythagoras, when he was asked what time was, answered that it was the soul of this world.

Philip being arbiter betwixt two wicked persons, he commanded one to fly out of Macedonia and the other to chase him.

After Cæsar routed Pharnaces Ponticus at the first assault, he wrote thus to his friends: " I came, I saw, I conquered."

When Demosthenes was asked what was the first part of oratory, he answered, " Action;" and which was the second, he replied, " Action;" and which was the third, he still answered " Action."

Cato said, " I had rather men should ask why my statue is not set up, than why it is."

The people of Asia were all slaves to one man, merely because they could not pronounce the word, No.

Alexander wept when he heard from Anaxarchus that there was an infinite number of worlds; and his friends asking him if any accident had befallen him, he returns this answer: " Do you not think it a matter worthy of lamentation that when there is such a vast multitude of them, we have not yet conquered one?"

Like the man who threw a stone at a bitch, but hit his stepmother, on which he exclaimed, " Not so bad!"

Pythias once, scoffing at Demosthenes, said that his arguments smelled of the lamp.

Demosthenes overcame and rendered more distinct his inarticulate and stammering pronunciation by speaking with pebbles in his mouth.

Cicero called Aristotle a river of flowing gold, and said of Plato's *Dialogues*, that if Jupiter were to speak, it would be in language like theirs.

Even a nod from a person who is esteemed is of more force than a thousand arguments or studied sentences from others.

It is a true proverb, that if you live with a lame man you will learn to halt. It is indeed a desirable thing to be well descended, but the glory belongs to our ancestors.

When Alexander asked Diogenes whether he wanted anything, " Yes," said he; " I would have you stay from between me and the sun."

When asked why he parted with his wife, Cæsar replied, " I wished my wife to be not so much as suspected."

For my part, I had rather be the first man among these fellows than the second man in Rome.

Go on, my friend, and fear nothing; you carry Cæsar and his fortunes in your boat.

Zeno first started that doctrine that knavery is the best defense against a knave.

Lysander said that the law spoke too softly to be heard in such a noise of war.

Agesilaus being invited once to hear a man who admirably imitated the nightingale, he declined, saying he had heard the nightingale itself.

The old proverb was now made good, " The mountain hath brought forth a mouse."

Pompey bade Sylla recollect that more worshiped the rising sun than the setting sun.

Whenever Alexander heard Philip had taken any town of importance, or won any signal victory, instead of rejoicing at it altogether, he would tell his companions that his father would anticipate everything, and leave him and them no opportunities of
performing great and illustrious actions.

He said that in his whole life he most repented of three things: one
was that he had trusted a secret to a woman; another, that he
went by water when he might have gone by land; the third, that
he had remained one whole day without doing any business of
moment. ᴈ ᴈ

For water continually dropping will wear hard rocks hollow.
To conduct great matters and never commit a fault is above the
force of human nature.

A Roman divorced from his wife, being highly blamed by his
friends, who demanded, " Was she not chaste? Was she not fair?
Was she not fruitful? " holding out his shoe, asked them whether
it was not new and well made. " Yet," added he, " none of you
can tell where it pinches me."

Archimedes had stated that, given the force, any given weight
might be moved; and even boasted that if there were another
earth, by going into it he could remove this.

Geographers crowd into their maps parts of the world which they
do not know about, adding notes in the margin to the effect that
beyond this lies nothing but sandy deserts full of wild beasts and
unapproachable bogs.

Anacharsis coming to Athens knocked at Solon's door, and told
that he, being a stranger, was come to be his guest, and contract
a friendship with him; and Solon replying, " It is better to make
friends at home." Anacharsis replied, " Then you that are at
home make friendship with me."

Themistocles said that he certainly could not make use of any
stringed instrument; could only, were a small and obscure city
put into his hands, make it great and glorious.

John Alexander Dowie

EV. John Alexander Dowie is sixty years old. He, himself, explains that there is no record of his birth, as his parents were not legally married. He says his mother was of a royal family, but he does not say who she was, nor does he give her name. As to his father, he knows nothing, but ventures the assertion that he fell in the charge of the Six Hundred at Balaklava, and so far, no one has successfully denied the assertion.

That Dowie does not know who his father was is shown in that he wrote to one John Murray Dowie, claiming him as his long-lost parent, and deposited himself as it were, on the John Murray Dowie doorstep. Later both parties swore halibis, and filed charges, disclaimers and demurrers.

At Madison Square Garden, John Alexander Dowie recently read some of the correspondence that passed between them and commented on it. Only he did not explain that all this happened many years ago. The "attack" on him by his ex-father, John Murray Dowie, won Elijah much sympathy, and needless to say no one went out during the explanation.

After revealing the mist that hovers over his begetting, Dowie advanced to the front of the stage, raised his white-robed arms aloft and cried, " Who cares who my parents were! I am the child of God, sent to deliver you a message! I am the son of God!" And the audience arose, and cried, " Amen, Amen!"

Strong men who have a blot on their 'scutcheons are very apt to be proud of it. It sets them apart, they are peculiar, born out of the needs of the hour. Dowie bided his time before proclaiming himself a reincarnation of Elijah; and those who have eyes to see and ears to hear, know full well that if the wind blows steadily from the right quarter, 'Lige will proclaim an Immaculate Conception. It is coming as sure as rent day, and the waiting is only to catch the Zionites in the proper mood. And if ever a child was born of one parent, I am perfectly willing to believe it could occur again. John Alexander Dowie is quite consistent.

In his article on Dowieism, Dr. Buckley said, " This man is a natural leader—he could succeed in anything he might undertake. Later on, Dr. Buckley says Dowie is a fraud, a fake, a hypocrite, a charlatan. To this, Dowie replies: " If I can succeed in anything I undertake, what is the necessity of my resorting to fraud?" And he scores thirteen.

The naturalist beholds unity in diversity, and the man of insight perceives that Dowie and Buckley are very much alike. That is why they so hate each other. Stags go after stags, and when a bull wants to fight, he selects a bull, or more properly, when he sees another bull, he wants to fight.

Dowie is on Buckley's preserve, as much as was the Wall Street beggar on Tom Lowry's, when he touched that worthy for a quarter. Buttinsky Buckley lowers his antlers, and makes you think of Landseer's engravings.

Dowie and Buckley are both orthodox Christians. Both believe that God made the world in six days and rested on the seventh; that he made a perfect man and woman, and was so mad because they disobeyed his orders that he cursed them both, and cursed all their descendants as well; that, as years went by, he grew madder and madder—more disappointed in his job, and finally drowned all the people on Earth, but eight. Later on, everybody got so tarnashun bad that even God himself could not forgive them, and so God's eldest Son came to Earth, born of a virgin, and was accepted as a sacrifice.

Everybody who believes in the Son will be saved, and those who do not will be lost.

Dowie and Buckley both believe all this; and while the fight between them is on, Rev. Dr. Henson leaps lightly into the ring and twists Dowie's tail so hard that Dowie quits B. Buckley, much to B. B.'s relief, and goes after Henson. Henson calls on Parkhurst for help, and as Henson retreats from the ring, Dowie dubs him a bath-tub Baptist, which means that Henson puts his candidates under water but once, while Dowie immerses his three times.

Between these four men there is small choice—all are needlessly orthodox, sublimely assertive, dictatorial, quibbling, full of J. Pluvius argument and East-wind reasons. They fling the rhetorical stinkpots with great accuracy, and when Dowie quotes from Buckley's argument against allowing women a vote in the General Conference, and a moment later shows how Parkhurst is the avowed enemy of the friendless woman, he gives one man a jolt on the jaw and the other a knock-out in the region of the solar plexus.

"My wife is my equal!" shouts Aleck, and caresses the matronly woman who sits near, on the platform. "Women vote in Zion; and I am the friend of every woman, good or bad; I am the friend of the evil-doer, not his enemy; I am the brother of the proscribed and the outcast; I am the brother of my people; I am the Father of my people; I am the friend of my people!" rings the voice of Dowie, as he waves his arms in the direction of his choir, where sit dozens of black men and women, mingled with the whites. And the hosts of Zion lift their banners aloft and cry, "Amen! Amen!" ✒ ✒

Dowie's methods are simply those of Benjamin Fay Mills, before he experienced a change of heart and became a Philistine. Dowie is just like the professional evangelists—he knows his people and he works upon them, and no doubt they react upon him. No Christian can reasonably criticize him, excepting as a matter of syntax, prosody and etiquette.

Whenever a man like Dowie appears, his performances are not so much proof of his own power, as they are a revelation of the stupidity of his followers. The weaknesses of the many make the leader possible—and the man who craves disciples and wants followers is always more or less of a charlatan. The man of genuine worth and insight wants to be himself; and he wants others to be themselves, also. Discipleship is a degenerating process to all parties concerned. People who are able to do their own thinking should not allow others to do it for them, lest their think pores close &~ &~

Religion should be a matter of individual experience. Religious denominations that own property, pay salaries, collect funds; that dictate the conduct of their believers and supervise their actions, are very much alike. Dowie's religion is the manifestation of a very old idea—the supremacy of the priest, the temporal power of the pope. Dowie supplies the creed and he furnishes employment, which is better than the others do. He has his uniformed soldiers to enforce his orders, and all who do not obey absolutely have to hike. If Dowie had the power, he would have stocks, ducking-stool, whipping-post and gallows—all these things for the good of the individual and the glory of Zion.

A man in the back part of the hall calls, " louder! "

Dowie stops instantly and shouts, " Guard, put that man out! " And not a wheel turns until the man is evicted.

People in the gallery hang their overcoats and wraps over the gallery railing. Dowie orders in a voice of wrath, " Remove those rags! " Two men sheepishly haul in their wardrobes—the rest of the wraps remain. " Remove the rags—they will drop soon, and will start a panic here—pull in the ulsters! " Four big guards walk toward the offenders and the coats are removed. " Sing Five Sixty-Two," rings out the shrill voice of Elijah. And the song is sung with a vim that shakes the rafters.

Out in California I saw men shoveling oranges into an immense revolving seive. Down below were eight different bins, and a certain size of orange gravitated without fail into a certain bin.

Each denomination catches a certain size and shape of head. A dogmatic religion is a plan for supplying a religious belief done up in cans. It saves you the necessity of evolving your own—somebody has done the work for you.

A man who can think for himself has no business inside of a denomination ✒ ✒

Should he stray into a sect, he will soon find his error and get out. Or, if he stays inside and tries to revise and reform the sect, he will be put out. Zionism has her guards ready to bounce the intruder ✒ ✒

Believe and pay—that is all you have to do.

Love, art and religion all trace to the same source in our natures—where one begins and the other leaves off, no man can say. But this I believe is true: If you are in love with your work, your sense of sublimity will find sufficient gratification there, and you will have no use for Dowie, Parkhurst, Buckley, Henson, or Pope Pius. All these are middlemen—if you are big enough, and you will go to God direct, and you will find him everywhere; and especially wherever men are doing good and useful work, that place to you will be a sacred chancel.

When the Mennonites and Quakers were forced to give up their preachers and churches or go to the stake, they discovered they could do without priests, and that piety still existed in their hearts. Since then they have had no professional priesthood.

" When the psalm sings instead of the singer,
When the script preaches instead of the preacher,
When the pulpit descends and goes instead of the carver that
 carved the supporting desk,
When I can touch the body of books by night or by day, and
 when they touch my body back again,
When a university course convinces like a slumbering woman
 and child convince,

When the minted gold in the vault smiles like the night-watch-
    man's daughter,
When warranted deeds loaf in chairs opposite and are my friendly
    companions,
I intend to reach them my hand, and make as much of them as
    I do of men and women like you."

A formal religion is an awful loss to the world in that it excites
the sense of sublimity, and then grounds the wires. The divine
passion leads to a prie-dieu when it should lead you to a work-
bench or to an easel.

Just as long as men are slaves to fear, somebody will give them
peace by a promise of sweet rest in heaven. If you have no home
here, Dowie's promise of a mansion in the skies is alluring.
Dowie appeals to the bereft, the oppressed, the persecuted, the
defenceless—those who are the unfittest. His glowing health and
his fighting attitude fixes their attention. Dowie has sublime
faith in himself, and we always believe in the man who believes
in himself. Dowie's people confuse Dowie with God, and God to
them is merely Dowie with whiskers a trifle longer.

Five years ago a Buffalo banker told me that Dowie's financial
schemes could not last much longer—the Chicago bankers were
going to throw him out. Since that prophecy the Buffalo banker
has busted, and although the Chicago bankers threw Dowie out,
he turned a handspring and fell on his feet.

The New York papers that came out in headlines with the declaration that Dowie was on the verge of bankruptcy, the next day
contained the news that Mrs. Dowie had sailed for Australia
with a chest containing seven million dollars in gold.

Just now we hear of his financial difficulties: accommodation
extended to others he can not get, but Dowieism will not go down
as long as Dowie lives. New York people send missionaries to
China; Dowie sends missionaries to New York.

The president of the Oneida Community once said: "Give me the charge of thirty strong men and women of average intelligence or three hundred, or three thousand, and I can make all rich." This man's father did the trick—he simply set the people to work, regulated their lives, including their love affairs, and took charge of their savings, and all grew rich. And the present president of the Oneida Community is the son of his father.

Dowie sets his people to work. They cut out tobacco, beer, oysters and pork. They live modestly, but have enough. Dowie takes charge of their savings, and all are prosperous. There is no poverty in Zion, and there is no poverty anywhere where people work and where there is no strong drink and tobacco.

Dowie is ahead of Buckley and Parkhurst there. Presbyterianism and Methodism do not brand smoking and beer-drinking as deadly sins. Oysters are supposed to favor peterosity, and meat heats the blood and also tends to filidoscacity; so Dowie eschews the one, and eliminates the other as much as he can.

In Zion there is no waste—all work and work to a purpose. The three thousand Zionites who went to New York, paid their own way. The round trip was twenty dollars—they had the money —and those who worked in New York City got paid for it. Dowieism is n't bad—it is good for those who want it.

When they get ready for a better religion, they will moult Dowie, as the bird sheds its feathers when it begins to grow a better plumage ☙ ☙

Parkhurst is the antidote for Dowie; Buckley dilutes both, while Mary Baker Eddy neutralizes all, as we neutralize strychnine down to a useful stimulant for those who think they need it. If any one of these denominations had the power, they would place me where I would ornament the stocks; have Ali Baba hanged in chains before day-dawn; Hugh Pentecost's ears would be cut off and Felix Adler would be treated as thinking Jews have usually been treated.

Let's all thank God for the opposition of forces that makes life and liberty possible. Before Martin Luther's time, Rome stood as a solid, unbroken sheet of ice; the good ship, Free Speech, could not navigate, and progress was impossible. Savonarola, Erasmus, Wyclif, Huss, Tyndale, Ridley and Latimer had tried to open the channel, and all had paid the penalty. Between the various denominations and sects there is small choice, but all are useful or they would not exist. They minister to the people who need intellectual crutches, and the number of them competing with each other, grinding on each other, heaving, sinking, seething and struggling, keep the ice broken up so Washington can cross the Delaware.

The simple truth is, Dowie is a very much better man than any of these microbes who berate him.

Dowie is a bigger man than Dowieism—bigger far than Zion City. He is big enough to know his people, and the mesh he uses is just the right size to catch the fish he wants to catch—the rest go through or bound over the bobbers, and the bullheads, as usual, stick to the mud and pass under. Dowie is all right—or partially so. There is not a single phase of Dowieism that is not recognized and preached by some one of the Eminently Respectable and Prominent Cults. Yet the members of the Cults aforesaid agree, like the Chicago papers, in nothing but this: a hatred and contempt for Dowie.

Dowie's weekly paper is a bouquet of violets compared with any issue of any daily newspaper in Chicago. These papers with their details of woe, grime, crime, blood and death, to say nothing of personals and medical advertisements that no gentleman dare read aloud, all claim the privilege of referring to Dowie as a toilet room rodent.

Beware of the paper or person that mud-balls people. The epithet a man applies to another usually fits himself best. We describe that which we see.

All the people who disparage Dowie you will find are in competition with Dowie.

Dowie urges his people not to buy nor read the Chicago daily papers. All wise men must admit that this is good advice; and it succeeds in drawing the fire of the enemy. We are advertised by our rabid enemies no less than by our loving friends.

Dowie buys two thousand acres of land and lays it out in town lots. Straightway the virtuous dealers in Cook County swamp are terribly shocked that a preacher should combine business with religion.

Dowie starts a savings bank and pays six per cent on deposits. The Chicago Clearing House refuses to do business with him, and all the jonfarsons and leeches cry out in alarm for fear the dear people will be victimized; the Chicago Board of Trade cautions the public to 'ware o' Dowie; and Cornwell, financial expert, explains that six per cent means discord in the music of the spheres. All this with the potent fact before them that banks derive their income on what their money earns, while Dowie has an income outside of his banking that would allow him to pay twelve per cent interest and still hold his reserve of two millions good ⌘ ⌘

Judge Tuley, a church member says, " The chief asset of Dowie-ism is human credulity," a remark that sounds singularly like Voltaire's. " The chief asset of the Christian religion is superstition." Indeed, Judge Tuley's remark applies to every religion, good or bad. Ex-Secretary Gage of Chicago said in his last official report, " The commerce of the world is carried on through faith." Credulity is a good thing.

Dowie has the emotionalism of the Methodists, but they repudiate him because, they say, " He believes in Christian Science." Our Mary Baker G. Eddy friends say he is full of " error " in that he is a Methodist. The doctors hate him because he cures folks without their help. The Presbyterians despise him because he has stolen their faith. The Baptists scorn him because he is so much like them. The Unitarians will have none of him because he is orthodox. The High-Church folks ignore him because he combines their ritual with his own. The M. E. Church South cut him because he does not draw the color line. The Prohibitionists and W. C. T. U. refuse to affiliate with him because he includes tobacco, oysters and pork among the unclean and forbidden things. The Theosophists and Reincarnationists repudiate him because he is a Christian.

Through a sudden and terrible accident, a few weeks ago, the daughter of John Alex. Dowie was fatally injured. Half of the surface of her body was burned to a crisp—death was inevitable. In a few hours she passed away.

I need not dwell upon the place which a beautiful and intellectual young woman of twenty-three fills in the heart of a father of sixty. The feeling is something essentially loverlike—Shakespeare has hinted at the tenderness of the relation in the story of King Lear and his daughter Cordelia.

A thousand people attended the funeral, and standing by the open grave Dowie delivered an address—an address tragically, fearfully self-contained, with that reserve which only a sorrow too great for tears can know. The breaking heart of the man would have hidden itself away, but the public position of all concerned made a private funeral out of the question. No daily paper mentioned the address—no religious periodical quoted it. I give the following short extract from the stricken parent's words: She said, " Father, will it be long? "

I said, " Not long, dear."

" Lord, take me," she said.

And we prayed for it at last, because we could not bear to see her suffer any more.

Then I sang, " Lead Kindly Light."

Then we repeated the Shepherd Psalm:

" The Lord is my Shepherd "—She said it so strongly—" I shall not want. He maketh me to lie down in green pastures; He leadeth me beside the still waters."

I could hear her murmur, " Beside the still waters."

The still waters were there. She was beginning to see the green pastures ❧ ❧

" Yea, though I walk through the Valley of the Shadow of Death, I will fear no evil."

And that was all we could hear.

She closed her lids and was sleeping.

I would let none weep.

She opened her eyes and smiled and then she slept.

I sang to her the song I have sung so many times to those who were sleeping in Jesus, and when I had finished she departed without a sigh, without a tremor.

My hand was upon her head and my hand was upon her body and I felt no quiver.

And now I stand here and I have no daughter on earth.

I had only one. You must all be my daughters, daughters of Zion. I have no daughter.

Admiral Togo

DMIRAL TOGO recently made a tour through the United States as a guest of the Government. The Admiral has done something beside supplying a name for one hundred thousand dogs. Togo is five feet two inches high, and weighs one hundred twenty pounds in the shade. He belongs to the Samurai caste, that is, the aristocratic fighting class. Bred for war, he is in fact the great original boy scout. The Samurai stand for the entire list of military virtues which Thompson Seton has put before the world so vividly; that is to say, loyalty, truthfulness, honor, integrity, health, self-reliance, and the silent and prompt obedience of orders.

America as a country suffers from the proclivities of the genus buckwheat—that is, the native villager, who talks all day to everybody on any subject and seldom says anything. This kind of man lives either in his garret or in his sub-cellar, and a good deal of the time is talking through his roof.

All people who revel, roll and wallow in their emotions are cast down in defeat and exultant in victory. The Samurai accept everything as it comes and count it good—even death itself. And life itself is a small affair when it comes to giving it away in a good cause. This gives you a type of man that is pretty nearly invincible. He can not be stampeded, bribed, bought or panic-stricken ๑ ๑

When Togo was asked if a fighting mental attitude did not tend to inefficiency in practical affairs, a slight ghost of a smile passed over his stolid face and he replied: " Life itself is a fight. Our enemies are inertia, indifference, selfishness, and love of ease and pleasure. To overcome these enemies requires the fighting attitude. When a man ceases to fight he is a dead one. The same virtues that cause a man to succeed in war when applied to business will make him a success there. The Samurai now are going into trade. The aristocracy of idleness is passing from Japan, just as it is passing from America. We are becoming a world of workers; and we discover that the qualities which make a good soldier also evolve a good citizen."

Here Togo relaxed into his habitual and becoming silence. It was a dignified and beautiful silence, self-sustained and self-reliant ᴈ ᴈ

While the man is in his sixties, he looks forty; and it is this absence of nerves, the quiet physically economic attitude, that saves him.

To lose your temper, to fling epithets, to raise your voice, are to Togo all trails to Tophet.

It is coming across the best minds in America that if we had sent missionaries to Japan in order to learn of the Japanese, instead of trying to convert them to our social and religious system, it would have been just as well for the Japanese and a good deal better for us.

Nations must get acquainted with one another, just as individuals should, in order to have a fair and proper understanding. Electricity and quick transportation have practically made the world one.

Once, in the Mitre Tavern in London, Doctor Johnson and little Oliver Goldsmith sat at a table. A man came in and took his seat in an opposite corner. Johnson leaned over and said to little Oliver, " Goldie, I hate that man."

And Goldie answered, "Who is he?"

Doctor Johnson rolled and rocked in his seat, sputtered, winked, and then said, " Goldie, I do not know who that man is; but if I knew him I would love him."

Most of the hate of the world has come through not knowing people ᴈ ᴈ

The quiet intelligence, appreciation and courtesy of Togo and his suite have been a great enlightener to a vast number of people in high places.

Togo looks like a quail in a stubble-field. There is nothing of the big, pompous or wonderful in the man. He does not travel with a brass band. He accepts everything, is grateful for everything, sees no slights, expects no insults.

Togo was able to withstand the cannon-balls of the Russians, but Boston codfish-balls and a few volleys of beans laid him low. The only criticism the Admiral had to offer on America was a gentle suggestion that banquets belong to the age of the savage, and he was slightly surprised that we placed so much emphasis on our eating ❧ ❧

Togo was deeply interested in the Arbitration Treaty, signed between the United States and Great Britain and the United States and France. He said that he proposed to lay the matter before his own Government when he returned, and he believed it was very probable that a similar treaty would be signed between America and Japan.

Madame Montessori

NOT long ago, in Chicago, I attended a monthly meeting of school principals.

On this particular occasion, an address was given by Ella Flagg Young on the subject of "The Ungraded School."

In these schools, instead of placing so much stress on books and memorization of rules, the children are simply kept employed, and their occupation is changed from time to time before any one thing becomes monotonous or wearisome.

It was found that many of the children were suffering from malnutrition, and it was believed that many of their mental difficulties arose from physical ills.

A luncheon was provided in the middle of the morning, and the subject of dietetics and oral righteousness had close attention.

¶ Attached to these schools was a supervised playground, and in some instances school-gardens. Much of the time was spent out of doors

" It was discovered," said Mrs. Young, " that it required a better quality of teacher in this work than in teaching children who were normal."

Mrs. Young ended her very interesting talk with the wonder why the same methods, the same care, and the same fine insight into the needs of the pupil could not be brought to bear in all the schools of Chicago, instead of favoring the children who were regarded as unfit.

Doctor Marie Montessori is an Italian schoolteacher. Her first business was that of a nurse.

She held a government position and had the care of defective children

This brought the question of education sharply before her mind. The conventional methods not being satisfactory for abnormal

children she devised a method of her own. A little later it came to
her as a great gleam of light that her methods in teaching
abnormal pupils was the best possible plan also for the normal.
Doctor Montessori has now established in Italy, under Government supervision, a chain of schools in which her methods are
being carried out. It promises to be as big an evolution in school-
teaching as was worked out by Arnold of Rugby—and then died
with him. Doctor Montessori builds on the work of Froebel and
Pestalozzi. Pestalozzi was a Swiss, born in Seventeen Hundred
Forty-six and dying in Eighteen Hundred Twenty-seven. Froebel
was a German, born in Seventeen Hundred Eighty-two and dying
in Eighteen Hundred Fifty-two.

The work of both these masters was carried on independently of
the government, and both were visited with the hostility of the
ruling classes.

Froebel and Pestalozzi held to the divinity of the child; and while
they did not openly make war on the dogma known as " Total
Depravity," yet most certainly they never repeated the dictum
that the child was conceived in sin and born in iniquity.

Within a few years the entire civilized world has ceased the whip-
ping and beating of children, and this through the acceptance of
the doctrines of Froebel and Pestalozzi. This is the way that
social evolution takes place—by being accepted by those who
successfully fought it.

First, we say the thing is contrary to the Bible.

Next, we say it makes no difference one way or the other.

Third, we say we always believed it.

Men fight for a thing and lose, and the men they fought take up
the issue that they opposed, and carry it to victory under another
name ๑๑ ๑๑

Switzerland and Germany are now taking the lead in matters of
education; and Doctor Montessori, Swiss by parentage and
Catholic by birth, is uniting with the government to bring about

the things that the governments of Italy, Switzerland and Germany once fiercely combated.

The primal care of Doctor Montessori is for the health of the child. She quotes Herbert Spencer, " The first requisite is to be a good animal." She recognizes that the child has to pass through the same stages that nations pass through. The child has the savage, the nomadic, the agricultural, and the commercial periods. " Happiness," says Doctor Montessori, " is the greatest asset in life."

Happy people are those who are employed in useful and congenial occupations, and such are always well.

The business of Doctor Montessori in her schools is to keep the children pleasurably employed.

She gives the child the right to freely explore its environment. Every baby, as soon as it can creep, begins to investigate. It tests everything, tastes everything, tries everything, and makes itself acquainted with everything in the room. Then it travels to other rooms. It goes upstairs, and perhaps rolls downstairs. But again it tries. There is something up there that it wants to see. Children want to climb ladders, climb trees, climb heights. They want to see the top of the house, as well as the cellar. This natural bent of curiosity and desire to know, to see, to understand, is the basis of education.

Doctor Montessori never uses a negative except in cases of positive vice or present danger. She never rebukes a child for rudeness or impoliteness. If the child is doing the wrong thing, she gently encourages it to do something else. If the child wants to stand on a chair in order to see out of the window, by all means she lets the child work out his own problem.

If there is a band playing on the street, all of her children get up and run to see the band and hear the music. The impulse to know what is being done, to be familiar with your surroundings, is one of the elements of power.

It may be regarded as strange to some to know that various parochial schools are adopting the Montessori methods, putting in school-gardens with out-of-door schoolrooms, and "busy work." It will appeal to some as a new criticism when the Church declares that the public schools are not progressive. The Montessori System is practically the Modern School of Francisco Ferrer. It is only a question of time before Ferrer will be canonized ❧ ❧

In a Montessori School, the children work, talk, play, prepare their meals, make their plans, learn to write incidentally and accidentally through desire and not through compulsion. Doctor Montessori takes children from two years old and up. She utilizes the services of the older children in caring for the young—thus carrying out Froebel's idea of the "Little Other Mothers." This is the natural way, in a big family where there are no servants, for there the older children care for the younger ones. Thus they get an education out of their work, at their work, which is the natural way, after all.

Walt Mason

ICHELANGELO and Leonardo da Vinci were born within a few miles of each other, and at about the same time.

Four hundred years have passed, and the whole whizzing Planet has not produced a single man to equal either Michael or Leonardo in their respective lines. They are still like that honest man in Peoria—without competition.

In Emporia, Kansas, where the Santa Fe stops for meals, live two world-beaters who work in one shop. These men are Will Allen White and Walt Mason.

White, he got a-going first. He has a distinct literary style, and the reason is because he has a distinct mental make-up. His cosmic make-ready is peculiar, individual and incisive.

He sees things at his own angle and detects differences which the rest of us discover for ourselves after he has told us. He has compared society in Emporia to society in Gotham in a way that puts Joe Addison and Dick Steele in the line for second money. His wit is sure but unlike that of Swift, it is kindly.

And now comes the janitor and general utility man, of the Emporia *Gazette,* Walt Mason, and puts White on the bum—almost. White has three names like Henry Cabot Lodge, and the writers who warm the benches on Boston Common. Walt is as democratic as if he came from Horace Traubel's town. He is full of wise saws, modern instances and prunes, and his wit burbles and gurgles like a Kansas creek where the bullheads gambol. Walt Whitman wrote poetry that did not rhyme; Walt Mason writes prose that does.

Here Walt has opened up a brand-new vein of literary pay gravel. The stuff was first run by White in the *Gazette* as padding. Soon people began to talk about it. Then country editors copied it. Next the New York *Sun* stole it. Now syndicates ask for it, because readers want it.

One of these little—'er—ah—poemettes, read on the trolley going down town in the morning, makes you smile all day. You clip it and pass it along, and the next morning scan your paper for another ఴ ఴ

'T is a busy age, my lords. The turgid and profound are good to stuff bustles, and to recommend. But the stuff we read must be short, sharp, good-natured and brief.

We have heard that there is nothing new in literature; that is: on the bookish bourse there is nothing doing, but here walks in a fellow out of a Fred Harvey biscuit bazaar at Emporia, and puts Boston to the bad. What right has a man in Emporia to have thoughts and to be a stylist, anyway!

They say that Walt is making a small barrel of money. My hope is that he will not make too much. As it is, he is a generous, human, charming and chummy gentleman, with baggy breeches, besmeared with printers' ink, and all unconscious that he has done anything. He prides himself on his editorials treating of economics and sociology. The poemines he calls pot-boilers. I think that they are much more. Walt Mason is a big man, who does good things so simply that we say " anybody can write like that." Suppose you try it?

Walt shows you things in right proportion, corrects your perspective and lends a right focus. His stuff exercises your liver by making you laugh. The old Bible prophets were beiliakers—the modern prophet is a working man, and a humorist.

Such is Walt Mason of Emporia.

I present a few specimen bricks by way of sample.

Sometimes—although of course it 's nonsense—your uncle wildly yearns, to be like all those sable Johnsons, who punish gents named Burns, and who thenceforward roll in rhino, and still for more insist; and then your uncle murmurs: " I know—the greatest gift's a Fist." Sometimes—of course it does n't matter—he blows a half a buck, to hear some big spellbinder, in language run amuck; the orator seems fat and wealthy, and talks in many tongues; and uncle says: " His graft is healthy—the greatest gift is Lungs." Your uncle likes athletic matches, adores the Marathon; and there in ecstasy he watches tired runners totter on; and when the winning one is given bouquets instead of eggs, to this conclusion uncle 's driven: " The greatest gift is Legs."

O let us toast, in many flagons, the noble fleet of water wagons, that journeyed proudly home! In vain the muse with language wrestles to find bouquets that fit those vessels, the monarchs of the foam! The Critic said, before they started, that all their joints would soon be parted, and all their rivets shrunk; their armor-plate was made of leather, their decks were merely glued together, and all their guns were junk. The Critic (was n't he a bounder?) predicted that the ships would flounder, when they encountered spray; the beams were rotten as the armor; the Admiral was but a farmer, who should be pitching hay.
Now chroniclers shall tell the story of how our ships in pomp and glory, went sailing round the globe; but where 's the prophet, sick and ailing, who threw a fit before the sailing, and howled and tore his robe?

If you should chance to mention Death, most men will have a grouch; and yet to die is nothing more than going to your couch, when you have done your little stunt, performed the evening chores, wound up the clock, blown out the light, and put the cat outdoors. The good old world jogged smoothly on before you had your fling; and it will jog as smoothly on when you have cashed your string.
King Death himself is good and kind; he always does his best to

sooth the heart that 's sorrowful, and give the weary rest; but there are evils in his train that daunt the stoutest soul, and one of them may serve to end this cheerful rigmarole. I always have a haunting dread that when I come to die, the papers of the town will tell how some insurance guy, paid up the money that was due to weeping kin of mine, before the funeral procesh had fallen out of line; and thus they 'll use me for an ad, some Old Line Life to boom, before I 've had a chance to get acquainted with my tomb!

Said Abe (the Nation's greatest man): " I do the very best I can; and if my course is erring quite, no argument can make it right, and if in righteousness I 'm strong, no sophistry can make it wrong; so, be the critic, foe or friend, I ll do my best until the end." The fact is galling to relate, but some of us can not be great; our ways obscure we all have to tread, and hustle for our daily bread; our pictures never may be seen in Who 's Who book, or magazine; but if, upon the Day of Doom, we came cavorting from the tomb when sounds the final trumpet's notes—we won't be herded with the goats—if we can say (and make it good): " We always did the best we could!"

In that hour of supremely quiet, when the dusk and darkness blend, and the sordid strife and riot of the day are at an end; when the bawling and the screaming of the mart have died away, then I like to lie a-dreaming of my castles in Cathay. I would roam in flowery spaces watered by the fabled streams, I would travel starry spaces on the winged feet of dreams; I would float across the ages to a more heroic time, when inspired were all ages, and the warriors sublime. At that hour supremely pleasing, dreams are all knocked galley west, by the phonograph that 's wheezing: " Birdie, Dear, I Love You Best."

If old Jim Riley came to town, to read a bundle of his rhyme, I
guess you could n't hold me down— I 'd want to hear him every
time. I would n't heed the tempest's shriek; I 'd walk ten miles
and not complain, to hear Jim Hoosier Riley speak. But I would
not go round a block to see a statesman saw the air, to hear a
spellbinder talk, like a faker at the country fair. For statesmen are
as thick as fleas, and poets, they are far between; one song that
lingers on the breeze is worth a million yawps, I ween. If John
McCutcheon came to town, to make some pictures on the wall,
I 'd tear the whole blamed door—way down, to be the first one
in the hall; you could n't keep me in my bed if I was dying there
with the croup; the push would find me at the head of the procession, with a whoop. But I won't push my fat old frame across
a dozen yards of bricks, to list to men whose only fame is based on
pull and politics.

Golden Rule Jones

Come lovely and soothing Death,
Undulate round the world, serenely arriving, arriving
In the day, in the night, to all, to each,
Sooner or later, delicate Death.
Praised be the fathomless universe
For life and joy, and for objects and knowledge curious,
And for love, sweet love—but praise, praise, praise!
For the sure enwinding arms of cool, enfolding Death.
Dark Mother, always gliding near with soft feet,
Have none chanted for thee a chant of fullest welcome?
Then I chant for thee, I glorify thee above all,
I bring thee a song that when thou must indeed come, come
    unfalteringly.
Approach, strong deliveress,
When it is so, when thou hast taken them
I joyously sing the dead,
Lost in the loving, floating ocean of thee,
Laved in the flood of thy bliss, O Death.
From me to thee glad serenades,
Dances for thee I propose, saluting thee, adornments and feast-
    ings for thee,
And the sights of the open landscape and the high spread sky
    are fitting,
And life and the fields, and the huge and thoughtful night.
The night in silence under many a star,
The ocean shore and the husky whispering wave whose voice
    I know,
And the soul turning to thee, O vast and well veil'd Death,
And the body gratefully nestling close to thee.
Over the tree-tops I float thee a song,

Over the rising and sinking waves, over the myriad fields and the
 prairies wide,
Over the dense-packed cities all, and the teeming wharves and
 ways,
I float this carol with joy, with joy to thee, O Death.

HEY called him Jones—Sam Jones. The name is
plain, almost as plain as Brown—John Brown.
Yet there was only one John Brown, and there
will never be another. One was enough, but we
needed the one. There was only one Sam Jones,
the world needs ten thousand, but it is quite useless to advertise for them.

The last time I saw Sam Jones was at Lily Dale—just a year ago.
We sat on the shore of the little lake one drowsy summer after-
noon, and he recited the poem that is printed above. There was
a moment of silence when Sam had ceased to recite, and then he
asked, with a smile, " Do you know why I like that poem of Old
Walt's? " ♣ ♣

" Not especially—why? "

" Because Death is calling to me—I am getting on good terms
with the Mother of All. You saw me walk on my hands today—
you saw me kick the hat off that tall man's head—these things
are nothing. My weight has decreased forty pounds in three years,
I eat two meals a day, or one—I have gone without eating for ten
days at a time. I am getting acquainted with the World of Spirit.
I do not discuss this question with most people because I do not
wish to disturb them, but I am loosening my hold on this earth
and pluming my wings for flight."

The news of his death was no surprise to those who knew him.
I am inclined to think that this untaught child of Welsh parents,
born in biting poverty, nurtured in adversity, and turned out to
buffet his way alone in factory and field ere his body was half-

grown, will live in history when all of the twenty-four presidents we have had, save one, are forgotten.

Such a man as this requires perspective—seen at close range, he looks extravagant, odd, fantastic. His political enemies can not forgive him the stern truths he expressed; the preachers find it hard to appreciate one who scorned their soft platitudes and who saw through their pretended piety. To this man, a religious organization was an anomaly—a contradiction: an individual may be religious, an organization—hardly! You might as well capitalize a syndicate for making love, as to organize a corporation for praising God.

The politicians wished to use Jones of Toledo for their selfish ends, but the man was bluntly, stubbornly honest—absurdly honest, one critic said. The religious element wanted him to stamp out vice and drive the wrong-doers from the city—but alas! it seemed to them that he sided with the sinner.

When a man was brought before him for stealing bread from a baker's wagon, he fined every person in the court-room ten cents, and himself a dollar, for living in a land where a penniless man had to steal or starve. The fact that the man was a wrong-doer was no reason to Jones why we should make him an outcast. If he was a rogue or a fool—and these were synonyms to Jones—why, the man needed our friendship most. This shows the absurdity of Jones—but I am painting the man at his worst. When a woman of the town was arrested for relieving a customer of his watch and wallet, Jones questioned the man, and when it was found the accuser was a respectable man of family, he refused to listen to a word against the woman, simply saying to her, " Go and sin some more!"

And then the Mayor added, quietly, " Vice can not be exterminated until the respectable element quits paying good money to surreptitiously support it." He then fined the man ten dollars, on his own confession, for patronizing a house of ill-fame.

In 1902 the legislature of Ohio enacted a law forbidding any one to act as police magistrate or judge who had not passed a regular examination and been duly admitted to practise law. This enactment was for the special benefit of Sam Jones—they said that he was dispensing with justice. This was not exactly so; what he dispensed with was law.

Samuel M. Jones was elected Mayor of Toledo four times. Even when the Democrats and Republicans made a deal and combined on one candidate to beat the Golden Rule Man, he won. When he ran for Governor of Ohio he was defeated. He won in his own city because he was beloved by the poor, the plain, and the ignorant. The fact that he was elected by the submerged one-half, can not be denied. The submerged did n't understand Sam Jones any more than we understand God, but they believed in him. To Sam, we were all submerged, more or less, and those who claimed to have reached the sunlight, really had n't.

Sam Jones planned, at the expense of the city, a comfortable and safe place where working women could leave their children— a sort of club house for overworked women—with a competent matron in charge.

The demagogs were shocked. They lifted a howl of dissent that could be heard in Toronto—" What business has a working woman to have a baby?" they asked with injured accent. And not waiting for an answer to their conundrum they began to talk about the downtrodden taxpayers.

Sam said that if the city could provide palatial places where thieves and other rogues could be locked up, fed and looked after, it should also supply a place where poor women could go and give their children a bath.

And Sam had his way.

Sam had no sympathy with cruelty, injustice, poverty, and misery, even admiting that these things were hoary with age. In my various talks and walks with him, I noticed he discussed principles, not persons—things, not individuals. And this characteristic, be it noted, is the distinguishing mark of greatness. " He always talked of things not people," said Huxley in his eulogy of Darwin.

Samuel M. Jones recognized no enemy—men understood him or they did not, and in his letters of "Love and Labor" he says, " If I were not as limited, my life would be so luminous that all men would see the truth I seek to express." Those who heard Jones' lecture on Walt Whitman will remember his emphasis on, " I am as bad as the worst, but thank God I am as good as the best."

❧ In working as a day-laborer in the oil fields, while yet in his twenties, Sam Jones invented certain appliances for pumping, which he had patented. He offered to sell his patents to his employer, but failing in this, he started to manufacture them on his own account. The business, beginning in a very small way, prospered, and as the years went by Jones became rich. At his death he was worth upwards of a million dollars. Yet he gave away, yearly, large sums to worthy and unworthy causes. He maintained a pension list of over forty old people who had worked for him, and was continually giving time and money to alleviate distress. Yet he realized the absurdity of charity as a means of permanent good, and was sorely perplexed because he could do so little in going back of the disease and curing the cause.

He fully realized that the only way to help people was to give them an opportunity to help themselves.

Education is a conquest, not a bequest—it can not be given, it must be achieved. And the value of education lies not in its possession, but in the struggle to secure it. He longed for a time when the state would supply the opportunities of the higher education to every youth, and prophesied a day when every college would be a workshop, every workshop a school, every church an art gallery, every pulpit a free forum for the full expression of truth, and every priest a worker as well as a teacher and student. To him the thought that education should always be associated with the young was in itself an indictment—the solace of study should be the heritage of all, to the end of life. In conducting his own business, Jones sold shares to any of his workers who had been with him five years, at par, and guaranteed dividends. His was the first factory in Toledo to adopt the eight-hour day; he always gave a Saturday half-holiday, and at Christmas time there was a five per cent dividend paid to all helpers on their year's wages. The man who attempts to better the condition of his helpers, dividing profits with them, must be very great and good, if the milk of human kindness in his soul does not turn to bonny-clabber.

To help men who do not want to help themselves, and to benefit those who look with suspicion and hate on their benefactors, is the task that confronts the generous employer. To give money, medicine, clothing or food, is nothing; to war with waywardness and get the man to help himself is the vital problem. And patronage will never answer—you must do good by stealth, and be ever prepared to have your best motives traduced and vilified. The history of profit-sharing is a tale of contempt, told often in the saloon, by the man who has received the dividends.

To educate people who do not want to be educated, and to place in clean and sanitary homes, families who prefer a slum—that is your task. But the man who expects gratitude does not deserve it—the reward for a good deed is to have done it.

One year, after paying a bonus to all of his workers, Jones was waited on by a committee who demanded to see his books in order that they might ascertain whether they had received their full share of the profits.

" Well, did you show your books? " I asked.

" No, I dared not—you see it was an off year and the real fact was, that we had lost money, and the 'dividend' was paid out of my own pocket."

These things were not told in way of complaint or for publication, but they show the courage and patience a man must have who sets out to help the proletariat.

" Endure, persist, hope and keep sweet," was the motto of Sam Jones ❧ ❧

Jones was great enough to face life without blinking—to know the worst in humanity and yet not to lose faith in his fellows. Ingratitude and misunderstanding are things to be reckoned with, and the man who complains of them is in the kindergarten wearing the check apron of innocence.

" Why should I complain of the dullness of my helpers? If they knew as much as I do, and still possessed their skill, they would be owning enterprises of their own, and I should be working for them," said Sam Jones.

It is a peculiar comment on society, when in a country that calls itself Christian, a man is regarded as erratic and unreliable because he practises the Golden Rule.

Mayor Jones sought to bring the Golden Rule to bear in his public life and in his private business. He did not side with wrong-doing, but for the wrong-doer he had a profound sympathy. " I want to give my love to those who need it most," he used to say. And again and again he would repeat the words of Whitman, " I do not feel for the wounded soldier—I am that man! "

He had the power to put himself in the place of the other man, and behind the sinner he saw a long train of conditions and events that had pushed the man on and on, and finally forced him over the brink. In his dealings he always endeavored to do for others as if he were the others.

But Sam Jones did educate his workers, and gradually there grew up around him a body of able and intelligent men who prospered with the business, and who now look after it as if it were all their own. He had a universal quality, and knew how to act in harmony with persons of very different character from himself.

There was never a strike in Sam Jones' factory, and the success
of the business—and this is true of all successful enterprises—lay
in the fact that the leader bound to him faithful, loyal and loving
helpers who did his work for him. Napoleon won his battles
through the valor of his marshals—" I 'll win the height for you
or I 'll not return," said Ney, amid the smoke of Austerlitz. In
due time Ney returned, and Napoleon silently kissed his cheek.
There can be sentiment in both war and business.

In his career, Sam Jones reversed the usual program. Aspiration
and ideality usually belong to youth—we stand on the threshold,
with a volume of poems under our arm, and look out over the
hilltops, before we go forth and take the world captive, and
re-create it—making all things new.

We go forth all right, but instead of taking the world captive,
it captures us. We are like those good people who go to the South
Sea Islands with intent to civilize the natives—if they remain,
they become South Sea Islanders. Instead of introducing the
fashions of Piccadilly they adopt those of the beach, and pounding
on a hollow log takes the place of Grand Opera.

With the successful man of business, care multiplies with acqui-
sition, and the things he owns, own him. And so the De Goncourts
wrote, " If a man is not handsome at twenty, strong at thirty,
rich at forty, wise at fifty, he will never be handsome, strong,
rich or wise."

Pictures of Sam Jones at twenty show him as an underfed, over-
worked, shy youth, with a tuft of chin whiskers, and small intellect or aspiration.

At thirty-five, history was to him a blank, the poets unknown,
science unguessed. He never wrote an article for the press until
he was forty; he never made a public speech until he was forty-
five ✎ ✎

He died at the early age of fifty-eight, and was known as a
practised and skilful orator; a ready writer; a good authority on

history; a student of science and an appreciative critic of the world's great literature. So there you have Sam Jones—inventor, successful business man, mayor of a great city, lecturer, author, student, critic, philanthropist.

But these are not enough to distinguish a man or set him apart in God's *Who's Who*.

Sam Jones will live, because, during the last ten years of his life, he was born again. Mahomet was a business man until he was forty-five, and had he died then we never would have heard the cry, " Allah il Allah! there is no God but God and Mahomet is his prophet."

Instead of caring more for money as he succeeded in making money, Sam Jones cared less. The long, clutching, shaky fingers of the miser, with the tremulous voice of uncertainty and fear, were never his. When his voice weakened, it stopped and stopped forever. Even when his body slackened its pace, his spirit was so strong that his voice was clear, musical and vibrant. My sheep know my voice.

Voice is the index of the soul.

" If I could give away all my money so it would be kept where it was giving men work and was doing good, I 'd give it away—all I want is my board and clothes," he once said to me. And those mild blue eyes, and the honest voice made doubt impossible. Gradually the man developed a Yogi-like contemplative quality— a passion for purity. He lived within himself—he believed in his divinity. Like Spinoza, we might call him " a God-intoxicated man." He lived in the world—he fought the world's battles, but he was not of the world. The world did not take him captive —he cast off its manacles and broke its fetters. He felt that he was afloat on the reeling sea of life—that he was a manifestation of some great, mysterious Power that was using him for unseen ends. And that he was so poor an instrument for the use of Deity, depressed him—so much was to be done, he could do so little.

His soul was stained with world-sorrow—the pain of the millions who are born but to struggle and die, dug deep into his vitals. ❡ The fear of Death was not in the formula that made Sam Jones. Death was to him the deliverer, and life he often regarded as a jailer that holds us captive. This view does not tend to longevity— this nostalgia of the soul does not make for length of days. It is a fever that consumes.

I have heard him repeat Beecher's words: " When I die do not place crepe—the emblem of gloom—on the house, but rather hang a basket of flowers at the door as an emblem that a soul has passed from death unto life."

And again he would quote the clown in *Twelfth Night*, " The more fool, Madame, to mourn because your brother's soul is in heaven." ✍ ✍

Gladly would Sam Jones have given his life for his race—he yearned for his kind as a mother yearns for her babe.

He had in him a strain of the madness of the old Hebrew prophets. He was Malachi and Isaiah, Koheleth and Daniel, Walt Whitman and Tolstoy by turn. He lacked the placidity and poise of the self-satisfied—he hungered and thirsted after righteousness. And he disappeared from our sight.

He is not here.

Ibsen

LOOK at his face!—that mask of iron stained with acid *∂∞ ∂∞*

Look again!—the iron and the acid are gone; it is now a wind-chilled mountain tarn, a marvelous mirror of the great Northland that reflects storm-riven, leafless pines that swing wildly to and fro on the edge of the precipices and snow-capped mountain-tops that thrust their rebellious heads in defiant challenge to the bleak, cosmic prospects. Has any dramatist, save Shakespeare, ever held together within himself so many complex tendencies as Henrik Ibsen? The real Ibsen lay in ambush behind the paradoxes of existence; each play screened a separate Ibsen; he was the soul of each one of his characters, but could not be identified with any of them.

He was a mystic, a poet, a philosopher, a dramatist, and he was each one of these things, utterly. He was a mystic because his imagination had shot beyond the masks of matter, beyond the "stream of tendency" that molds those masks, into the supercerebral, where the intuitive substratum of man catches upon the hypersensitive, spiritual plates, gleams and presages from a Third Empire—welded of flesh and spirit, but where neither rules *∂∞ ∂∞*

Nietzsche preached an Overman. Ibsen mapped out his empire. This prophecy of Ibsen's appeared in *Emperor and Galilean,* one of his earliest dramas, and is found again in the last drama, *When We Dead Awaken.* In the latter play he did not leave the earth-twisted souls of Rubreck and Irene, the lovers who ascended the mountain together, in the snows of the pass to be picked by the crows.

The rising sun gushes full upon their cold bodies; but their souls are borne away by the Eagle of the Dawn.

Ibsen was a poet, because in him burned the immortal loves and hates, because he possessed the power of transfiguring the thing he touched, of translating the ordinary into the extraordinary. His ear caught the clangor and clash of Law. He was ecstatic, exalted and flung his rebel spirit at the sneering stars. He thundered, and passed.

He was a philosopher, because he was impersonal, an interpreter of life, answering no questions because Life answers none. Incisive, psychologic, with a grim humor—a humor that bit, etched and silenced—replying to all questions after the conclusion of each play by planning another play, he preserved an indifference that deceived, as all philosophers deceive.

The aloofness of the philosopher is merely the white heat of emotion—a passionate desire not to show passion. The art consists in seeing that the mask does not drop off.

He was not a master dramatist because he was a master technician, but because he realized more vividly than any other dramatist who has ever lived that the heart of things is Conflict, that the God of things as they are is a god of war; that Man is in desperate straits here upon earth.

Crucifixion is dealt out to those who dare the social ruling order. And death, the death of the bug that slept itself to death in a rug, awaits those who venture not forth into the land of spiritual adventure ❧ ❧

Life is a sealed book. Who understands? Forth from the night-time of the Unconscious comes that spectral shape, Man. Back into the night-time of the Unconscious is he hurled after his short parley with Destiny. And the historian of this pitiful incident in Eternity—what has he to say? There is an enigma; if he can depict its character in a single work of art he has chronicled all Time has to say: he has posed a riddle.

From Æschylus to Ibsen there is but one theme—the conflict of the will of man with the blind forces that seek his destruction;

the desperate charges of Intelligence against stupid Circumstance. Ibsen saw this conflict with the clarity of Sophocles and Shakespeare. There is clash of battle in each play. The world-war is carried on in the most insignificant towns in the Scandinavian peninsula. The great question, How may I survive? rises for solution at each minute into the mental and physical world of the humblest of Nature's creatures.

Brand and *The Master Builder* are two plays that show us two stupendous Wills that seek to batter their way through the myriad menaces of a hostile environment; in *Brand* the blows of the mighty hammer of Purpose can be heard against the granite heights by those in the valley below. Behold Solness on the dizzy summit, for just one second! So far and no farther— too high, too high he climbed! He is whirled off his footing into space. The rest is silence and a sublime defeat. What is the moral? we asked of Ibsen when the old war-lord of individualism was alive. He smiled ironically and turned away—he was not in the counsels of Omnipotence.

In *The Wild Duck* the problem is: How may we follow our ideals and still be happy? Can husband and wife live happier with a lie existing between them than if they stood mortised in the truth, though it is an unpleasant one? The woman has " sinned" before marriage. The husband knows nothing of it. The idea enters a mutual friend's head that it would be a good thing to tell the husband the truth and thus found a marriage on absolute frankness. The result is a catastrophe. Ibsen flings this question into the face of humanity: Truth—what is it good for? Man can not exist without his lies. Truth mocks and slays. Absolute frankness in love is the death of love. Even great truths must be lied about before they become currency. And what currency! Like paper money, they become tainted in the handling.

Again the problem appears in *The Enemy of the People.* Tell the truth and the world will pelt you with stones. Calvary taught it nothing. The mob must have its pap. When truth comes in contact with the pocketbook, the pocketbook fights with the strength of the fiend—and wins. Herr Stockmann told the municipality of the watering-place in which he lived that the springs the tourists drank from were poisoned. His house was stoned. But he was not dismayed. He alone is great who can stand alone. Keep a closed mouth in the presence of a remunerative lie—or take the consequences. Make your choice!

In all his plays there sits the Sphinx with her riddle. Answer it who may. Man has been called a god in ruins. Ibsen saw in him an evolving devil. A martyrdom awaits those who lift the standard of rebellion; but it is only in rebellion that man becomes great. Your enemy is your friend who stings you into action. "At times there are moments when the whole history of the world appears to me like a shipwreck; the important thing is to save yourself." Ibsen flung this doctrine of egoism at a world saturated with the flabby doctrine of altruism. The one thing needful is to find yourself, affirm yourself in the face of all opposition. " The kingdom of God is within you." When you offend yourself, you offend the divine. Life was given you to live, not to sacrifice. Nature knows nothing of self-sacrifice; she immolates the weak. Self-sacrifice is great when it is a means to the end of self-glorifi- cation; but self-sacrifice as an end in itself is mutilation—an instrument for perpetuating ugliness.

A man can not better society in any better way than to teach the lesson of strength by example. Let the weak look to the founda- tions of the houses in which they live. " Mint the gold within you," Ibsen wrote to Brandes. Will you mold yourself in bronze after your own ideal or become a little pewter image that can be bought in the market-place by the first cow-herd?

The man who treats life ruthlessly is the great man. Men, like races, survive because of their strength, not because of their good- ness. Persistence of force is persistence of strength; the way to achieve immortality is to deserve it. The strong, full-blooded man has discovered Nature's meaning.

Man, in his pride, believes he is subduing universal forces to his will when in reality he is doing the will of universal forces. It is as though the lightning-rod believed it had willed the lightning from the thunder-cloud, when its magnetic qualities only drew it thither. So all Nature finds a magnet in human strength. It voices its thunder through individuality.

Be true to your dream of power and sweep forward with your destiny, Ibsen thunders. Nora Helmer leaves the house of her husband when she discovers his perfidy. She had found that she had a soul to cultivate. The Doll's House in which she lived collapsed in a night. She discovered that she could not be an ideal mother until she became an ideal woman. She had been only a wife. It was necessary to be something more. She was first of all a human being. She went forth in search of herself.

Sudermann's Magda has uttered that magnificent challenge, "I am I!" Nora Helmer cried to the night, "I am—who?" There can be no liberty for the soul so long as it works within the limits of its ancestral conscience. Endless liberty implies endless ejection, the steady, vigorous, unashamed exploitation of what is within—the lengthening of the shadow of the Ego against the eternal wall of circumstance. All greatness violates; all heroism slays &➤ &➤

The revolution that Ibsen preached was a spiritual revolution— a revolt of each man against his lower, conventional, mechanical nature. The problem of individual growth is how to keep at bay the waves of suggestion from external objects and internal corpses that threaten at each minute to overwhelm the mind. How may I use myself? There is a nucleus of inner forces come to consciousness in the brain which we call the I; it is the organ of personal identity; an organ within an organ, a magnet toward which all things converge for judgment. To allow this center to be over-

ruled is to be " lost." To immortalize it in dream and act is to be
" saved." ๑ ๑

Ibsen would not compromise with his age. He was a terrible task-
master. He lived up to his doctrine of heroic egoism. Is it easy to
live thus? Is it a philosophy of self-indulgence? Does it degrade?
Look at his face!

Stevie Crane

STEVIE is not quite at home here—he'll not remain so very long," said a woman to me in 1895 ❧ ❧

Five years have gone by, and last week the cable flashed the news that Stephen Crane was dead. Dead at twenty-nine, with ten books to his credit, two of them good, which is two more than most of us scribblers will ever write. Yes, Stephen Crane wrote two things that are immortal. *The Red Badge of Courage* is the strongest, most vivid work of the imagination ever fished from the ink-pot by an American ❧ ❧

" Men who write from the imagination are helpless when in the presence of the fact," said James Russell Lowell. In answer to which I'll point you *The Open Boat,* the sternest, creepiest bit of realism ever penned, and Stevie was in the boat.

American critics honored Stephen Crane with more ridicule, abuse and unkind comment than was bestowed on any other writer of his time. Possibly the vagueness, and the loose, unsleeked quality of his work invited the gibes, jeers, and the loud laughter that tokens the vacant mind; yet as half apology for the critics we might say that scathing criticism never killed good work, and this is true, but it sometimes has killed the man.

Stephen Crane never answered back, nor made explanation, but that he was stung by the continual efforts of the press to laugh him down, I am very sure.

The lack of appreciation at home caused him to shake the dust of America from his feet and take up his abode across the sea, where his genius was being recognized, and where strong men stretched out sinewy hands of welcome, and words of appreciation were heard instead of silly, insulting parody. In passing, it is well to note that the five strongest writers of America had their passports to greatness viseed in England before they were granted recognition at home. I refer to Walt Whitman, Thoreau, Emerson, Poe and Stephen Crane.

Stevie did not know he cared for approbation, but this constant refusal to read what the newspapers said about him was proof that he did. He boycotted the tribe of Romeike, because he knew that nine clippings out of every ten would be unkind, and his sensitive soul shrank from the pin-pricks.

Contemporary estimates are usually wrong, and Crane is only another of the long list of men of genius to whom Fame brings a wreath and finds her poet dead.

Stephen Crane was a reincarnation of Frederick Chopin. Both were small in stature, slight, fair-haired, and of that sensitive, acute, receptive temperament—capable of highest joy and keyed for exquisite pain. Haunted with the prophetic vision of quick-coming death and with the hectic desire to get their work done, they often toiled the night away and were surprised by the rays of the rising sun.

Shrinking yet proud, shy but bold, with a feminine longing for love and tenderness; mad gaiety, that illy masked a breaking heart, at times took the reins and the spirits of children just out of school, seemed to hold the road. At other times—and this was the prevailing mood—the manner was one of placid, patient calm and smooth, unruffled hope; but back and behind all this was a dynamo of energy, a brooding melancholy of unrest, and the crouching world-sorrow which this life could never quite unseat. Chopin reached sublimity through sweet sounds; Crane attained the same heights through the sense of sight, and words that symboled color, shapes and scenes. In each the distinguishing feature is the intense imagination and active sympathy. Knowledge consists in a sense of values—of distinguishing this from that, for truth lies in the mass. The delicate nuances of Chopin's music have never been equaled by another composer;

every note is cryptic, every sound a symbol. And yet it is dance-music, too, but still it tells its story of baffled hope and stifled desire—the tragedy of Poland in sweet sounds. Stephen Crane was an artist in his ability to convey the feeling by just the right word, or a word misplaced, like a lady's dress in disarray, or a hat askew. This daring quality marks everything he wrote. The recognition that language is fluid, and at best only an expedient, flavors all his work. He makes no fetich of grammar—if the grammar gets in the way so much worse for the grammar. All is packed with color, and charged with feeling, yet the work is usually quiet in quality and modest in manner.

Art is born of heart, not head; and so it seems to me that the work of those men whose names I have somewhat arbitrarily linked, will live. Each sowed in sorrow and reaped in grief. They were tender, kind, gentle, and each possessed a capacity for love that passes the love of women. They were each indifferent to the proprieties, very much as children are. They lived in cloister-like retirement, hidden from the public gaze, or wandered unnoticed and unknown. They founded no schools, delivered no public addresses, and in their day made small impress on the times. They were sublimely indifferent to what had been said and done—the term precedent not being found within the cover of their bright lexicon of words. In the nature of each was a goodly trace of tincture of iron that often manifested itself in the man's work. They belong to that elect few who have built for the centuries. The influence of Chopin, beyond that of other composers, is alive to-day, and moves unconsciously, but profoundly, every music-maker; the seemingly careless style of Crane is really lapidaric, and is helping to file the fetters from every writer who has ideas plus, and thoughts that burn.

He is dead now—Steve is dead. How he faced death the records do not say; but I know, for I knew the soul of the lad. Within the breast of that pale youth there dwelt a lion's heart. He held his own life and reputation lightly. He sided with the weak, the ignorant, the unfortunate and his purse and strength and influence were ever given lavishly to those in need. *He died trying to save others.*

So here's to you, Steve Crane, wherever you may be! You were not so very good, but you were as good as I am—and better in many ways—our faults were different, that's all. I don't know where you are, Stevie, but when I die I hope I will face Death as manfully as you did; and I hope, too, that I shall then go where you are now. And so, Stevie, good-bye and good-bye!

Thoreau

IF Emerson and Poe were America's two most significant writers, Whitman and Thoreau were her two most significant figures.

Thoreau was the perfect rebel. He began the "spiritual revolution" long before Ibsen preached it to Brandes.

Without bitterness, without a touch of melancholia, without the slightest evidence of regret he retired from the little world of "practical life" to the infinite universe of Mind and Nature. His cosmic nonchalance was as sublime as the faith which engendered it; his mysticism was the mysticism sprung from the deeps of wonder; his unsociability was not misanthropic, but arose from the fact that he had found another kind of sociability than that demanded by the world; he had become the crony of the Great Comrade. He chummed with Night and Day, and found much to say to the Oversoul.

The law of adaptation to environment—that an organism can survive only on condition that it makes peace with the hostile forces that envelop it and that tend to its destruction—is contradicted absolutely in the case of a mental original like Thoreau. Genius must adapt itself to its heredities, to its instincts, to its inner urgings, and stand forever opposed to its physical, social and religious milieu.

Revolt is dissent from environment. All geniuses—seers, poets, prophets—are revolutionists, and from the moment of their birth they are engaged in a constant war to conserve for their own interests the things that are in them. Their greatness is determined by non-adaptation to their environment. For this reason geniuses are shy and retiring. It is their instinct of fear. Once they become molded by their environment they are lost. All things conspire against them. When they mingle with the herd they put on the mask of mediocrity—often the mask of vulgarity—to throw the hounds off the scent. They insulate themselves in non-conductors, and so pass over the deadly coils in perfect safety.

Thoreau would not herd. The come-and-go of life he recognized as a kind of issueless migration and hibernation. Life in large cities to him was merely the delirium of momentum. People in cities move like fish—little fish—in water or like rats in a cage: guts and gulleys that lead nowhere. These great spectacular cities are a whirl of drunken mænads—a fine study in the propulsive power of delusions. Christ, Heraclitus and Thoreau took to the Desert; the Best finally break into silence. Color, variety, odor, the rise and fall of gladiators battling for the nickel that one of them has dropped in the gutter, the cavalcades of the commonplace—these interests for a little while; but the cry of the Best is for harmony, expansion, and so they take to Dreams—the delirium of contemplation. Here Thoreau was king.

We say dreams are fantastic and absurd; hence they mean nothing. But our daily life must seem absurd, nonsensical, inutile, comic, to one looking on from a higher sphere. A dream is no more irrational than is life as De Maupassant, Heine and Thoreau found it. As absurd as the gestures of harlequins are the deeds we do in dreams; and just as absurd are the deeds we do in this dream called life, wherein mere sequence is confounded with rationality.

❡ As to traveling—who had traveled more than Thoreau? He had been places that few people could visit. He had seen things that could not be seen in Europe.

The illusion of traveling—that I can escape myself by moving from point to point—arises from the belief that when you move the body you move the mind. The earth is in perpetual movement around the Sun, and in a year's time it has been in millions of different points in space, but it is always enveloped in its own atmosphere; it can not escape its character. All much-traveled people are blase—they have discovered the illusion of movement.

¶ You think stoicism cowardice when it is the greatest of all affirmations. If you refuse to move, evermore you will find yourself flinging off satellites, even universes. Create, watch, understand. Of all fallacies, none is greater than " Seek and ye shall find." Seek NOT and ye shall find. Resign yourself to your demon. Sit still and listen and receive. Men live most in sleep. You are always in your atmosphere—like the earth, you are always swathed in your genius. Little people must travel. I travel. Kant and Thoreau did not have to.

Thoreau conceived the Soul to be a kind of infinite static eye. The soul was everywhere, partook of all things, was the eucharistic wafer. Thoreau moved from center to center, not from place to place ᴓ ᴓ

His great Truth: drop anchor anywhere, and it will drag—that is, if your soul is a limitless, fathomless sea, and not a dog-pound; never mind your sails—furl them, and bank the fires in the engine-room; sit in the crow's-nest and follow the anchor—from this flowed his nonchalance. Nothing evil could possibly befall him. The soul should be agile—always prepared to move. No retreat in the mind is safe against the sudden incursions of the great ancient fatalities that lurk in our unfathomable being. Rather, the deeper we build in the soul our mansions the more we lie open to those things that lie deeper than all dreams, deeper than all conceivable depths. You may make your citadel proof against the hurricanes from without and the lightning-bolt above, but there is no art yet found to frustrate the forces that work from beneath. Beware of the ancient fatalities that lie depth on depth within you.

The drowning man by his frenzied struggling only beats the waters still higher above his head and so makes his fate more certain. So in our struggle against circumstance we set up newer and newer, higher and higher, waves of emotion and of passion that but submerge the understanding and the soul's eyes all the quicker. Lie still and float. Assent to the order of things smashes the tyranny of that order. Approve all that comes to your hand—then cast it away and think no more of it.

Thoreau knew of these fatalities; so he set his soul as one sets a steel trap.

The active man hunts for his destiny—literally, he " pursues his calling." It is as though the motes that float in the sunlight were to hunt for the sun. Utopia is here and now—it is a condition. If you wait you shall be claimed by your rightful owner; move ever so slightly toward your destiny and you move from a higher to a lower level. You may seek all your life for the things you need, but if those things you seek do not need you, you will end lamed and mutilated. The man who forces the Northwest Passage will be forced through it seeking something else or while seeking nothing in particular. They who " pursue their calling " pursue the echo of it.

Like Spinoza, Thoreau was an adept in cosmic mathematics. Dissolution is a backyard view of evolution—the mathematics of growth and decay are the same. Growth adds two and two, and makes four; decay divides four by two and makes two. The evolution of a pimple, the involution of a bud, the dissolution of a sun follow one law.

Accident is always perfect, thought invariably bungles. You are carried to port by currents that are on no chart.

If the effects of all our acts could be followed out in all their ramifications for one hundred years, it would be found that the day-long idler had done less harm to his fellow-men than the most industrious man in the community.

Thoreau reached for nothing. Success always satirizes our dream of success. Possession leaves us startled—to have a thing is to have it not. The very rich and the very poor always look bored—disillusioned—for their states of mind are exactly the same. They both circle about the same flame. But there is a mind that circles about its own light—its parallax, aphelion and perihelion.

Whether it appears in Benares or Walden, Athens or Weimar—now or not now—the place where it stands is the center of duration, the core of all values. It possesses, but has no possessions; it succeeds, but has no definite successes.

Drowned in the infinitude of space, clamped between times, crawling from one straitjacket of circumstance to another straitjacket of circumstance—howbeit we view it—no matter in what terms we apprehend our mortal state, the one tremendous fact remains that we are conscious of this state, that there is that Consciousness which is not drowned in the infinitude of space, clamped between times, and does not crawl from circumstance to circumstance. It is that which sees our mortal state! This was the basis of Thoreau's riant mysticism.

He laid traps for himself; found himself to be the Divine Adventurer. Man's whole life from the cradle to the grave is only a partial history of himself. The whole of Self is never circled. There are crypts and vaults that have never been forced by the boldest, peaks that have defied the bravest, and possibilities that have forever remained impossibilities. Our dreams are an arc of the Ego; our waking another arc, and the adventure after death another arc. But who shall piece these arcs together and calmly view his own completion from that Center which stands inviolate to all change and motion?

Thoreau's soul wending its way leisurely along the highways of reverie was sometimes suddenly jostled by a great Personage that vanished and was lost in the crowded mental thoroughfares before, startled and amazed, he could turn full upon It.

Mysticism is to feel the mystery of a thing before you have examined the thing. The sense of mystery was Thoreau's first and also his last sense. The five material senses were but the tentacles of that original sense, tentative guesses at a solution of the Enigma.

Wonder rises with insight. The characteristic of the superior mind is amazement, while the inferior intellect is only capable of worship. Amazement begets poets, seers, philosophers. A life-long wonder at everything that is presented to consciousness is a lifelong growth, the soul's candidature for unseen, undreamed of modes of existence; while worship, being essentially a moral attitude toward that which knows not us, professes, impliedly at least, to have found a solution to the Great Mystery. Hence, this solution is a stoppage, an end, decay—stagnation, senescence. If I fly to the zenith I am still at a nadir; if I fly to the nadir I am still at a zenith. And the law that holds in the physical universe holds in the mental universe. My good may be an evil; my evil may be a good—for neither term has anything to do with dis-coverable ultimates. The bottom of the sea is the top of a moun-tain; the top of a mountain is the bed of a sea; my highest thought is only a stalactite in this Mammoth Cave of wonders which the glow-worm of consciousness has illumined for a moment. We may have as many ideas about a single object as that single object is capable of change—which is an infinite number. Who can put his finger on the top or the bottom of a cylinder that revolves quicker than any eye can follow? The mystic of Walden never was foolhardy enough to put his finger there. He watched it go round with delight.

To him it was not so wonderful to be immortal as it was to be alive. To be after death is no miracle; to be at all is. If I can not unriddle myself in this Now, how can I hope to do it in a Then? Merely to find myself consciously thinking Here is more extra-ordinary than merely to go on thinking forever somewhere else. Truth is a matter of perspective; it is a relation of distance, not of "fact" and conception. At a certain point geometrical axioms will seem to be absolute truths; move a pace higher and they become relative truths; move still higher, into the supersensuous world, and they are seen not to be valid at all. Imagination demolishes logic. Before I can speak of Truth I must first find out where I stand, whether I am standing anywhere, and whether the thing I call my truth is not a passing, necessary illusion, whether it is merely a tool or a " find," whether it is a thing I really see or merely part of a perspective.

Culture is not to be measured by book-learning nor yet by experience. It is the manner in which we confront books and experience. It is a frame of mind. It is an attitude. Thoreau would have been a highly cultured mind had he never left his native town or had he never read a book.

The soul awaits the great Event, the great Romance—the Unique Adventure. It never comes to pass, for it has missed it in the expectation. Thoreau expected nothing. Here and now was the Great Event. Life was the Unique Adventure.

Jean Jacques Rousseau

TWO hundred years ago a man was born who was the father of the Nineteenth Century, the grandfather of the Twentieth Century and the godfather of all revolutions.

He was Jean Jacques Rousseau. In many respects Rousseau was the most extraordinary man that ever lived—a man of whom Disraeli said, " If history had no Rousseau we should have to invent one."

Rousseau is one of the few men whom nobody cares to believe in, but whom everybody must believe in. He is one of the few men whose writings, with the exception of the *Confessions,* are obsolete, but to whose pen nearly every philosopher and thinker pays tribute.

This is because Jean Jacques Rousseau, like Voltaire, Paine, Ingersoll, John Brown and Lincoln, was not a man but an incarnation, a fatal event in the evolution of the race, a Voice that had to be promulged.

Men who are wrong are just as necessary to the world as those who are right. What a man thinks does not count, but the time, place and manner of his thinking do.

Three-fourths of Rousseau's opinions and doctrines are rubbish in the right place. He was generally wrong, but he smashed what needed smashing. He unriveted chains, he unlocked bolts, he dissolved a whole aristocracy, he blew in the ramparts of the Bastile, and he wrote the history of his life, which founded a literature entirely new in the world.

And he did all this as every great man does what he is ordered to do—grabbed the things nearest to him and used them.

Sentimentalist, educationist, communist, lady-killer, baby-killer, gentleman, woman suffragist, mollycoddle, dreamer, a cash-down spender and borrower, democrat, aristocrat, and sociological faker par excellence, this extraordinary man stands in history with Leonardo da Vinci and Benvenuto Cellini. He, like they, epitomized the aspirations and the humbugs of the race.

But his work, his achievement in thought and in the movement for human liberty which must immortalize him forever, was his denial of the divine rights of kings. He completed in France what Cromwell began in England. The divine rights of kings! It was Rousseau who in his *Social Contract* compounded the political " 606 " that forever drove that worm-eaten belief from the human mind ❧ ❧

Society is a contract, said Rousseau, a sacred contract entered into by every peasant at his birth with the ruling power, and woe betide the ruler that breaks the contract. Rousseau, of course was wrong, but he was right then and the doctrine is still legitimate to use today when the Kaiser starts to pull the old bunk.

❧ In society there is no contract. As in Nature, the fittest survive and the weakest go to the wall. And that is right and good. But Rousseau, of course, had never heard of Darwin—and Darwin said he did n't care a tinker's tink for Rousseau. Some day somebody is going to say the same thing of Darwin—times change. Rousseau's cardinal contention was that man in a state of nature is a benevolent animal. Today we know that Rousseau was wrong. In primitive societies the strong man took by natural right the leadership of the tribe. The craftiest, the most intelligent man in the tribe became a priest, a medicine-man, a lawyer. No man is any better than it is necessary to be. As society evolved, an incalculable number of changes and readjustments took place, but the law of deference to strength and brains never was obscured ❧ ❧

Rousseau's benevolent savage is a myth. His psychology was bad. It is a fundamental instinct of the individual to award to the superior man—morally, mentally or physically—the highest prizes of life.

Rousseau's democracy came out of his fundamental principle that all men are originally good and equal. But today we know that democracy is only a word. It has never been practised or practicable. The people rule—through rulers. And the man who has the most to say about the rule of the people is a tyrant with false whiskers.

In America, instead of Grand Rulers, we have Bosses. An aristocracy of mind, an aristocracy of character, an aristocracy of craft and graft—we will never get beyond the aristocracy principle. Socialism itself would become an aristocracy of officeholders and the boss would be supreme.

Rousseau was thus a sentimental democrat. He was all feeling. He thought with his nerves. He was a superb creator, but he could not think. A sublime egomaniac, he was the incarnation of the will-to-produce through the emotions. The will-to-produce, to create, has never been affirmed with greater tenacity and with so much energy as by Rousseau. He was always in a condition of feverish exaltation.

He was an elementary force, like Hugo, Wagner and Whitman, and dazzles the imagination like a volcano in eruption or like a geyser lashing Antæus. Victor Hugo said Rousseau was a new kind of genius, for he created a new way of feeling.

To create naturally, to create spontaneously in the empyrean of thought and action, to create new sensations, to create in his own interior of life by incessant flagellations a la Saint Augustine and Tolstoy—that was the secret of Rousseau, of why he carried in him the germs of a thousand revolts, a thousand poems, a thousand fantasies and a thousand bitter memories.

Creation! Creation! It is that passion that makes man a god. The world is forever in gestation, and so is the brain. The brain is a matrix. In Rousseau not to create was to die. There was nothing serene or coldly intellectual about him. Emotions and images, feelings that moved like lightning, a frantic mental rhyme, a passion that hurried like maddened waters—all this produced great crises in his life when he appeared insane—was insane no doubt ❧ ❧

Genius scorns its own safety. Parturition is the neighbor of death. Those who are normal, sane and healthy see clearly. Rousseau was insane, and so have been the great minds of all time, from Buddha to Nietzsche. Insanity in genius is a super-abundance of health; while the perfectly sane man is invariably stupid, and always uninteresting.

Rousseau's life itself was a romance written by a mad demon. Born with an infirmity, strangely sensitive and clairvoyant even as a baby, he was at seven years abandoned by his father who had allowed him to stuff his head with romances. Put into a boarding-school of a Protestant pastor in Geneva; taught Latin, history, geography; battened, crammed and rammed with learning, at nine he began the study of Euclid.

At eleven years he was an engraver. The man to whom he was apprenticed beat him. Here, according to himself, he learned to steal, to lie and to give lectures. At twelve he poses as a stoic between erotic dreams.

At sixteen years he fled from Geneva and became a tramp. In Savoy he encountered Madame de Warens. She sent him into an asylum in Turin, where he goes over to Catholicism. And so it runs to the end of his life.

He lives whole lives in a single day. No feeling, no crime, no sensation is foreign to him. Life for Rousseau was an experiment. Living was an experience.

All experience after it has filtered through and refined itself in the mind of the first order is good. In the perspective of memory the solid angularity of all our pains and " sins " is melted in a shining ether. The ego puts an aureole on everything. Even penance and remorse are luxurious; they are methods of glorifying our transgressions. In the great menstruum of the emancipated mind, in spite of that terrible bleat from his heart, everything is fashioned into gold. The real philosopher's stone is the brain.

Rousseau was unscrupulous. So was Cæsar, Bacon, Bismarck and Webster. A man who makes a promise has blasphemed. He sneers at Fate and Destiny. Every promise is kept for an ulterior purpose, just as every debt is paid in order to contract another. Rousseau was elemental. He did what was expedient. Like Bismarck, Rousseau might have said, " If I lied I meant it." In Rousseau's *Confessions* there are a thousand and one lies. It is the liar's *Arabian Nights*—not lies in the usual sense of the word, but feats of the imagination, a record of the things Rousseau was going to do, thought he did, or ought to have done.

And these things are just as important as the things he did. The practical has no greater importance than the imaginary, and what I intend doing is more important than what I have done. Unaccomplished purpose is a promise of immortality.

Rousseau with Voltaire was a reservoir and the alembic of all the past world. To those two minds the past massed itself for judgment—and got it. His brain was, in fact, a universal brain. The Baltimore and Chicago Conventions talked Rousseau, whether they knew it or not. Rousseau was latent in Cromwell. He was there as instinct, as tendency. In the dullest brain this Call is buried, but it lies so deep under strata of custom and convention that its strings are never felt.

Rousseau was a lock-picker of inner doors. He was a psychic seismograph. He registered in his sensibilities the earthquakes in the souls of muted millions. In France today the school-children chat about " Jean Jacques." Two hundred years from now he will still be the mighty " Jean Jacques."

France never forgets her great. And the world can never forget France. With all her vagaries, she is the Torch of the world. Voltaire, Rousseau, Hugo, Millet, Rodin—we can do without the rest!

Edgar Allan Poe

PAINE tells us that all genius can be explained by environment. As a certain soil only will produce lemon-trees, so a certain social and racial soil only will produce a certain type of poet, musician or painter.

But Poe upset this interesting theory. His work is exotic in America. He came from Mars, where people do not have to work, economize and keep sober.

Terror and beauty were the twin goddesses that baptized the soul of this strange genius, Poe. His life was an excursion into the weird. And the weird is the beautiful, plus the strange. He dwelt on the borderland that divides sanity from insanity. He caught gleams of a remoter, super-lunar world that blasted him when he looked or listened. He fumbled with the keys to strange doors; he haunted the corridors of white temples set in dreams; he held conference with strange creatures of air and light that no one else could see; he saw behind the veils of matter into the ghost-world. Poe was unanalyzable. He was the victim of an obscure mood that lies beyond the experience of ordinary men. In reading his tales or poems we are shot into terra incognita. We feel an Atmosphere, but we see nothing plainly. We verge on the lunacy that legends say lurks in mountain moonshine. We have the sense of being haunted. We feel lost in a giant Nightmare that fascinates like the beautiful, sinister eye of a snake. We lay down *The Fall of the House of Usher, Elegia,* or *The Raven* to touch the furniture or listen to the ticking of the clock and thank God that we are still real and sane. The victim of an obscure mood, his soul was stroked by subtle fingers on ghostly bodies. His heart pumped into his brain the most pathetic figures that ever haunted the cells of a brain—those brain-cells that entombed a million prenatal despairs that were the catacombs of his Lenores and Helens.

What were those " sheeted memories of the past " that squeaked and gibbered at his heels all his life? His face as depicted by Valloton is the ghastly face of a man who has seen the forbidden. Whence these gnawed and upturned dead faces that drifted past on shoreless seas of sinister green? And those cunning, black eyes that flashed on him from their sunken sockets? Hallucinated! Hallucinated! we say—but all great art is the product of hallucination, of a vivid, violent, inner vision that passes before the mind's eye like a bolt of lightning over the mountain-tops.

Like Hecla's torch that flames in an imperial solitude did this strange visitor to earth, Edgar Poe, live and die among men. ⁋ One night, many years ago, in Philadelphia, the celebrated painter, John Sartain, was sitting in his library, when Poe, wild, disheveled, bruised, ran into his room and declared he had seen on the walls of the prison, where he had spent the previous night, a host of angels clad in moonlight, that blew from wreathed trumpets wild blasts towards the heavens. Has not the poet, too, his Via Dolorosa?

His poems take us to one region only—" bottomless vales " and " boundless floods " and " chasms and caves and titan woods." They are excursions in No-Man's Land. Had he discovered the El Dorado of the spirit? Had he forced the Northwest Passage from matter to the supermaterial?

We wonder in what ethereal sphere his soul had been molded, and why it got itself flesh and came here to this prison-house to chant and get buried after forty-four pitiless years of life. The glamor of another world hung over his soul. He seemed out of place in the flesh. A strange brotherhood are these hallucinated beings. They come into life laden with inextinguishable griefs, and stand as one removed from death. They are gray of heart and ashen-hued of brain; they are tethered to the unseen, and you shall sooner dissever the sun from its fires than see them walk the ways of men.

Poe's soul was cradled in a filmy ecstasy. All reality was a blasphemy. He preferred half-lights, doors ajar, curtains that swung in what he believed to be a mystic unison with the breeze, flames that flickered in ebon censers, waters dyed in shadows. The mystery of man! And the mystery of the world! They are hieroglyphs, and no one will ever decipher them.

The dark tarn of Auber, in the *Misty Mid-Region of Wier,* was to Poe a real place. Stagnant pools and fetid heaths were the places where his spirit delighted to linger. He could see in darkness better than in light.

His poem, *Silence,* tells of a region where he kept tryst with " corporate silence." Corporate silence! What a thought! Is not the universe itself silence that has found a body? And is not silence the ghost of noise? Somber, sinister, brooding silence! Silence that can never be silent, murmuring its drowsy secrets in the ear, forging the minutes into the eternal, forever-recurring hours, weaving its arras of dreams!

Poe trod strange Jungfraus of silence. There are deep lethean lapses, lustral silences in which the soul seems to rest from its Sisyphean labors.

Ulalume is his most remarkable and characteristic poem. It haunts like an unremembered thought. Here at least are the Blessed Isles, here the lotos-land of the distraught—star-dials and the alley titanic, and the realms of the boreal pole. *Ulalume* is the last word in poetic mysticism. It is the soul of Poe cadenced. The bitter pessimism of the man! To him the universe was an epic scrawled by a bug. *The Conqueror Worm* is a vision of the world and all the nothingness of it. There is the same philosophy at the bottom of it that penetrates *El Magico Prodigioso* of Calderon. It is life viewed from the trenches of despair. Men build their houses or dreams, and the worm gnaws at the foundation. As life grows longer it grows shorter. We travel from mother to mother-earth; and the flesh that we love so well is spun into dust. Man has his banquet, and is banqueted upon in turn. Mystic, pessimist, poet, mathematician, a man drunk with beauty and love, a bringer of strange tidings—Edgar Allan Poe signals and beckons from his tomb.

Emerson

OU are spinning like bubbles in a river, you know not whither or whence, and you are bottomed and capped and wrapped in delusions," says Emerson, the Skeptic, in his essay on Montaigne. The universe at any given moment is but a dissolving state of consciousness. Behind the arras of dreams there stands a Dreamer, and that there is a Dreamer and a dream are all the skeptic can affirm.

Skepticism is a system of arriving at provisional universals by skipping the particular. It holds to no one thing, but affirms an All. As a particle of salt is dissolved in water, so is a particular fact dissolved in its eternal Idea in the mind of the sage. Your object standing there in space, tangible and movable, has no more substantiality than the gorgeous color-bands woven by sunken Autumn suns. They are part and parcel of the cosmic mirage.

❡ All things seen are but projections of the seer; all truths are aspects of the Truth; each brain is a facet of the Universal Mind. The universe itself is but an arc of the uncircled eternal. The skeptic works by elimination.

The arch-skeptic is the arch-believer. He may smile indulgently at all your facts ranged neatly in their pigeonholes; but there is a Fact at which he will not smile. He is awed by himself. He will not believe his eyes, because there is an unlidded Eye within his soul that sweeps the infinite spaces. He will not believe his ears, because there ring upon the spiritual tympanum the whispered vibrations of the Law that is not dependent on the atom. He believes little in the rule of thumb and finger. Two and two may make four and an eighth on Jupiter. An extra cerebral convolution might have made it so on this planet.

The " order " of the world is an order built of chance. Did the reverse hold true of every " universal " law, we would as dogmatically assert the " fixed order " of things; and we would get along just as well, or better—or worse.

Our reasonings are expressions of character; our divinations are related to temperament, and our widest scientific generalization is but the orbit of the strongest sun-midge. Processes are eternal; facts are the ephemera of Time. Emerson held to the Processes; what the Processes promulged he spurned. Our speech is mere cavil. No action is whole and completed. Our real thoughts are untongued. The heart has no lips. Our passions are but the jagged shards of an earthen vessel broken by too much usage. We are doomed to the unutterable. There is repetition, but no " order " in the universe.

Up to the steep Matterhorn of these negations the skeptic soul of Emerson toiled till it reached the pinnacle—the Oversoul that canopies all negations; the Oversoul that is unarithmetical and may not be numbered. There he dwells to this day—like the pinnacle of Mont Blanc, still, snowy and serene.

" Life is a bubble and a skepticism," he says in a passionate paragraph. Things reel and sway and pass beyond the senses in the minute. Men lay snares for the Present and are caught in their own traps. Youth girds itself for a battle that is never fought; manhood dreams of an old age that never comes. Childhood is best enjoyed when 't is past. The descent from anticipation to realization is sheer, and our actions are rounded by a leer. Like Faust, we are damned if we bid the present moment stay, and we are damned if we bid it go. Rest is stagnation; motion is dispersive. We are lost either way. If you are as coarse as Belial, or as ethereal as Shelley, you are doomed to doubt.

Systems, codes, conventions, moralities are put forth in trust and faith from the larval brain of man, and Time grinds them to smut. As the aspiring flame from Hecla's crater is lost in the pits of night, so are our highest exaltations lost in the swash of the durations. Nothing is fixed. All things are travailing at birth or are entering on the death-spasm. Nothing that is born or dies can be final, and that which is not final is not true. The temporal order is apparitional. Governments are organized instincts—and instincts are sexual and stomachic. That which stands through eternal change is the law of change, and this, too, is tethered to the inner man.

" Time melts to shining ether the solid angularity of facts," says the great Transcendentalist. And this applies to moral as well as to physical facts. A proper perspective shatters differences. Good and evil differ in time and clime. Shall I choose this or this—and how shall I know that that which I choose is true? What is right in Constantinople is wrong in New York.

Cain and Mary of Magdala are necessary ingredients in cosmic economy. Evil and good are spiritual systole and diastole. There is a vice slumbering in every virtue. Comparative sociology tends to weaken the safeguards which conscience imposes. Time melts scruples, and the conscience of twenty is not the conscience of sixty ❧ ❧

Patriotism depends on the accident of birth. If a man is born in a stable, is he bound to ride a horse all the days of his life? Theft is a matter of numbers: there are statues to Napoleon, but none to Jack Cade. Civilization is the closet where we hide the racial skeleton. Our vices are ancient virtues; virtues are vices that shall be. Altruism is a subtle mode of achieving egoistic ends. Self-sacrifice is the oblation of self to self. Religion is a mood, and philosophy, after all, is but temperament intellectualized. Note the Sherman Act!

A history of human opinion would be a history of mankind's errors. The Galilean system is no whit better than the Ptolemaic. There is an increment of mystery—that is all. What difference does it make whether the earth goes around the sun or the sun goes around the earth, if we have not solved the mystery of motion? What difference does it make whether matter is an expression of mind or mind an expression of matter, if we can define neither term? The gods of the peoples are metamorphic, and scarab and Jove are but names. The telescope of Galileo increased the distance between us and the stars. Microscope, retort and crucible are not as useful as flint and spear and battle-ax *○* *○*

Each brain is a premise, and what you believe, that is so. Civilization boasts that it has given us social order and humanized us, when in reality it has but subtilized the various forms of aggression. All things tend to complexity and perplexity. The simpler a thing is, the nearer it is to perfection. The Black Fellow can realize his ideals. Lord Byron could not. Highly elaborated cerebral processes beget highly elaborated aspirations. Simple natures start from simple premises, and a highly complex civilization is but a device for increasing human ills.

Emerson tells us that society never advances or recedes. It forever stands. He is skeptical of all " progress." In " Compensation " he riddles the Occident's pet illusion. The Eastern sage repeats the syllable "Om" a thousand times, and is self-hypnotized. The Western gascon bawls " Progress," and is hallucinated by the idea that he is moving in a straight line. There is social dilatation, but progress is an illusion. Mankind is like a blind horse traveling around a circus-ring. To acquire " knowledge"—in its Western sense—is a process of sharpening the claws the better to grip your fellow-man's throat in the competitive struggle.

If you pursue things, Time will devour you; if you stand still, you will devour Time. Emerson's law of compensation tallies with that profound saying of Seneca's, " For it is all one not to desire and to have." This is the essence of skepticism. It denies that any one thing is better than another, and affirms the identity of opposites. Rest on the Oversoul and watch the water-flies flit over the darkling currents of life. Bid no thing go; bid no thing stay; welcome the good and bad—and stand still.

Action is founded on fear—the fear of one's self, the fear of silence, the fear of being alone. Action is an opiate, not a stimulant—it drugs the introspective self. Those who sleep, dream, meditate, achieve all that action unconsciously aims at and never attains —peace, calm, the lustral redemptions. Molt hope and fear and you enter the realm of the sage. The particular no longer usurps, and life in the supersensible begins. Opinions become brain-myths, and "forward," "backward" and "progress" the patois of fishwomen ꙮ ꙮ

The skepticism of the mystic is born of the idea that all things eventually flow back to their sources. The ages have solved nothing. The same fundamental problems that confronted Æschylus confronted Ibsen. The soul of Plotinus is revivified in Maeterlinck. Œdipus and Hamlet were undone by the same inscrutable Fate. Job's piercing shrieks were echoed back from the mouth of Manfred-Byron on the heights of the Jungfrau. The sublime vision that overcame Buddha amid his purple sins sublimated the soul of Tolstoy; and the furies that lashed Orestes with serpent whips scourged Oscar Wilde to his doom.

Marriage, society, government are still open questions. Imago or butterfly, the spirit persists forever. You can not leash the spirit of Emerson to a system, nor hitch his star to a benzine-buggy ꙮ ꙮ

Pessimism is a sublimated, transcendental optimism. The pessimist's ideals are so high that he will not, can not, conform his spirit to this world—the drifting cinder of a burned-up Asgard. Pure optimism is cerebral vacuity tempered by a stomach.

Emerson disbelieved in the temporal order. Like all the mighty brotherhood, he was at war with the petty and the transitory. In the realm of Space, Time and Circumstance, the worst always happens because the bond-servants of the triple chain are always hoping for the best.

"The Transcendentalist" was a lecture delivered at the Masonic

Temple, Boston, in January, Eighteen Hundred Forty-two. It is the great challenge to things as they are. It is not the challenge of the skeptic, but the challenge of the pessimist. It breathes the positiveness of all negations. What is worthy? asks Emerson. Your charities are sycophantic, your governments but organized theft, your civilizations a long train of felonies, and your boasted virtues but sleazy vices.

Life is a degradation, and the man lives in the slime-pits of lust. " Much of our labor seems mere waiting; it is not that we were born for." His thought is that of Buddha, the Man of Galilee, Marcus Aurelius, Seneca, Plato, Amiel, Schopenhauer, Nietzsche. These have all agreed, in diverse ways, on the essential sordidness of practical life. Life on the terms given us is an insult to the soul of man. Hurry us from this " Iceland of negations" into newer, deeper infinitudes, past these mephitic atmospheres! How came we to Molokai? We are the " butt-ends of men," the tailings of gods, celestial sawdust, leavings of past deviltries. I will none of it, cries our Hamlet of the white tunic in sublime disdain.

Nor could that subtle-seeing eye be deluded by the vesture of things. " Thou ailest here, and here," said Goethe, sticking his finger into mankind's age-long sores. "And thou rottest all over," said Emerson. These mechanical inventions—the gewgaws of a senescent race—shall all be destroyed and leave posterity with as little knowledge of them as we have of the lost arts of Egypt, a civilization that is not yet cold in death. The seas shall sob their litanies over the places where you now higgle and haggle for your dole. Your temples and shrines shall become sun-food, and you shall sooner count the stars than number the nothings of daily speech ೞ ೞ

Things will be neither better nor worse in times to come; they will be both. The balances are always kept. Evil will never grow less so long as men cling to the temporal order. Ixion is bound to his wheel, and while the wheel goes round there is no help for man.

The things that are tangible are the things that are evil. Good is a negation. Transcendentalism is a negative good. It aims to release the individual. In the Spent Dynamic alone there is hope. On the crest of the final equilibration will man find rest. Life is a series of undulations and " illusion is God's method." Facts are mere bell-buoys on the stream of infinite being. The objective world is gelatinous. Transcendental pessimism seeks another order ✍ ✍

The equilibration that Emerson dreamed of—is it aught but a wraith on the storm-billows? All motion tends to equilibration; yet a state of equilibration can not be preserved; motion begins again. And so are we played upon. The Pythagorean Harmony, the Spencerian Equilibration, the Emersonian Oversoul—are they not identical?

But we will wait. Patience! Our work is not here and the sidereal days are not for us. Passion born of fire, and thought born of pain, and beauty born of sex, and death born of life, mean nothing to us. We smile at your amblings and loathe your chicaneries. We sit with our hands folded waiting a call. If our souls were created for nothing, then to nothing we will return. " If I am the devil's child, I will live unto the devil." We will wait for eons; the waves of unguessed cycles shall foam upon unwombed worlds, and spit us forth in vestments new and strange; and still we shall wait the call of the Infinite Counselor. And if it come, we shall know; and if it do not come, we shall know too.

Francisco Ferrer

T sunrise on the morning of October Thirteenth, Nineteen Hundred Nine, at Barcelona, Francisco Ferrer was shot, by order of a court-martial appointed by the Spanish Government.
The trial had been speedy and secret.
The charge was a simple one of treason.
No charge of violence or of leading an insurrection was proved. It was simply that Ferrer's published articles and speeches had incited to riot. Thomas Jefferson fixed in our Constitution that treason should not in the United States consist in anything you might say or print, but solely in what you might do.

In Spain, as in all monarchical countries, the idea of lese-majeste prevails, and to criticize the king, in either his office or his person, may be punishable by death.

This is even so in England, but happily the English have a sense of humor, and public opinion would never allow there this tyranny over the individual.

There is quite as much liberty of speech in Great Britain as in the United States, for Public Opinion rules.

And the consensus of Public Opinion in every civilized country, even Russia, is one of horror at the death of Professor Ferrer.

Spain today stands indicted at the bar of Public Opinion, and her punishment is the execration, contempt and pity of the thinking men of the world. Even the Pope went into his chamber and refused to touch food on the day following Ferrer's death.

Count Tolstoy telegraphed a hundred words of deepest pain and regret to King Alphonso.

Men of valor, scientists, poets, decorated by the King of Spain, sent back their stars.

Scholars by the score wrote to the Academy of Science, at Madrid, asking that their names be stricken from its rolls.

The newspapers in Spain are silent—they have to be—save for the few hypocritical and studied editorials in defense of the Government. The Conservative Party, which is the Clerical Party, argues that Ferrer struck at the very heart of the Church and of the Government in his writings, and they print extracts to prove their point.

They say that all nations have the right, and it is their duty, to destroy the avowed enemies of the State and of religion.

This is the good old argument of dogmatism, that the State is right—" The King can do no wrong"—and religion is a holy thing handed down to us by God Almighty, and to criticize it is to merit death. " A traitor to God and a traitor to his Country," is a Sixteenth-century cry.

Bruno, Copernicus, Galileo, Savonarola, Huss, Wyclif, Latimer and the rest of the men known as "martyrs," died because they put their own thoughts above the thought of entrenched authority. When Ferrer was sentenced to die, he could not and did not believe that the order of execution would be carried out.

Ferrer was essentially a non-resistant, he was a man of peace, his weapons were ideas, and his shield was the armor of truth. His life was lived in the sunlight. No charges of conspiracy were proved. The secret conclave and the stealthy plot were to him unthinkable. He lectured, he wrote, he established manual-training schools. He quoted Tolstoy, John Ruskin, Emerson, Walt Whitman, Booker T. Washington, William Morris. He established ninety-six schools for the handicrafts, claiming that the youth of Spain—boys and girls—should be taught to be useful.

He was a rich man and he used his wealth without stint in the cause of the plain people.

He said that idleness was a crime, and that our souls could be saved only by human service, and not by prayer. He declined to allow priests to introduce religion into these schools.

He believed in a religion of service, not of services.

He declared that kings and queens should be reverenced only as they possess competence, love and pity, and not because chance has thrown them into this position of power. He condemned conscription, and the appropriation of money for war; and especially did he deprecate the making of war by one nation on another beneath it in intelligence. He condemned the use of strong drink, and always and forever his appeal was for Economy, Temperance, Industry, Beauty and Use.

Naturally in all these things he criticized the Grand Dukes—or the hereditary reigning class—and he smote the prelates who lived fat on the labor of the people, offering prizes that were not theirs to give, and issuing threats they could not execute.

That is to say, Ferrer supplied the proofs for his own condemnation. Could Emerson or Whitman have stood up and pleaded not guilty? ❧ ❧

From the point of view of the Clerics, this man deserved death. An excuse came when a mob uprose against the established order. As if a riot should occur in Chicago and the police would seize Clarence Darrow, Horace Traubel, Bolton Hall, Charles Ferguson and William Marion Reedy and throw them into the donjon-keep, and apply the Third Degree. Ah, yes, the Third Degree, that little cross-section of the Spanish Inquisition which we still retain and use here in America, the land of the partially free and the brave more or less. For shame—merciful Christ! for shame! So Ferrer smiled when they passed sentence of death upon him. He thought the world had gone beyond that. He was sure they were only trying to frighten him.

But outside the walls, his daughter knew the temper of the Clerics. She hastened to Rome, saw the Pope in person, and begged him to interfere and save her father. The Pope, too, felt sure that Spain would realize the weight of Public Opinion and not go back to a medieval procedure. So he simply sent a mild telegram to King Alphonso, suggesting clemency.

The daughter saw the King and he allayed her fears with hypo-critical promises.

The day of the execution came, and Ferrer heard the iron-shod feet of soldiers coming to his cell.

They ordered him to prepare for death.

For a moment nerves gave way, and this gray-haired teacher of sixty collapsed.

But it was only for a moment.

He refused the services of the priests in attendance. He even asked them not to raise the crucifix over his head. He declined the strong drink, and said, " I die sober and I die sane. I ask for no forgiveness, and I make no apologies! "

He was led forth to the place of execution. His request that he might face the firing-line was refused.

His eyes were bandaged and he was turned to the wall, his back to the soldiers.

His last words were, " Long live the Modern School!"

The order to fire was given, and Ferrer fell.

What was a man but a moment before was now a mutilated and torn mass of flesh, blood and bones, tumbled in a heap.

Did this dispose of Francisco Ferrer?

Oh, no, you can not get rid of a man of ideas by killing him. His spirit abides, and his soul goes marching on.

Spain thought to kill Ferrer. What she did was to arouse the world of Public Opinion on the divine right of free speech.

The death of a man, any man, is a little thing, but the effects of that death, and the lesson of it, may be burned into the hearts of millions, may sear the pages of history, and shake the thrones of tyrants until they shall topple and be swallowed up by the sea.

❡ And so it seems that a mass-meeting was held in Paris in memory of Francisco Ferrer, to protest against his martyrdom, and to plead in behalf of free speech.

Such meetings were held all over the world. I had the honor of attending one such at Carnegie Hall, New York, and mingled my voice with that of others in behalf of freedom of speech, and in protest for the death of Francisco Ferrer, good and great

After the meeting in New York, the audience quietly dispersed, each going his respective way.

But in Paris it was different.

Several of the speakers were avowed Anarchists. Some called themselves Socialists. The audience was wrought up to a high pitch of excitement, and when the people filed out they moved a solid, raging, howling mob down the boulevard.

They broke every street-lamp on the route, smashed windows, broke in doors.

Coming to the park they destroyed the seats, and were piling them up preparatory to setting fire to them when the gendarmes charged the mob, and broke their scabbards over the heads of the leaders.

That closed the " Ferrer Demonstration." Some days after, another Ferrer mass-meeting was called and the police promptly barred the doors of the hall and called the meeting off.

Then there were cries and howls from divers and sundry concerning repression of the people and the violation of the rights of a free people

As I understand it, street-lights are beautiful and beneficent. They aid the people—all of the people—on their way. The beggar or the merchant, the child or the soldier, the working girl and the millionaire, all are benefited.

Is the cause of the dead teacher, Ferrer, helped by destroying the lights and smashing windows?

Park benches are useful alike for tired people, and those out of a job. Also, park benches are useful and convenient for Anarchists and Socialists who do not and will not work. Is freedom's cause helped by burning property which all the people need?

The fact is, this lawless rabble seized upon the death of Ferrer as an excuse for disorder.

The event gave them a chance to lift the lid off hell.

Civilization was unmasked, and the savage surged to the fore. Ferrer stood for progress, but the Paris mob stood for dissolution and disorder.

When a man was burned at the stake at Cairo, Illinois, a few weeks ago, and the flames licked the clothing of the poor wretch, well-dressed and respectable women danced around the funeral-pyre in glee, while others, perhaps of a more practical turn, ran for kerosene. The devil was loose, horns rampant, tail akimbo.

℃ Recently, Emma Goldman and several Anarchists went into court, in Philadelphia, and asked for an injunction restraining the police from interfering with their meetings.

As all the world knows, Emma Goldman is the chief anarch of her time. She believes that law and government are instruments for the suppression of the individual, and she says so. Yet, she declares that she does not stand for violence. And it must be said that in much that she says and does there breathes a fine spirit of humanity ✎ ✎

But in her contempt for the police, the agents of law, she has over and over incited her auditors to deeds of violence. Go ask the cities of Pittsburgh and Buffalo what they think of " peaceful Anarchy!" Street-lamps, windows and park benches go by the board when Anarchists become zealous. The activity of an Anarchist is in the line of destruction and not creation, and murder is not to him strange nor wrong.

Is that all?

Not exactly. Berkmann was a convert to the revolutionary teachings, and was so convinced of the beauty and righteousness of the philosophy that he procured a pistol, a knife and a dynamite-bomb, and went to the office of Henry C. Frick in Pittsburgh, with intent to murder and destroy.

Fortunately his aim was bad and he merely wounded several men. This philosophic Anarchist was captured and given a long term in prison. The excuse now made for Berkmann is that he was mentally unbalanced, having been overwrought by dwelling on the wrongs of the poor and the crimes of capitalism. However, no one can meet Berkmann and think him insane. He holds the same opinions now that he did when he tried to kill Frick, only then he carried them to a logical conclusion.

Czolgosz, who killed McKinley, shot truer and was sent to the chair ∞ ∞

So please note that now come our Anarchistic friends who scorn and repudiate law, and invoke the law to give them protection in the matter of free speech in order that they may destroy law. These Anarchists quote Thomas Jefferson and cite the Constitution, the highest legal document in America. That is, they demand the right to stand under the protecting wings of the Constitution, while they tear it to tatters.

And certainly we all believe in free speech, and the right to hold and express an individual opinion.

But when this speech incites the weak and the volatile to destroy street-lamps, break windows, burn park benches and go after our captains of industry and officers of government, with deadly weapons and murderous intent, we say that speech then becomes assault, and the tongue a deadly weapon. Berkmann is a living certificate to the effectiveness of Anarchistic teaching.

Emma Goldman and Berkmann once applied to the Superintendent of Carnegie Hall in New York for leave to preach the beauties of Anarchy therein.

Andrew Carnegie who built this hall was a partner of Henry C. Frick. That is to say, the enterprise and initiative of Frick helped make Carnegie Hall possible. Having tried to kill Frick, the very folks who endeavored to murder him, now go to him and ask to rent his hall in order to denounce him!

And this brings us around to the decision of the judge, who having listened to the able plea of Emma Goldman in Philadelphia in behalf of free speech, and agreeing with very much that she had to offer, disposed of the question by saying, " There must be a limit to the use of language. And while the expression of an individual opinion is proper, yet when purposely or otherwise the expression incites others to deeds of violence, the limit is reached, and the duty of the police is then to take steps to protect the lives, persons and property of the public. The prayer for an injunction is denied." ʂ ʂ

Incendiarism is setting fire to property. But if you see a man piling hay against your house, and pouring on kerosene, even though there be neither smoke nor fire present, you have a right to protest, and forcibly.

Upon the police falls the responsibility of protecting property and keeping the peace. For the courts to restrain the police from interfering with a speaker who has in the past by his words incited to deeds of violence and lawlessness, does not seem sensible or right. There is one thing quite as sacred as free speech, and that is the rights of the people to go about their peaceful occupations, and to enjoy the fruits of their toil.

Not long ago I was talking to a zealous Marxian on the subject of free speech, and the preaching of discontent. In the conversation I voiced some of the sentiments I have here expressed, as to the necessity of placing a limit on inflammatory utterances. His answer was, " If I had my way, any one who argues against free speech as you do, should be suppressed."

His ancestry was Celtic.

In law, the lie is the first blow. That is, you can assault a man with a murderous tongue, the same as with a murderous weapon. If a man stands in the street and uses language that may cause some one to throw a brick through my window, he is not exercising a right or a privilege within the intent of the law, and the police should interfere and restrain the worthy talkissimus, even though he claim to be a messianic philosopher.

In a "free society"—that is, a society without law—would there be more free speech than now?

Not exactly.

The man who lifted up his voice against certain people or certain things would be suppressed as quickly as would an Orangeman who got numerous on the seventeenth of March.

The assault of the tongue would find a quick limit, for Fingy Connors would forge to the fore, and fix bounds to both speech and action. Free speech would be limited by Fingy to what he thought proper and right.

In every community there are lawless, careless, slipshod folks with small grasp on the truth that one man's rights end where another's begin. These people cut their initials in places that would be better unadorned; they may pull up flowers by the roots; lift gates off their hinges; strew papers on the street; shout and yell when honest men are asleep.

Along railroad-lines we see where this type of person has used the signs for targets and filled them with bird-shot. Depredations of this small, but annoying sort are seen by the traveler from Maine to the Gulf of Mexico.

In the elevated and subway trains in New York, rowdyism on Saturday and Sunday nights recently became intolerable. The loafers insulted women, frightened children and often assaulted men. They roamed through the cars, knocking off hats, sprinkling ink, and passing out language that was atrocious.

The employees were powerless.

To stamp the thing out, one hundred men were selected from the police force. These men, mostly young, mingled with the crowds on the cars from six to ten o'clock. They wore citizens' clothes, and often shabby garments. But they were men who could hit quick and hard.

When lawlessness started, they took a quick hand. On all station-platforms were policemen to receive prisoners.

Several hundred ruffians were seized, subdued, handcuffed and locked up.

One offender pleaded the right of free speech, and got a calloused fist in his mouth by way of reply.

Now, in a state of Anarchy, if hoodlumism started, what would we do?

Well, we would endure it for a time, and then the better class of citizens would pick out a few hard-hitting men, and appoint them a committee to enforce decency and order. If Anarchy prevailed, I would post a notice on my farm that any one shooting my chickens and destroying my trees would be allowed to do it three times, and then he would get his block knocked off, or get shot so full of holes he would look like a pepper-box.

Other peaceful neighbors would join with me, and we would pass rules as to what was allowable and what not.

Then we would hire a stocky man, freckled, with bow legs, to see that these rules were enforced.

So then we again have law, for law simply formulates the will, wish and desire of the many.

Fra Junipero Serra

AMONG the world's great workers—and in the front rank there have been only a scant half-dozen—stands Fra Junipero Serra. This is the man who made the California Missions possible. In artistic genius, as a teacher of handicrafts, and as an industrial leader, he performed a feat unprecedented, and which probably will never again be equaled. In a few short years he caused a great burst of beauty to bloom and blossom, where before was only a desert waste.

The personality of a man who could not only convert to Christianity three thousand Indians, but who could set them to work, must surely be sublimely great. Not only did they labor, but they produced art of a high order. These missions which lined the Coast from San Francisco to San Diego, every forty miles, were Manual Training Schools, founded on a religious concept.

Junipero taught that, unless you backed up your prayer with work, God would never answer your petitions. And the wonderful transformations which this man worked in characters turned on the fact that he made them acceptable and beautiful. Here is a lesson for us! He ranks with Saint Benedict, who rescued classic art from the dust of time and gave it to the world. Junipero is one with Albrecht Durer, Lorenzo the Magnificent, Michelangelo, Leonardo da Vinci, Friedrich Froebel, John Ruskin and William Morris. These men all taught the Gospel of Work, and the Sacredness of Beauty and Use.

Junipero was without question the greatest teacher of Manual Training which this continent has so far seen. Without tools, apparatus or books, save as he created them, he evolved an architecture and an art, utilizing the services of savages, and transforming these savages in the process, for the time at least, into men of taste, industry and economy.

That this miracle of human energy and love could not endure, and that after Fra Junipero had passed out, there being none to take his place, the Indians relapsed into their racial ways, was to be expected ◆ ◆

When Junipero reached California he was fifty-three years old. He died at seventy-one, so his life's work was compressed into the short space of eighteen years.

On Mount Rubidoux, at Riverside, there has been erected a giant cross, eighteen feet high, in commemoration of Fra Junipero. Here he often used to come and pray when the sun went down. This heroic cross outlined against the sky, with its setting amid the mighty rocks, is a most impressive sight, symboling to us the seeming barrenness and sorrow of the man's life. Yet down below, stretching away on every hand, are smiling, peaceful orange-groves, from which, blown on the night breeze, come to us the sweet perfume of perpetual blossoms.

Thus, with the life of this unselfish soul, in spite of seeming failure, his prayer for beauty has been answered.

In the great "Sunset Cross" has been set a bronze tablet, and upon it there are these words:

The Beginning of Civilization in California
FRA JUNIPERO SERRA
Apostle
Legislator
Builder
To Commemorate His Good Works This
Tablet Is Hereby Placed.
Unveiled by William Howard Taft, 27th President of the
United States, October 12, A. D., '09

The guiding spirit in this good work of keeping alive the best in the mission spirit is Frank A. Miller, Master of the Mission Inn. ⁋ No visitor to California should fail to visit beautiful Riverside and see with what lavish love the Millers have expressed, without being slavish imitators, this passion for beauty that once filled the heart of Junipero.

Even President Taft, jaded from much sightseeing, was thrilled by what he saw at Riverside. At the "evening meal" at the Mission Inn, where Bishop Conaty told a little of the life and work of Junipero Serra, the President listened with marked attention and a misty something came to his eyes, which had not before occurred on the whole trip.

The closing words of the Bishop's address are too earnest and heartfelt to be lost:

"Mr. President, we are here tonight, not to ask any favors at your hands, for you have granted to us all that our hearts desire in Southern California. We are not here tonight to give you advice; you have had lots of it, and you are wise enough to make the selection yourself as to which advice you will follow. But we are here to ask you to unite with us in honoring the memory of a great and good man, a man who understood what a true man understands and does—his duty to his fellow man. We are here tonight to honor the memory of Fra Junipero Serra, founder of the Missions of California, a man who crossed the ocean in days when oceans were perilous to cross, that he might help even the poorest of God's children, the most abandoned of the races on the continent, the savage Indians of California.

"I know, Mr. President, that back of that man in his brown habit, as he moved, footsore and weary, year by year, visiting his Missions, I know that behind him and in him was the spirit, the character which developed, in its highest form, that which makes true men and which makes life better worth living because they have lived—a missionary without selfishness and of true character ✿ ✿

"Mr. President, this community and this State of ours are honored by the fact that you, as the Chief Executive of our Nation, and as the first citizen of the Republic, today unveiled a tablet to the first citizen of California; that you, Mr. President, by your act have given to the world the seal of your authority upon that fact, that good men should never be allowed to die and that good names should always be held as the most priceless inheritance in which a people can glory.

" Mr. President, you have unveiled today the bronze that commemorates the memory of Junipero Serra. No more pleasing tribute can you give to California than the high honor you have paid this day to the memory of this truly great Franciscan Educator, Apostle and Builder. Our Landmark Club is ninety per cent non-Catholic. And thanks to that spirit, the friends of the Mission are one in preserving for California the sweetest of her inheritances, keeping bright the jewel in her crown—the Missions of the Franciscan fathers.

" And, Mr. President, thanks to the Master of the Inn whose life has been devoted to the preservation of those memories, we are his guests with you tonight and give our loving tribute to the memory of that gentle and noble man, Junipero Serra."

Talmage

ON the death of Talmage the metropolitan newspapers, for the most part, disposed of the man with a squib. Those that gave him half a column or more did so with intent to cheapen, disparage and belittle.

In 1889 the New York *Sun* that befogs for all, gave Talmage the most tremendous avalanche of abuse that was ever heaped upon any living man in America. The article covered just one complete page of the paper, and must have been months in preparation. It was a lawyer's brief, worked out with infinite care, with intent to indict the man before the bar of public opinion so he could never again show his face. The writer followed the great preacher from boyhood, step by step, from that shabby little toll-gate house kept by his father and mother in New Jersey, where hardship, toil and deprivation crouched. Sleuth-like it sniffed out his secret faults, enlarged his lapses, gave base motives and selfish intent, filled every hiatus with suspicion, and showed how chicanery, trickery and deceit had been the things upon which the most famous preacher in America had built. The final chapter of the indictment left Talmage accused, by inference, of burning his own church in order to conceal crimes that the virtuous *Sun* was too considerate to expose.

But the roast tipped to t' other side, and Dana was damned, not Talmage. A clever writer, with a lawyer-like ability to seize all the facts, or pretended facts, on one side, and make the most of them, can riddle the reputation of any saint in the calendar. But unless you already hate a man, abuse will not avail. People said, " Talmage may have his failings, but he has at least a few good qualities, and he should certainly be given credit for these." Dana forgot that men are great for what they are, and not for what they are not. Having shown the worst Talmage was, he was in duty bound to reveal the best. There is where Dana's diatribe came tardy off and made the judicious grieve. A more skilful logician would have made a pretense of being unprejudiced and have masked his malice with a show of reason—not so Dana.

The result was a great wave of sympathy for Talmage. Instead of being squelched he was elevated to the position of martyr. Never was he so popular. And then began the syndicating of his sermons in thousands of newspapers, so that he was followed weekly by not less than six million readers. When he lectured the buildings were so taxed that often the meetings were adjourned and the speaking was out-of-doors. Thus at Kansas City, one Sunday morning, I heard Talmage preach from the grandstand of the race track to ten thousand people.

Talmage taught " the blood of Jesus;" he believed in the miracles; he upheld Moses as a historian and teacher of science. This sort of dogma is not ours; but mixed up with his theology Talmage revealed a deal of tender sympathy, and brought the Man of Galilee very close to vast numbers of tired, over-worked and heavy-laden people. He pleaded for tenderness, gentleness, patience, love and kindness to those who are nearest you. His was a doctrine of cheerfulness, cleanliness, order and decency. He never spoke in public without bringing in the mother who once held you in her arms and rocked you to sleep, kissing away your childish troubles. For the old, the infirm, the sick, he was an Eye, an Ear, a Trumpet and a Voice from the hilltops.

And who dares say that Talmage was all wrong—was he not right in these things? We should be gentle with the weak, considerate with the erring, patient towards the young, and the white-haired mother who once carried us in her arms should now receive our kindest love and care—here is where no one can disagree with Talmage. Grant that these things are trite, admit they are commonplace, yet they should be said and said yet again. Did Talmage " harp on one string? " I am glad, for he ministered to millions who needed him—ministered to those who were not ready for any music but this one-stringed harp.

On the death of Talmage I bought a copy of the *Sun*. I said, " Here is an opportunity for his old-time antagonist to say a judicious word—a kind word—the hatchet of the dead Dana will be buried in the grave of Talmage, and over the mounded turf the *Sun* will cause thyme and mignonette to blossom, just to show that the malice of this little life is meaningless, and beyond the tomb the strife of earnest and o'er-wrought men has no place." So I bought the *Sun*—the *Sun* that tans for all. And instead of the spray of mignonette, I found a bunch of cockle-burs and nettles, tied round with a creeper of poison ivy.

The article was evidently written by a Sophomore while the line-o' type man waited at the bottom of the stairs.

In the bare stickful of comment there were the words " faker," " hypocrisy," " deceit." And then followed that very thread-bare story about Talmage preparing a series of sermons, heading each with the place where delivered, and distributing these sermons to the newspapers. The damning count followed that the sermon supposed to be delivered at Birmingham was not given at all, because Talmage changed his route and did n't go to Birmingham. It also said that the man baptized in the Jordan was a tramp whom Talmage seized by the neck, pulled into the creek and ducked—and then gave him a quarter and a kick at parting.

Hurrah for the *Sun!*

In the days of Dana every man on the *Sun* wrote just like Dana, hated just like Dana, and liked the things that Dana liked. But Dana is dead, and now this man he hated has followed him across the Great Divide. Only one man is now on the editorial staff of the *Sun* who worked there when Dana was alive, and yet you will still see the labored effort to " write like Dana," and keep alive a tradition upon which the mossy marbles rest.

Talmage will live in history. The story of Christianity in America
can never be written and Talmage left out. His place will never
be filled, and it is not necessary it should be. But the memory of
the man will never be smothered with silence, nor damned by
disparagement. He was what he was.

The secular press denounced him because he did the things it
everywhere does: it wrote his epitaph with a sneer dipped in
aqua fortis. The religious papers give him scant praise, and
Zion's Herald, of Boston, openly affirms that Talmage once
drank " bottled stout " after giving a lecture on temperance at
Glasgow. The *Sun* that rots over all, also prints the story; but
the *Herald* gives the name of the host who supplied the stout
and information—with no word of comment concerning this host
who entertained his friend and afterward " exposed " him. As for
for myself, I'd rather get rip-roaring, fighting, beastly drunk,
than reveal for ridicule the lapse of a friend with whom I had
broken bread.

Talmage was not a drunkard, he was not a wine-bibber—no one
ever accused him of excess. The most they could say was that he
was " inconsistent." To recount that on this occasion he tasted
wine, and on that drank " bottled stout " is small, mean, quibbling
and absurd. To tell of these things is worse than to do them.
Talmage preached total abstinence, and he should have been a
total abstainer, but if he, at rare intervals, broke over the rule
in the house of a supposed friend, it ill becomes us little men to
gloat in glee over his faults.

Would you like to go to Heaven with a man like that with whom
Talmage drank bottled stout? He would lure you on with
ambrosial **XXX**, and then run and tell St. Peter you were a Tank
from Grand Rapids.

But surely the Sophomore of the *Sun* is worse than the
Zion's Herald Scribe. The Scribe may go to Heaven, but the
Sophomore will yammer forever between the worlds, fit neither

for Heaven nor Hell. He is a sinner who nails a man because he is another. The Devil, at least, is a gentleman, and he would be ashamed to associate with the spawn of earth who would drink with his friend and then gibber and squeak over it among the unco gude. There are a few things beside holy water the Devil abhors: a fight between enemies delights his soul, but disloyalty in friendship he will not stand for. He demands that his own shall stand by him, and each by each other, or hike for stellar space.

It seems that it remained for the " infidel " and the outsider to pen the passing word that will probably be accepted as posterity's verdict concerning T. DeWitt Talmage. Hate and disparagement will die, lavish praise will be forgot, but the encyclopedia of the year 2000, I prophesy, will quote William Marion Reedy, who says:

"A great force, a tremendous vitality, has gone out of the world. A voice that spoke to millions is silent; a fount of thought that flooded the country for many decades is dried and barren. Whatever the verdict upon DeWitt Talmage's theology, his rhetoric, or his logic, there can be no question of his power. He dominated the place he filled, the public that sat under him. His mind dominated millions of other minds. A tower of vitality, he showered that vitality copiously. The cool, close logician may convince the chosen circle; it is the man of impassioned appeal that sways the multitude. Huge of voice, vast of mouth, everlastingly in motion, tongue and foot, hand and brain, he held captive some of the largest English-speaking assemblages that have ever gathered in the temples of our time. Following upon the steps of Henry Ward Beecher, he lived in a period wherein he stood unique, a survival of exuberant strength, a dean of a faculty fast fading from this generation. Much of the Beecher fortune fastened itself to his career. Beecher had his enemies, his assailants, his scandals; Talmage did not escape. The man who swayed the

Brooklyn Tabernacle to its very pillars was almost convicted of deceit, heresy and falsehood, and, afterwards, in England, was publicly accused of intemperance. This was the occasion for his tremendous shout: 'Another lie nailed!' The church militant was what he never ceased to represent. He clamored and fought, fought and clamored, for the greater light to fall upon the minds of the millions. His sermons, aside from the people they impressed directly, at first hand, went out upon the land in print until there were few corners of the wildest lands where the most benighted countryman did not read, weekly, a Talmage sermon. The reading of that Talmage sermon was for hundreds of thousands the single link to questions of the better, biblical life. God and man, church and prayer, came into countless American homes only through the sermons of Talmage. As a great, commanding figure, he survived into a period of lesser men. He was a man of iron, and of brass; the blare of his brazen rhetoric deafened a world. Puny, placid reputations shrink before these triumphant tyrants in the world's arena; small things, small cavils, spiteful detractions, shrivel and disappear. There remains the memory of a huge, vast-bulking figure; a figure that kept millions at attention, and kept fresh and vivid to the multitude that purest well of English, the Bible." ❦ ❦

WU TING FANG

Wu Ting Fang

IT looks now as if Wu Ting Fang, our old college chum, will be the first sure-enough President of the Republic of China.

Doctor Wu is the canniest Chink that ever came over the cosmic pike.

He has certain qualities that make him akin to Benjamin Disraeli. He is clever, witty, rapid, satirical, patient, ambitious, and possesses purpose, plus. He is a man who mystifies everybody and is deceived by none.

Wu Ting Fang is a walking certificate as to the effectiveness of American journalism. Twice has he been Minister from China to the United States, also to Spain and to Peru. When he first arrived in America, he wore English-made clothes, a chimney-top hat and a top coat. He carried a cane, and his manner was that of the educated cosmopolitan.

And why not? The father of Doctor Wu was a convert to Methodism. He became a member of one of the Mission colonies, and was spoken of as a " rice Christian." In this colony, Wu Ting Fang was born, and little Wu spoke English before he did Chinese. When a youth, Wu was sent to England, and for a time was at Oxford ๑ ๑

When Doctor Wu first came to America he was forty-five. Very soon after landing here he discarded Christian clothes, and wore his shirt outside of his trousers. We are also told that he evolved a pigtail in a single night.

About this time Li Hung Chang appeared on the American horizon. Li was a genuine Celestial—Wu an imitation. Li could not speak the English language, and did not want to. He had, however, a very able interpreter.

Li, it was, who set the example of propounding those delightful, executive-session questions. For instance, Li Hung Chang asked

George H. Daniels what his salary was, and then followed this up with, " How much do you steal and yet not get caught? "

He asked the ladies as to how many children they had, why they did n't have more, whether they were on good terms with their husbands, and did they love their lovers more than their husbands. If so, why?

Then it was that our old friend Wu Ting Fang got the cue, literally and poetically, and evolved into the guileless Heathen, who looks at everything with wide-open, curious eyes, to compare inwardly the things he sees with the things at home across the sea. All of the questions asked by Li Hung Chang were repeated by Wu Ting Fang.

When Doctor Wu asked Doctor Chauncey M. Depew how many wives he had, the reporters got busy and the wires flashed the embarrassing interrogations. Wu Ting Fang was great copy! Of course, no white man, or any other man wearing English clothes, could have had the brass-plated effrontery to ask these questions; but a man in Oriental costume, protected by a seemingly imperfect knowledge of the language, could interrogate in a way that would put us all to the bad. Doctor Wu delighted in getting some one to talk to him in pigtail, thus, " No checkee, no washee," and then answer them in faultless English.

It is a well-known fact that a foreigner with an innocent outside is received by many ladies in good society, with a fearlessness that the ladies never manifest in dealing with an equal of the genus gent.

The East Indian pundits have innocence to incinerate, and are usually regarded as incapable of guile. The Vivakenanda Rootabaga is looked upon as very wise, and ninety-nine per cent pure. Their curiosity is all flavored with a sweet desire to know.

And this was the pose of Wu Ting Fang, the man educated in London, and versed from babyhood in Western ways.

Wu Ting Fang, in his youth, professed the Christian faith, but he sloughed it with his Christian clothes. Now he is a Confucian, and it was delightful to see the naive way in which he discovered spots on our religious sun, and found that Emerson only echoed the high ethics of Confucius. I saw a preacher take two hours to explain to the innocent Wu the Westminster Creed. And the wily Wu listened as if it were all news.

Americans are a pioneer people. There is much here, no doubt, that is very rude and crude and absurd. Wu Ting Fang pricked our bubbles without our discovering what had been done until after he was gone.

The man must have gone home every night, locked himself in his room, and laughed aloud at the way he had taken in American Society. Yet we might have known that he was not so unsophisticated as he seemed, for he was constantly springing our American slang and voicing our idioms.

I was once seated near him at a banquet. On the other side of the table was a lady whose dress was very much decollete. There was nothing about this to shock Wu Ting Fang, who had attended banquets in England, France and America for twenty-five years or more, but he gazed at this lady without a sign of emotion on his face and finally addressed her, asking, " How does it happen that you are overexposed and underdeveloped? "

He had the whole table in a roar by interrogating the Toastmaster as to how many wives he had. He questioned the guests as to their methods of life and their hopes and ambitions, making little side remarks all the time, which, of course, were for the press, and which the reporters were not slow in picking up. He shook hands with the waiters, seemingly thinking they were guests. ⁋ The dishes brought on the table came in for criticism, and he compared them with the dishes he was used to at home. Most of the things he refused to eat, simply pecking at them and making remarks about them, for our great amusement.

All of this was straight play-acting.

There was always a great temptation, on meeting Doctor Wu, to open up negotiations by firing at him questions, this in self-defense, for his was the choice of weapons.

A fair, innocent, little dimity thing in pink and white once said, " Doctor Wu, what is the difference between marriage in China and marriage in America? "

And Wu replied, " In China, you see, my dear little girl, the bride never sees her husband before they are married, while in America she never sees him afterward." A lady once asked Wu where he would live if he had his choice.

He replied, " Madam, I would live in Ireland."

Very naturally she asked, " Why? "

" Because Ireland is the only country in the world where the Irish have no influence."

" Mr. Wu," said a Chicago man, " I hear there 's a movement in China to cut off those pigtails you fellows wear. Why do you wear the fool thing, anyway? "

" Why," responded Wu, eyeing his man as he spoke, " why do you wear your fool mustache? "

" Oh," replied the other, " I 've got an impossible mouth."

" Er—so I should suppose, from some of your remarks," said Wu.

He was dining one night beside a bishop, a clergyman of high standing, who wore an emerald-ring which he prized highly for its history as well as for its beauty.

" Will you let me see your ring? " Wu asked.

The bishop gladly passed the trinket to him.

Wu examined it critically, and then returned it, saying:

" It is the best imitation emerald I ever saw."

The bishop was slightly startled. He asserted it was genuine, and had been used in England by churchmen for two hundred years, and had always been considered a flawless gem.

" Nevertheless," Wu replied, " it is an imitation emerald."

Some time later the bishop met a gem-expert in New York and

showing him the ring, asked his opinion of the gem. The expert looked it over and told him it was an imitation. Some time after that the bishop again met Mr. Wu, and he told him what he had done.

" I have reproached myself for having told you," Wu remarked.

" I 'm glad you did tell me," replied the bishop. " Else, I might have transmitted a lie to posterity."

" You would have been in good company in doing that," said Wu, and the incident was at an end.

A Washington correspondent, when trying to interview him, was met with the question: " How much do you earn a year? "

" Oh," he replied evasively, " I earn about twice as much as I am paid."

" Indeed," replied Wu. " Do you find it difficult to save anything on your twenty thousand a year? "

Wu always likes to have the last word, and he usually gets it—he says the last word first.

The man, nevertheless, is a strong and able individual. He is filled with the idea of Republicanism. At heart he is a democrat. He has an exquisite sense of humor. He knows more about Christianity than most Christians, and he sees the sham in our institutions. At the same time, he is able to appreciate the best, and out of the mass of our enterprises, which we claim as democratic, he perceives that the trend is right, proper and altogether beautiful. The good that is in America he is trying to transfer to China. There is no doubt that we have a deal to learn from these people across the sea. If missionaries had been sent to China in order to learn from them, instead of trying to inoculate them with our ideas, America would have been better off and probably China would not have lost anything.

In China, the conventional, high-class mandarins regard Doctor Wu Ting Fang with suspicion. His degrees and titles are to them ridiculous. This, however, is to be expected. The man is a radical.

Also, he is a cosmopolitan, and it is worth while to note that while he is in America he wears the Chinese costume, yet in China a good Stein-Bloch smart suit suffices.

Wu Ting Fang does not stand for war; his attitude is eminently that of diplomacy and peace, but he has not been slow to avail himself of the results of war and violence, and so today he looms large out of the misty conflict in China as the biggest figure in the Empire. He is big enough to advise the Prince Regent to resign; and he is big enough to name his successor. And this means that the people will name him!

Wu Ting Fang built the first railroad in China. He is an economist by nature. Industrialism has been his hobby, and it is interesting to know that in a recent visit to China of Charles M. Schwab, orders were given for American steel to be used in railroading, steamship-building and skyscrapers for China, all to the extent of something like twenty-five million dollars, this largely through the indirect influence of Wu Ting Fang, who never deals with his party direct, but always at second hand. It is a wonderful psychology, this thing of never showing your hand, but doing things by indirection.

When George Arliss gets through with the portrayal of Benjamin Disraeli, Earl of Beaconsfield, a good character for him to portray would be Wu Ting Fang. If nobody else volunteers to write the play, I will do it myself, submitting proofs to Wu Ting Fang, who possesses a fine literary appreciation, especially where his own ego is involved, although the idea is abroad that he only speaks English with a chopstick.

Buy your tickets for the concert!

Amiel

THE Nineteenth Century gave to the world three great skeptics: Ernest Renan, Henri Amiel and Robert G. Ingersoll. The skepticism of Renan was a gay skepticism. It capered all over the universe. The world to him was a playground. Was there no God? Well, what matter? Was the soul of man only matter highly refined? What difference did that make? Have we not archeology, history and philosophy to console us? The world is a beautiful red apple; let us eat it up before it rots on our hands. He was a brave, ironic spirit, with a touch of the satyr's glee in living. Ingersoll was the Almighty's jester, and the tinkle of the bells on his suit of motley could only be silenced by the sound of the splash of Charon's oars.

Ingersoll did his work so thoroughly and well that it will never have to be done again. He laughed the Devil and the clergy out of court. He quashed their claims forevermore. The Devil lived just as long as the clergy kept him alive, and now he survives only in merry vaudeville—thanks to Ingersoll.

Amiel was the saddest skeptic the European world has known. He bit the apple of untrammeled thought that Renan held out to him and he found a worm at the core. Amiel was the lordliest victim that the great Moloch, the Ideal, ever claimed. He was a regal soul, felled by Thought, possessing a brain that in its operations was as subtle as light, an interior eye that pierced all the veils of illusion. He lived a solitary god of futile dreams.

The *Journal Intime* is the minutiæ of his soul, jotted down at various intervals during thirty years. There is no book like it in the world. Montaigne, Saint Augustine, Rousseau, Maurice de Guerin pale their fires before this feat of introspective vivisection. The minds of the great self-revealers, if Montaigne alone be excepted, are surface minds compared to this tremendous revelation of a soul in its inferno, this epiphany of a God of Woe; this stricken Prometheus, chained to the granite walls of Necessity, his vitals picked by the vultures of Doubt.

He was a Hindu sage who had once reached Nirvana, but had fallen again into ways of the flesh. He was the victim of some terrible parental mistake. Surely he was not conceived in joy. He himself intimated that he was a victim of tired sheets. He was a spectator who stood on the banks of the river of Time and watched the hurried flow of all the baubles of earth—himself included—over that troubled surface. He was a man petrified by a vision of the Infinite. Half of his soul lay immobile in Eternity; the other half trailed through the sewers of Matter.

Being a god, a bit out of focus, he yet saw all sides of all problems. He knew that an opinion on any subject excluded an opposite opinion. Hegel had said that all opinion was guilt. To make an assertion is to take sides. What side shall we take in an infinite universe? All things are in process of change. What is true in a world where nothing lasts, where there is a perpetual becoming, an endless, issueless striving, a rebeginning each moment?

To live is sin—that is the burden of Amiel's journal. And it is not the Sour-Dough of worldly failure that utters this. It is Wisdom's last word, the ripened conclusion of one of the intellectual giants of the ages. And has not that been the conclusion of the great thinkers of all time? Sophocles, Koheleth, Æschylus, Buddha, Lucretius, Plato, Hegel, Schopenhauer, Leopardi—have they not given utterance to the same thought? Did not Christ Himself say that Satan was Prince of this world? And yet Amiel doubted his doubts. Like Pascal, he suffered all things, groped through all the varying phases of his mind to find no exit. Pain alone was real to Amiel—all else was illusion.

" The world is but an allegory; the idea is more real than the fact; fairy-tales and legends are as true as natural history," he says in one of his entries. All matter is merely emblematic. The universe is a myth of thought. It is a dream within a dream. It is a shadowy projection of the unknown God. All action is a phantasmagoria, meaningless because it is transitory. Why should a man do anything if nothing lasts?

To him, Pain was the great Fact. " Those who have not suffered are still wanting in depth," he says. Happiness intoxicates, stupefies, numbs, slays. With suffering comes insight, and with insight comes resignation, renunciation, the stilling of the will, the merging of the individual soul in the World-Soul. It is the wisdom of Marcus Aurelius, the pagan who has so much to teach Christians

Amiel's type of mind was unique. He can be compared with no one. His nearest analogy is Hamlet. Indeed, Amiel was the Hamlet of his time, the man who picked all things to pieces and strewed the wreckage over the literary world—but not in a spirit of mere destructiveness. He wept as he destroyed; he lashed himself anew at each denial. His infidelity was a prayer. And when he asked, " Is there a God? " there was more faith in the question than in the dogmatic assertions of all the creeds.

He says the profoundest things with the ease and simplicity of a man relating an after-dinner story. " Isis lifts the corner of her veil, and he who perceives the great mystery beneath is struck with giddiness. I can scarcely breathe. It seems to me that I am hanging by a thread above the fathomless abyss of Destiny. Is this the Infinite face to face, and intuition of the last great death?" The last great death! Out of Karma's web, free of the wheel of illusion, beyond the reach of Maya! This, after all, was Amiel's elemental impulse. He dreamed of the Lost Land, the great unmapped territory that lies beyond matter and motion. He turned constantly to this mystical dream with passionate yearning. He was like a child lost in a woods who dimly remembers his home.

Like all minds of the first order, he had no love for science or scientific methods. He says succinctly, "Science is a lucid madness occupied in tabulating its own necessary hallucinations." Minds of the first class see, they apprehend in a single mental glance; the scientist, with his crucibles, alembics, and measuring instruments, plays on a surface of things. He is the eternal dupe of appearance. Philosophic skeptics alone are never duped. They know the underlying principles of all things. What do details matter? Born in a scientific era, Amiel saw about him thousands of men setting forth on their voyages of discovery. But he knew there was nothing to discover. Science deals with facts. The seer knows there are no facts. There is only change, illusion, endless motion ✒ ✒

The Ideal! The Ideal! Her victims are as numberless as the sands of the sea. The immortal Mocker—who will slay her? She takes the savor from our mouths and robs us of life itself. Amiel's great, sad soul was a hermit in an alien universe—a hermit tortured by dreams of fair infinite negations.

There has never been but one Amiel—there will never be another, have no fears. The Good God knows that one is enough.

Sir Joshua Reynolds

I N NORTHCOTE'S *Life of Sir Joshua Reynolds*, the author says, "The Founder of the British School of Painting first saw the light on the 16th day of July, 1723."

Of course, what the learned biographer means is that the man was born. Still there is plenty of precedent for using that expression concerning seeing the light—it comes down to us with the mellow tinge of time upon it, a little frayed at the edges, but still stout and capable of service. And so if my friend Prof. Harry Peckaboo, and the ready writers of the Chicago Renaissance, still continue its use, 't would be a carping quibbler who would say them nay.

Sir Joshua Reynolds came from a long line of clerical ancestry, which Emerson once said, with probably no special thought of himself in mind, is a very good start for poet, painter or philosopher. There was a straight line of clergymen on Sir Joshua's father's side for five generations, and on his mother's side it was the same with the exception of a single break in the apostolic succession. The grandfather of Sir Joshua, Rev. Asa Potter, left a small mildew on the escutcheon by marrying Miss Theophila Baker, daughter of the Vicar of Bishops Nymmet, without the consent of the worthy vicar.

Now the vicar had intended the girl should be the wife of another clergyman, a widower, who had a "living" worth twice the one on which the Rev. Mr. Potter only held a second mortgage. But love had its way, as love has before and since, and the young clergyman and the vicar's daughter disappeared one moonlight night, and were married over at the little ivy-covered church at Stoke Charity ❧ ❧

When they went back home in a week to seek blessings and crave forgiveness, they found the door locked upon them, and a fierce voice from an upper window ordered them begone. The vicar disinherited the daughter and publicly disowned her. And this was the bride whose first born daughter became the mother of Joshua Reynolds.

Sir Joshua was always a little proud of his pedigree, and once in a melting mood of confidence at the " Turk's Head," told Dr. Johnson, Goldsmith, Burke, Garrick and Boswell of how his grandmother had insisted on her right to wed the man she loved. Old Ursa Major's squint little eyes grew very misty, and he blew his nose violently on a big red handkerchief as Reynolds continued the tale.

The Rev. Asa Potter died only five years after his runaway marriage and left his wife with three children. The vicar still refused to take his daughter back into favor, and the poor widow cried her eyes into blindness, and soon followed her husband.

" The eldest of those orphaned children she left, was my mother," said Sir Joshua, after a little pause.

" Hush-sh-sh-sh," softly whispered Boswell—" Dr. Johnson is going to speak!"

Old Ursa was swaying in his chair as though about to have an apoplectic fit. Finally he found voice in a sputtering burst of emotion ❧ ❧

" Sir!" exclaimed Doctor Johnson, " Sir! you are proud of your grandmother, and well you should be, but I notice you are not boastful concerning your great-grandfather who disowned her, and hastened her into an early grave. Sir, your great-grandfather pretended to love his enemies, and yet had only hate for his daughter, whose sole offense was that she had given her heart to a good man. Sir, I would like to have kicked your great-grandfather out of the pulpit and pushed his prayer book down his throat!" Dr. Johnson was slightly given to exaggeration in speech; but still the Rev. Stephen Baker did a foolish thing when he disowned his daughter. " Never darken this door again," they used to roar at the erring one. They talked in that strain in the good old days more than they do now.

To brand a child with disgrace is to disgrace one's self. The irascible old clergyman never thought of that; and he would have little patience with the philosophy of a modern prophet who says to his children—" Go where you may: commit what crimes you may: sink to such depths of shame as you may, but always remember that this is your home, and you still have one friend left."

When you go out to Windsor from London 't will pay you to walk out across the old arched bridge to Eton. You will then follow through the College Yard, across the wide campus and on down the hedge-lined road to Burnham Beeches.

And before you take the train back you will follow along the pathway, across the meadow and over the stile to Stoke-Pogis churchyard, where Gray wrote the *Elegy*.

There are many curious, old inscriptions in that place where heaves the turf in many a mouldering mound. But none is more curious than the one marking the grave of the Rev. Stephen Baker. Only a few steps away sleeps the daughter whom he spurned, and by her side her chosen mate.

Stretching away on either side are the toppling headstones to other members of the Baker and Potter families! all turned to dust long years ago, and their hate and their pride and their prejudice buried with them.

How sharper than a serpent's tooth is an irascible parent. 'T is foolish to quarrel: love while you can, and forgive while you yet may ✿ ✿

To pardon is the privilege only of the living.

Victor Hugo

SAVE perhaps Walt Whitman and Shakespeare, no poet of any century possessed a vaster imagination than Victor Hugo. Shelley's imagination was subtle, tenuous and gained in luster and glory through its very limitations. With Shelley one may die of ecstacy and be blasted by light from etheric suns, but one is never lost. In Shakespeare, Whitman and Hugo, one may be lost utterly. In these titanesque minds the Infinite put its sightless logic. With them, you are lost, drowned, unlodged—unless you know the highways over the constellations ❧ ❧

The brain of the scholar, of the savant, absorbs the culture of men. It is fed in libraries and museums. The brain of the poet absorbs the culture of the Time-Spirit itself. The imperial imagination of Victor Hugo penetrated the pores of the Infinite, and on the finite world it acted like a giant suction-valve. His culture, like the culture of the greatest geniuses, was a miracle of transubstantiation. Until it reaches the alembical imagination of the poet and seer, the universe is vegetative.

He seethed, and he made all Nature seethe with him. Whatever Leconte de Lisle looked at, died; whatever Victor Hugo looked at, lived. The academic tape-measure failing to reach around his form, they have said that he lacked unity, restraint, measure. He had the unity of Niagara, the restraint of lightning and the measured motion of the earthquake. When the capon looks at the eagle it no doubt believes the eagle insane. The only limit that the mind of Victor Hugo knew was death, and that, too, was to him a limitless limit, a lure, a promise. Whoever believes that chaos has its laws will understand Victor Hugo. Whoever believes that there is a discoverable unity in existence will never understand him ❧ ❧

The passion for unity is a symptom of fatigue. Hugo never grew tired of diversity. He reveled in difference. Life with its torrential and eternal multiplication of forms satisfied, and would have satisfied throughout an eternity, that gluttonous soul; and his passion for God was a craving for partnership. He sought out God in order to find out His secret. He, Victor Hugo, craved to make atoms, stars, hurricanes, Utopias, Hells, and Shakespeares. Since Prometheus, had Man ever such a glorifier? Was genius ever so worshiped? Hugo's hero is the human soul. The evolution of the human mind was the evolution of God. Mind was the pontoon that carried man from age to age. The Ideal was the aeroplane that carried man to the mystical Mansion in the Skies. Hugo's brain was a portable universe. He was always big with God and Man. He constituted himself the knight-errant of the race. All his life he stood sword in hand at some moral Thermopylæ. His arrogance was the arrogance of a Jupiter. He was melodramatic; but so is God. He raved and stormed and ranted; but so does the Jehovah of the Jews, in whose likeness he was uttered. His books are a carnival of words, but they have at their best the sovereign solemnity of the " I am " of the Lord.

The flaming veil of day, the somber drop-curtain of night—all are glorified. He is Pantheist, Deist, Pagan and Christian. He marshals atoms and epochs, thunders and Cæsars, battlefields and hovels before our eye with the gesture of a man who was the director-general of a Cosmos.

In his hands language became incandescent. Words were fennel-rods whence this Titan drew a creative fire. Words explain everything. The poet is Nature's sacred syllable Om. All thoughts and feelings aspire to be words. No thought or emotion can be completely realized until it becomes crystallized into a word, a phrase, an epigram, a poem. To name a thing is to isolate it, confer on it a soul, give it entity. If names, words, languages did not exist, it is doubtful whether number would exist. Words are worlds and

Hugo sat down and wept because there were no new verbal assonances to conquer.

From sound he squeezed blood and light and tears. With the cymbals of syllables he struck crashing preludes, passionate inter-mezzos, and tortuous postludes. There are sentences in Hugo's pages that are trumpet-calls from trans-stellar Sinais. There are paragraphs that are fulgurant fanfares of sound—nothing more. Sound turning sommersaults and becoming light and lightning. Vibrations changed into auroras and sibillant twilights, fused into sulphurous anathemas, dissolved into vaporous innuendoes. Victor Hugo was the Wagner of words.

Had Victor Hugo a religion? Had Shakespeare? Had Goethe? Had Wagner? Genius needs no religion as that word is used generally. It is sufficient unto itself. It sees into hell; it sees through hell. It sees into heaven; it sees beyond heaven. The plummet of its thought sounds all bottoms. It penetrates the soul of the atom, weaves itself into the mystery of the sea, and, vicariously, lives the life of seer and murderer. What dogmas shall genius hold when all dogmas come to it for interpretation? What has genius to do with belief, when it is conscious of miracle and mystery only.

Has God a religion? Does He believe in Himself? God falls from grace at each minute. He repented of Adam and lost faith in Him-self on the cross—" My God, My God, why hast Thou forsaken Me? " The religion of genius, like that of God, is to participate in whatever is, to partake of existence, to vitalize life. Genius can not sin; it can do no wrong. The passion for experience knows no morality. It absorbs and it emits. Goethe said, " I understand the murderer, for I am he." The mind of genius is a matrix. Verlaine and Christ, Hugo and Napoleon, are equals in the realm of the imagination ❧ ❧

The great tragedy of genius is its essential godlikeness. It has the instinct for omnipotence, omnipresence and omniscience. It has the vision of God, but not the attributes. It absorbs the Infinite, but it can only create the finite. It is homunculus with the will to be Jupiter. Shakespeare, Byron, Christ, Wagner, Nietzsche, Flaubert, Rodin, Michelangelo, had the passion for Creation. They remained artificers in words, sounds, marble, paint. Sublime cobblers! Samsons of comprehension, they strained at the pillars that sustain the Temple of Life—and the temple budged not. Brazen inexorable granite! unbreakable fetters of our eternal finitude! ✒ ✒

In the cosmic carnival of chance, the brain of genius, by its art, fabricates order and harmony. Beethoven and Shelley and Spencer unified their dreams. But genius can never fabricate the supreme thing, the one thing needful to be God. It can not create diversity without unity, it can not create a chaos, it can not strike from the keys of matter and motion that stupendous note of discord prolonged throughout an eternity that we call life. Only the insane understand God; and great genius just falls short of insanity—and godhood.

Sick in his impotency, Victor Hugo, in a divine rage, bespattered his God. The poem is called, " *Dieu eclabousse par Zoile.*" He accuses Omnipotence of monotony. The words are put into the mouth of Zoilus, but the thought—and the words—is the thought of Hugo.

Charlatan! Have done with this game of blind man's buff. We are sick of the eternal humbug called life. For once and for all let us tell the Almighty some facts about Himself. His work has neither beginning, end nor middle. His imagination is exhausted. He repeats Himself eternally. He wrote Himself out after the first seven days. Winter and Summer; night and day; birth and death; storm and sunshine. Eternal renewal! the poet chants. Eternal repetition! Eternal boredom! says the thinker. Each thing is made in the pattern of some other thing. The moon looks like an orange. The tree looks like a hedgehog. The river looks like a serpent. No invention anywhere. Sterility and stagnation everywhere. Motion itself is an illusion. Human beings invent strange perversions of natural instincts to bless themselves with new sensations. They die of ennui. The eternal blue of heaven is setting us crazy. We know hope to be a liar, and despair is as stupid as death. Still, we must to one or the other. In history God creates nothing new. From Herodotus to Carlyle it is the same scoundrel that holds the center of the stage and the same humanity that is mulct, revolts and is mulct again. He does over a Tiberius, replasters a Nero, regalvanizes a Robespierre. Since Cain not a new crime has been invented. His butchery at Kishineff is an old story in the Old Testament. The disaster at Messina is of no more importance than that of Pompeii. The same clay, the same men. The same natural causes, the same tiresome consequences.

The normal look on the face of every being over twenty-five is one of fatigue. All other looks are counterfeit. After twenty-five nothing can happen; before that our acts repeat our ancestral acts; after that we repeat ourselves. We are highly organized parrots and apes. We have the capacity to enjoy newer sensations, newer worlds, newer combinations on the old barroom checkerboard where we are the checkers. The human being is passionately in love with the unknown; but we have exhausted life. We are still young; life is stale, worn out, as commonplace as light, as wearisome as love. God is defunct; He is a tired old man, exclaims Victor Hugo. He has nothing more to show us, nothing more to tell us, nothing more to teach us. Euclid, Plato, Aristotle, Æschylus said everything—and they were secondhand.

There is, indeed, only one puzzle: Why is anything? And if God exists, of what use is He? Why does He exist? There are only three dimensions for us. Two and two—will they forever make that stale four? God, if Thou wouldst divert us, invent ten more dimensions for us. Point us the way to some marvelous planet hidden beyond our telescopes in your wrinkled ether, that we may emigrate there bag and baggage and refresh our bored brains and hearts. Or fabricate for us the unimaginable, the unguessable, the new macrocosm and the microcosm. Even we have invented marvelous myth and fairy stories. Canst not Thou do as much in Thy omnipotence.

If not, raffle off Thy stale wonders to the monkeys, O God! We have outgrown Thy nursery wonders. Have done! Have done! Pose! Pose! Pose! That is the cry that has eternally assailed the savage incursions of genius into the empire of the forbidden and its assaults upon the ramparts of the conventional God. Swine, cows, hens and goslings never pose. But they believe that the eagle perched upon its rock for a flight into the azure and the lion erect, expectant, do. The critical Poloniuses dispose of the satanism of Baudelaire, the trumpetings of Hugo, the Don Juanism of Byron, the protean attitudes of Heine, the kaleidoscopic multi-incarnations of Wilde, with the word " pose." It is the judgment writ in Lilliput.

Genius without pose is not genius. All grandeur becomes self-conscious. All superior beings seem to be acting a part. What is called pose in genius is the manifestation of multiple and contradictory personalities. The simple, local, cut and dried minds whose thoughts, emotions and life-developments have been surveyed by their ancestors, and of whom they are merely a sparkless increment and not a vital development, are puzzled before the myriad masks that genius wears; they have the look on the face of the cow before the changing colors of the dawn.

Genius is both Cain and Abel, Lucifer and God, Hamlet and Falstaff, Munchausen and Euclid. Hugo had multitudes locked up in him. As Leonardo da Vinci struck every mental attitude, so Hugo struck every imaginative attitude. He was the sincerest man of his age. Did Francois Villon pose when he turned house-breaker? I believe he did. It was a splendid piece of irony. Sometimes the poses of genius are a sacred sport. To amaze the bour-

geois, to flabbergast the galvanized masterpieces of routine, to
turn sommersaults over the social Ark of the Covenant, to do the
supremely absurd and indecorous thing before the eyes of owl-like
commonsense: this is the sinister irony with which genius confronts stupidity. It is even said that Jupiter himself once turned
cow to astound the groundlings.

Genius is said to be morbidly egoistic. It assumes in fact, a still
higher form of psychological development than egotism. It is
impersonal. It not only believes in itself utterly, but it subdivides
itself *ad infinitum,* that it may worship itself under a myriad forms
and revels in its own luminous magnificences. It worships itself
in the third person plural. The brain of a Hugo, a Goethe, a
Whitman has a gigantic mirror at the top of it. Against it there
is flashed all the attitudes of its diurnal physical, moral and cerebral existences. Before that mirror congregate for rehearsal the
embryos of the things they dared not do and the flesh-and-
blood embodiment of the things they have dared to do. Before
that passionless, incorporate reflector the countless selves of a
genius are always on parade. It is the marvelous phenomenon of
self-consciousness, at the zenith of its earthly evolution. It is the
Self reviewing its own protean poses. It is the consciousness of a
mighty Sun that holds within its monstrous grip a countless
number of satellites.

Against Hugo as against Shelley they have hurled "Blasphemer!"
As though the mind could blaspheme! As though a thought
could be impious! As though a brain could ever do wrong! The
human mind invented God; the human mind is privileged to kill
Him whenever it pleases. There is only one blasphemy of which
the human mind is capable—that is, to exclude from it any
thought that knocks for entry. Genius is never so sublime as when
hurling its anathemas against the walls of heaven. Lucifer marshal-
ing his hosts against the Lord, Prometheus launching his thunder-
bolts from the Caucasus against Jupiter, Cain with imprecatory

glory of Japan were embodied in the young Emperor, who was then seventeen years old.

Before Mutsuhito was twenty-one, the old feudalism was broken up, and a Constitutional Government inaugurated. The systems of Great Britain, America, Germany, France, were closely studied and long reports made by various committees sent to the West. At one time Mutsuhito seemed intent on resigning his office as Emperor, and allowing the people to elect him if they would as President. The idea of democracy was strong in his mind, but he soon perceived that the glamor of the old could not be thrown away and discarded. He must build upon the past.

The reverence of Japan for their Emperor is the reverence which we of the West are supposed to feel toward Deity. The Emperor, with the Japanese, is a supreme being, the representative on earth of Deity. He is called, " The Son of Heaven."

In Japan, Shintoism is the prevailing religion. Its three principal points are the worship of Nature, the worship of heroes, and the worship of ancestors. Children worship their parents; grown-up people worship the Emperor as the Supreme Parent; and the Emperor worships his own ancestors.

The sacred and reverential awe which the Japanese have toward their government is something that Americans find it hard to understand ⅋ ⅋

Religion in Japan is absolutely a part of the State. Mutsuhito was big enough in brain to understand that he could do more good by reigning as the Supreme Monarch, and he himself establish Democracy, than to allow the people to inaugurate it themselves ⅋ ⅋

Throughout his twenty-first year we find him working to abolish caste. The Samurai, the heroic warrior class, were counseled to lay down their arms and go into business. Mutsuhito issued an address wherein he stated that business was human service, and it was just as necessary to supply things to people which they needed in their every-day lives, as to protect them from their enemies by fighting.

The Samurai spirit could manifest itself by running a factory, by keeping a shop, by farming, in the arts and sciences, and in teaching school, quite as well as in warfare. Fighting has long limited man in his mental activities. The more things we do in life and do successfully, the greater we are in spirit and the greater our reward will be in the world to come.

Where Mutsuhito got his eminently Emersonian philosophy we do not know; but he put it into practice, so that today you may go into a grocery in Japan and be waited upon by a Samurai. The ancestors of a Samurai would no more have thought of making themselves useful than would one of the Grand Dukes of Russia ➹ ➹

Mutsuhito introduced the system of universal education, based largely on American ideals. It was on his initiative that hundreds and thousands of young Japanese were sent out to all universities of Christendom, so there was not a single school of any prominence in the world where Japanese students were not in attendance. The expense of this teaching was borne by the Government. Harvard, Yale, Princeton, Cornell, Columbia, all have had their Japanese students for the past forty years. Vassar, Smith and Bryn Mawr have not been overlooked, and Japanese women have been in attendance at these.

It is supposed that women have no influence in Japan, where polygamy is legalized. But Mutsuhito knew perfectly well that the power of the sexes is very evenly divided, and that men learn from women quite as much as women from men.

The population of Japan when Mutsuhito took the oath of office as Emperor was about twenty million. Now it is fifty million. During his reign the whole political, social and economical system has been completely changed, and as intimated, no such revolution has ever occurred in any other nation in a similar length of time. Japan now stands side by side with the six foremost world-powers: America, Great Britain, Germany, France, Austria, Japan ✒ ✒

Beyond a doubt Mutsuhito was the best-loved Emperor in the entire world—this of course through the basic tendencies of Japan to work the apotheosis of their chief ruler, also through the genuine merit of Mutsuhito.

Some years ago I heard President Taft give a little impromptu lecture on the Japanese. President Taft came forward with the statement that he had met the Emperor of Japan on six different occasions ✒ ✒

President Taft described the Emperor as a very gentle, suave, yet strong and earnest individual. Mutsuhito knew what he wanted to do, and worked always with the intent of bringing the thing about. He had the crystalline mind. He was as keen in intellect as Elihu Root and just as silent and self-contained. With it all he was a poet and a musician. He studied the ways of the world, and he had ideals in the line of Government quite surpassing those of any other ruler in Christendom. He of all men was not dictated to by the law of mortmain.

When Mutsuhito was born, Japan was a shut-in nation. Foreigners could not get in nor Japanese get out. Japan in Eighteen Hundred Fifty was exactly where Great Britain was before the days of William the Conqueror. So we can truthfully say that Japan has progressed as much in sixty years as England, France and Germany have in ten centuries, or a thousand years.

By deliberate preference Japan was a hermit nation.

It limited the size of its trading-junks, it allowed no shipping to leave its coast, it barred foreign visitors, it crushed out Christianity as an arch enemy.

Perry had not visited Japan when Mutsuhito was born.

Military science in Japan in Eighteen Hundred Sixty-five was as primitive as that of the Romans before the days of Julius Cæsar.

Japan then had a literary language which the people did not understand any more than Americans understand Greek.

Also, the Japanese knew practically nothing about sanitation and right living. Well did Doctor Weir Mitchell say that the cause of long life in Japan in early days was on account of the scarcity of food, the rice being given out with mathematical exactness, and meat being out of the question. Now, however, we find the Japanese excelling in sanitation and in the knowledge of right living. They have professional schools and have made great strides in science. They understand modern industrial development, and know the science of schoolteaching better than we do.

¶ The Japanese are vegetarians, and they have proven themselves the greatest fighters in the world. Courage in our sense is not known—they are simply without fear.

Their principal qualities are their patience, their industry, their love of art, and their simplicity. They are economists. They know how to live and they know how to die.

The young Emperor is a monogamist, happily married, with a goodly family of children. He wears English clothes, speaks English with exactness, and reads American newspapers.

He is in absolute sympathy with the reformations inaugurated by his illustrious father. In stature he is small and slight, and, strangely enough, is of light complexion, and would pass most anywhere as a European.

His father, Mutsuhito, was not the son of the Empress. It has been stated that the mother of Mutsuhito had in her veins European blood, and that this reveals itself in the present Emperor, Yoshihito, who strikes back to his grandmother. Yoshihito is a very simple, plain, and modest little gentleman. He is rather proud of his blonde attributes, as his light hair and dark blue eyes set him apart as a genuine son of the sun.

Happily he has passed through the romantic and reckless age, and time has tamed him of any mad ambitions that he might have

had towards rule or ruin. He is personally big enough to sink
himself and listen to the advice of his elders. He is surrounded by
very able diplomats and statesmen, and there is no fear that
Japan will take a backward step. Mutsuhito had no desire to
make war on the West, as his strong army was only to preserve
the respect of the nations. His ambition was that some day war
and the implements of destruction would be unnecessary.

A similar sentiment is in the heart of Yoshihito.

Admiral Togo said, "The qualities that make a man a good
soldier in time of war make him a good citizen in time of peace."
The Japanese have some great virtues that we would do well to
take on.

America has nothing to fear from Japan, save competition in the
line of well-doing.

Marilla Ricker

NCE upon a day it was announced that Clarence Darrow would speak on "The Rights of the Poor." ❧ ❧

And feeling poor I decided to attend the meeting. Mr. Darrow began by saying, " I intended to speak to you about the ' Rights of the Poor,' but on reconsideration I can not find that the poor have any rights and therefore I will be obliged to speak on another theme."

❡ Have the poor no rights? Alas, none that are recognized. Respectable people, according to the gospel of Carlyle are those who ride in gigs; and according to our standard, folks who do not or can not employ a lawyer, have no rights. Go to a court of justice and ask for a little of their specialty and the first question is, " Where is your lawyer? "

Should you go to a court house without money, you can't get in; but if by chance others get you in, you can't get out.

Come with me to a police court!

All night the police have been gathering them in—drunk, disorderly, petty thieves, street-walkers and runaway boys and girls barely out of short clothes, all in together, pooling their depravity ❧ ❧

There is seldom any testimony against the offender but that of the officer who made the arrest. He has his story well in hand—he has told it so many times! He is bound to justify himself for making the arrest, for every convict adds to his honors.

Here they come, at the rate of one a minute.

Sometimes five minutes is given to trying a case, but rarely. The judge is in a bad temper—he was out late, too.

" Ten days—thirty days. What 's that? Don't talk back to me, six months! "

There is no habeas corpus for the man without a lawyer, and there is no lawyer for you if you have no money. Justice is a commodity and the price is high.

The names are called, and from the pen, the particular culprit is pulled or pushed before the Bar of Justice, just as we are told we all will be at the Last Great Day.

Dazed, sick, weak from lack of food, excitement, sleeplessness or fear—usually ignorant, what chance is there here for innocence with empty pockets! The hardened ones, who know the process, may put up some sort of defense, but for the accused person who is here for the first time the case is hopeless. There is no opportunity to communicate with friends, even if they somewhere exist, and the tears of protest and appeals for mercy, dumb or expressed, are taken as proof of guilt.

" Guilty or not guilty? " calls a hoarse voice.

" Guilty," replies the stammering tongue—" guilty! "

" Five dollars or ten days! "

" I mean not guilty! "

It is too late, a strong hand on your shoulder pushes you along to the pen on the other side where the condemned wait for the " Black Maria." If you have been here before, you do not mind, but if it is your first experience of this kind, horror fills your being and you know what it is to be spit upon and crowned with thorns.

℃ Often the judge means to be kind—he hesitates and sometimes lets the culprit go. But as a rule the police dictate the convictions and their business is to make a record. The idea of the place is that all are guilty until they are proved innocent—better that a hundred innocent should be punished than that one guilty man escape ✺ ✺

There is no justice for the man without money in a police court, any more than there are for him beefsteaks in a restaurant. Of course, we know that no person should be without money—that is granted.

But just now we are dealing with conditions, not theories. The

arresting officer is attorney for the state—the accused is as helpless as Christ before Pilate.

A sinner? Probably. Yes, and guilty, too,—I grant you that.
But a man or a woman, still—my brother and yours. Yes, and as
Old Walt says at sight of the culprit being hurried to his doom,
" I am that man! "

Now just suppose that you are in bonds, sick, sore and undone
from a sleepless night trying to rest upon a plank, amid the
howling, laughing, sobbing, cursing mass of humanity. You have
done wrong, to be sure, but your throbbing head can not think
of where and what it was—the past seems so murky and confused.
There are steel bars in front and solid iron walls on three sides.
Through the bars, now and then, some one in brass buttons
stands and stares, or talks in bantering phrase in a way people
never do to equals.

Equals? You are behind steel bars, and the only equals you have
are those in disgrace.

And as you stand there shivering, grasping the bars for support,
some one touches your arm and you look around.

But one glance into that face and your resentment oozes away.
It is a woman who speaks to you—she surely is not a prisoner
and how she got inside the cage you do not know. She does not
belong here. She is free—there is freedom in her very glance.
A singular looking woman, tall, mannish, commanding, with iron
gray hair. But the voice and manner are those of a woman—
motherly, gentle, sympathetic, kind. Still she does not seem to
take things very seriously—her self-reliance is contagious. She
has courage plus. " There seems to be a mistake somewhere—
tell me why you are here? "

Half a dozen prisoners are trying to talk to her, tugging at her
skirts, begging her to listen to them. You hear them implore her
by name, " Marilla! Marilla! " But she hears only you.

" That will do—never mind—don't lose heart, when your name

is called I will be there!" And she makes a memoranda in her note book and passes on to some one else. And there runs through your head a line of scripture you learned in your childhood and which never before meant anything to you, " I was in prison and you visited me!"

Finally, a hoarse voice bawls your name and you stagger out before the judge. The whole place seems to swim before your vision. There are confused questions and answers, and all you remember is that your Good Angel of Freedom is standing there saying, " Your Honor, I appear for this person and ask for a jury trial. I also request that bail be fixed."

Marilla! Who is Marilla?

I 'll have to tell you—she is Marilla—Marilla Ricker. She is no one else.

Cranky? I think so.

Wheels? By all means.

Bughouse? Beyond a doubt.

She has no predecessors—she never will have a successor; she has no duplicates, and the only person who looks like her is Marilla Ricker ❧ ❧

The worst that I can say about Marilla is that she is a lawyer. She was admitted to practice in the city of Washington forty-seven years ago. She was ninety-four years old last June, but she only confesses to sixty-four. However, as she was sixty-four thirty years ago, I figured she is ninety-four now, but I may be wrong in this, for Marilla says time is an illusion; and space, like the Democratic party, is a fallacy based on a hypothesis.

Marilla can not truthfully be called an infant prodigy.

Nobody living can remember when Marilla was any younger than she is now. And there be people who firmly hold that she is a genuine prehistoric—that she was never born and can never die. I first saw her in 1876 at the Centennial in Philadelphia, where I was told the Exhibition was in honor of Marilla's hundredth birthday. Her tongue now is just as ready as then, her laugh as catching, her wit as nimble, her insight as clear.

Unlike most women, she can listen as well as she can talk. She can look wise and can talk still more wisely. But especially she can listen in a way that will lead you on to tell all you know, and finally make you flounder in unseemliness. " Give the calf rope," is one of her working mottoes.

" Your Honor and Gentlemen of the Jury, I follow the example of the learned counsel on the other side and submit the case without argument," I once heard her say.

It should be explained that the " learned counsel on the other side " had made a speech two hours long, and had worn everybody's nerves to a frazzle.

The jury laughed. The judge snickered, buried his nose in a book and then stood up and ordered a nolle pros. in favor of Marilla's client ❧ ❧

Marilla is big enough to be called by her first name; great enough to waive form, ceremony and all cast-iron dignity.

Everybody who knows her loves her; those who do not love her do not know her.

And there are plenty of people who do not know Marilla, and never can because their mental processes run on a totally different schedule from hers; they are not on her wire. But this you can depend upon—she makes no effort to adjust her thinkery to that of people who delegate their thinking to others.

There is one word that looms up large in Marilla's lexicon, and that word is Freedom.

Her life has been a struggle and a fight—a fight to give freedom to others. And in giving freedom to others she has achieved freedom for herself. She has practised law for nearly half a century, and most of this practice has been in defense of accused people. Guilty or not guilty means little to her. " We are all guilty," she says, " for we have thought the thing and this person possibly was rash enough to do it. Had we been born under the same conditions and lived in the same environment we would have done the same."

Some go to church to watch and pray.

Marilla goes to church to watch. But I once heard her quote the prayer of St. Augustine: " O God, I thank thee that thou hast seen fit not to allow me to be tempted this day beyond my strength to resist."

And again, " O God, have mercy for the weak—thou hast made the strong able to take care of themselves."

The life business of Marilla has been to be a friend to the friendless—to be a friend even to those who were not friends to themselves ͽ ͽ

If a prisoner has money to pay a lawyer, Marilla lets him pay. But like Louis Agassiz, Marilla has had no time to make money; and in fact, she has often turned it away to defend men and women who had neither money nor friends.

" People who have no friends are those who need them," she often says. And also, " If a man is not a friend to himself, then he needs me." ͽ ͽ

And another thing that proves Marilla to be a very great and lofty soul is that she has no whine concerning the ingratitude of many of those whom she has helped. People who expect gratitude do not deserve it.

Once Roscoe Conklin successfully defended a man charged with stealing a tray of diamonds.

After Roscoe's argument the jury brought in a verdict of " Not guilty," and the judge discharged the prisoner. The poor man was so moved that he fell upon the neck of his attorney and wept tears of gratitude.

Shortly after, the man disappeared, and Conklin felt for his diamond stud—a thousand dollar brilliant, and found it was gone —clipped clean. Conklin raised a howl you could have heard clear to the White House. Marilla, who happened to be present, only laughed and said, " Roscoe, this is all a part of the game we are playing. Take your medicine. Everything we do, we do for ourselves. The Ego is the all. He has your diamond—you have your Ego and it is quite as dazzling as the diamond. Let the carbon go." He of the Hyperion curl tried to laugh but could n't. All he could say was, "Of course you laugh—it was not your diamond!" And Marilla in mock distress said, " It was the turquoise that Leah gave me!"

Possibly the fact that Marilla is comfortably rich and has been all her life, is a factor in her equanimity, which word by the way, Buddha said is the greatest one in any language. A fixed income gives a peace like a dress that fits in the back. But only wise people can keep an estate snug and intact, well reefed against stormy weather. Marilla is a financier—she invests money but does not waste it.

Marilla was married a thousand years ago, and shortly after, her husband passed away leaving her his fortune as he could not take it with him. They say he was a very worthy man of excellent mentality, a direct descendant of the great Gin Ricker Shaw. That he had discrimination and great good sense is sure, for did he not have brains enough to marry Marilla?

And then he showed a sensible spirit by dying at an opportune time, for had he lived he would have gone through life known as " Mr. Marilla," or " Marilla's husband." Only an archangel could be a mate for this woman, no archbishop could.

Marilla is as much bigger mentally than the average man as Dr. Buckley is bigger than an orang-outang.

Marilla has shaken the superstition out of her cosmos, and Dr. Buckley has n't. Marilla asks no reward here or hereafter for doing good. She believes that the penalty for a wrong act lies in the act, and the reward for a good deed is to have done it.

Marilla's life has been no sacrifice, even if she has toiled for the sinner. Her face has ever been turned toward the East, and beneath her corset beats a heart for all humanity—a heart lavish in its love and loyal as the planets that circle 'round the sun. That the woman has ever been a veritable Puritan in her life even her enemies admit. Her name has never been between the putrid lips of scandal. Everywhere she has friends, but no intimates. Neither her heart nor head has ever been in chancery. Freedom has been her watchword—she believes that even love should be free, which is quite different from a belief in free love. She sits at meat with publicans and sinners, and gamblers and thieves, big and little, call her Marilla. Women of the town cross the street to kiss her cheek and say, " God love you, Marilla." Bootblacks follow after her and say, " Let me carry your satchel, Marilla—it won't cost you nothing!"

She is one with the rogues, but she still is not one of them. She is one with the weak, the defenseless, the fallen—those who grope their devious way and stumble, or who slip and fall in the mire. She has no word of blame or censure for anybody, even the fools who misunderstand her. The rogues and fools all punish themselves—she does not have to. And she knows full well that the rogues and fools are one and the same.

In her sympathy Marilla is not maudlin. She does not try to usurp the place of Atlas. She does her work and forgets it. She says a good memory is a fine thing, but a fine forgettery is a finer. She does not ask the evil doer to repent—she asks him to forget. She shakes none of your misdeeds before you. She says, " If you have been a fool, forget it, for the world never will until you do."

To Marilla righteousness is only a form of common sense, and wickedness is a mistake.

Marilla does not advise you to wear your past for a chest protector; for if you do, she says you will soon equalize matters by wearing your future for a bustle.

Now here is a woman who knows every form of vice, crime and

misdemeanor. She knows the little thieves and the big ones, for has she not lived in Washington forty years? And yet knowing all sin and shame and vice in its every form, the wrong has never smirched her soul. She is an optimistic pessimist. Gentle, kind, moderate in judgment, sympathetic, she knows the best and the worst, and yet she neither believes in God nor devil, and in her belief there is no heaven nor hell save as we create them for ourselves every day.

The belief in a future heaven where you will be rewarded for your good deeds she regards as vicious and immoral, and hell to her is a place invented by priests for the sake of making people support them ᵰ ᵰ

Ali Baba says that a horse that will balk will also kick, strike, bite and run away when the breaching breaks.

Years ago when I used to go to the Baptist Church, I was taught that people who did not go to church used tobacco, and those who use tobacco, also swear, get drunk, and use the Seventh Commandment for a door-mat.

Marilla has not been inside a church for some twenty-seven years, excepting when the preacher was not there, because she says she wanted to save her soul alive. She has never gone forward to the mourner's bench and has never been born again. She is a doubter by nature and has been an infidel since babyhood.

And yet our orthodox friends who often are so hot after their enemies that they hate their friends, admit that Marilla is a combination of Penelope and Minerva, with all the frills of Phryne absolutely left out.

Marilla is the High Priestess of Free Thought in America—the archbishop of all infidels. She holds that the Christian religion as it exists today has nothing whatever to do with morality. In fact, her keen insight detects the strain of vicarious vice in Purity League prudes and all those good people who hire a hall and proclaim their purity with a brass band. Marilla maintains that the women who carry the chip of chastity upon their shoulder, usually have a heap to say about purity.

When Gran'ma Granniss takes the stage and pierces that silence with her falsetto against divorce, Marilla seconds your Aunt Susan, who replies that divorce means freedom for women, and liberty to those who are riveted to a beasticus for ninety-nine years. And boldly does she declare that the relationship of the incompatible does not spell morality.

Once Marilla went to England carrying a letter of introduction from Chief Justice Chase to the Chief Justice of England. Marilla called on his Lordship at his private Chambers. He was just getting ready to take the Bench, and was arrayed in one of those twenty-five dollar horsehair wigs and a Mother-Hubbard gown. He asked Marilla to sit with him on the Bench; so an impassive Jeems, who was Master of the Wardrobe, was called in and Marilla was soon clothed in her right mind and a dress like those worn by a bloomin' barrister, you know.

And so in raiment not gaudy nor expressed in fancy, Marilla accompanied his Lordship, and achieved the distinction of being the first woman who has held down the woolsack in England—a thing which, had it been known at the time, would have shivered the tight little island from John o' Groat's to Land's End.

Marilla was appointed a United States Commissioner by President Grant, and gave decisions that are quoted for their crystalline quality and rare good sense. At that time Washington judges were in the habit of giving cumulative sentences by which a man might be imprisoned for debt for life on some trivial offense. Marilla had a way of letting such prisoners go free, and giving her reasons why, that caused such procedure to become obsolete forevermore in the District of Columbia.

On the question of personal immortality Marilla has decided opinions. She cites that the Buddhists, among whom are many learned men of great spiritual power, constitute nearly one-third of the human race; and they not only do not believe in personal immortality, but hold on the contrary that it would be a curse. They regard the man who hopes for a life after death as beneath them morally, spiritually, mentally. Marilla puts the argument about this way: The belief in everlasting life was first evolved by savages, and then taken up by priests who promised an endless life of joy to all who obeyed their edicts. It is a most selfish and harmful doctrine, and by turning man's attention from this world to another, has blocked progress at least a thousand years ❧ ❧

She says that without this belief there could have been no demonology, no persecution, no hot opposition to science, no fighting of progress at every step, and no continuance of a superstitious dogma into a scientific age. ·

There is no idea so pernicious in its results as the doctrine of individual immortality. It has formed a leverage for the enslavement of mankind. It has filled the world with gloom and made of man a crawling coward. It has given chains and whips of nettles into the hands of priests since time began, and they have used their weapons for the suppression, repression and degradation of humanity. And all based upon the idea that man has a personal existence after death! So long as that dogma is preached there will be men who pretend to be able to control your place and condition in another world. Let the insignificant little priest in this insignificant little village withhold the rite of holy communion, absolution, or extreme unction from this one and that, and if they die tonight, their souls will wander in torment during all eternity! ❧ To unhorse the priest we do not have to prove that there is no life after death—all we need do is to stand strong on the living truth that we do not know anything about it, and that he knows no more than we do. We can then live our lives as if we were to live always, and if death is an endless sleep we have made no mistake. Right living here and now is the part of wisdom, and if there is a life to come, righteousness, honesty and truth are a good preparation for it.

Marilla's plea is for this world and for the men and women still on earth. Use this life right up to your highest and best—let this world be a better place because you are here. And if there is another world, right living here is the fittest preparation for right living there, but the more you live in the present and the less in the future the better off you are here and hereafter. The further you evolve here, the higher your status there. And the way to evolve now is to live now.

The man who repeats at stated intervals the peptonized formula, " I believe in the resurrection of the body," and who further believes in a material heaven, is the only materialist. Yet he is the person who dubs this man or that " materialist." This is on the same principle, exactly, that the party that steals your pickle-jar will forever after refer to you as a thief.

Whether we live again after death is not determined by our present belief on this subject. If we live again we 'll change our minds, should we now believe death ends all.

The soul of the infidel who scoffs immortality—if such there be— will live after death just as if he never scoffed, if individual immortality exists.

No sane man believes in annihilation—nothing is destroyed, nor can it be. Things change their form but not their essence. Coal soot is carbon, and so is the diamond. The diamond is only carbon that has had a peculiar experience—that is all. And it can be turned back into gaseous form and then into soot very quickly. There are three forms of immortality, taught by different sects. The first is a personal life for the individual after this.

The second is the idea that we are each and all manifestations of a Supreme Life. In other words that there is only one Life and we are all particles and parts of it. When we die, our spirits like our bodies return to their original elements and live again in the mass.

The third is a poetic form of immortality, and is that our influence lives, and as we have influenced people, so do they again influence others, and so we see how the influence of Socrates, Jesus and Emerson can never die.

Everybody in the world believes in one of these forms of immortality. The so-called scoffer does not scoff at immortality—he only scoffs at your particular conception of it.

Marilla believes in the scoffer, and points out that he has scoffed superstition out of many minds, and therefore has done much good. The thing that is too frail to stand scorn, should go down—and does.

Marilla declares that she has more faith in Kellar than she has in Mrs. Pepper. And while she fully realizes that we are surrounded by phenomena too subtle for our crude senses to fully comprehend, she thinks it an absurdity to attribute such phenomena to disembodied spirits—this being quite after the old idea of accounting for thunder by saying it was a manifestation of God's wrath.

The proposition, " If it is n't spirits, what is it? " is very bad reasoning ᵴ ᵴ

Dr. Richard Maurice Bucke, of the London Asylum for the Insane, once said that up to 1880, fully forty per cent of all alienation arose from religious mania. Since 1880, there has been in all asylums a marked decrease in religious mania owing to the spread of free-thought and the lessened emphasis on eternal punishment. But the idea of hell and damnation is quite as logical as the dogma of everlasting life, for it is all a bare assumption, anyway ᵴ ᵴ

And just so long as man is taught that he has an " immortal soul " that can never die, he is going to fear the future and speculate on his destiny in another world.

We can adjust ourselves to the known and cope with any difficulty we can see, even to going down heroically and gloriously before it in fair fight, but thought fixed upon a fog that conceals the unknown is a perpetual source of misery and dire unrest.

If love is the finest thing in the world, fear is the worst.

Apprehension paralyzes man's best efforts, and makes of a demigod a cringing cur.

Good work can only be done by people who have abolished fear —sublime thoughts come only as we put fear behind.

Fear is the precursor of all overreaching, grabbing and clutching for place, pelf and power.

Fear is the prompter of hate, untruth, duplicity, and is the very base and essence of jealousy.

The dogma of personal immortality, with its concomitant uncertainty as to your future, has flooded space with quaking fear, filled the sky with nightmares inexpressible, and horrors that are beyond speech. And especially has it clouded the sky of childhood, and polluted the days of innocence with black despair. But the worst feature of a belief in immortality is that it has given millions of rogues a lever by which they have worked both upon the fears and loves of mankind. All good spiritualists agree that fully one-half of all so-called "mediums" are frauds, and they also admit that most genuine mediums do not hesitate to amend and supplement their peculiar, psychic powers with trickery and untruth—giving their clients their money's worth —what they wish to hear and what they will pay for.

The entire dogma of endless punishment that was preached for nearly two thousand years has become so repugnant to humanity, that even the orthodox of the orthodox have abandoned it, and are quite willing to say " we do not know." And if pursued with the question what has become of all those millions of children, not a span long, which they and their predecessors consigned to hell, they admit they were possibly mistaken, and say that hell was only a theological necessity devised to make bad men good—and also to make them pay.

The mystery of death, codified by centuries of priests into a belief in an individual immortality has been the greatest single force of the Christian religion; it is still, in its finally drawn forms, the most vital bit of life possessed by the church. Examined in the light of results and of essential influence, there will be found on the credit side of this belief not one beneficent item, excepting the doubtful relief of the dying man who hopes for glory, and the questionable solace of the bereaved who hope to meet loved ones again in person. On the debit side there is every form of evil inflicted by church and churchmen from Constantine's time to our own.

The dubious credit account is utterly wiped out by the fact that there is a higher and more unselfish ideal of immortality, which demands no perpetuation of the individual as such, and requires no administration by church or priest. In this ideal, personality has no place. Instead there is the demonstrable certainty of the immortality and high purpose of the human race, of the immortality and ever-growing influence of good deeds and good lives, and of the living immortality of worthy and beautiful parenthood. In this ideal there is something positive, natural, noble, worthy of the sternest battle of life. Beside it, the mysticism of a personal, individual spirit life clutching for comfort and dodging pain, is weak and lifeless, fitted in every respect to be placed among the discarded beliefs and ideals, which originated in times crude, and savage ❧ ❧

It is true, of course, that some gifted men like Dr. I. K. Funk and Alfred Russel Wallace, seem to find evidence of the existence of disembodied spirits. But granted that they are on the high road to important enlightenment, still nothing whatever can detract from the satisfaction obtainable from the purely unselfish ideal of a practical and demonstrable immortality. Could the preachers hold up this ideal for a hundred years, as they have held up the dogmas of personal immortality for nineteen hundred years, what strides the world would make—what building for the future generations might be planned!

Marilla says, we want a religion that will pay debts; that will practise honesty in business life; that will treat employees with justice and consideration; that will render employers full and faithful work without grudging or scamping; that will keep bank cashiers true; officeholders patriotic and reliable; citizens interested in the purity of politics and the noblest ideals of the country. Such a religion is real, vital, effective.

But a religion that embraces vicarious atonement, miraculous conception, regeneration by faith, baptism and other monkey business; a religion that promises a heaven of idleness for all those who agree with us, and a hell for those who do not, Marilla regards as barbaric, degrading, absurd and unworthy.

You own prosperity, power, life, love, land and immortality just as long as you can hold on to them and no longer. Man is only a protozoan wiggling through a fluid called atmosphere: he is here but for a day and knows neither where he came from nor where he is going.

We are just as immortal as any one can be today. What boots it how much food there is if we can not eat! What will it matter to us about immortality if we have no sensation to feel pain at its loss? We have, every moment, all of the immortality we can use. Success is the most hygienic thing of which we know—the glowing, glorious sense of success! Hard work does not kill anyone unless it is accompanied with a feeling of failure. To work and believe that all your toil is for naught, that you are losing ground, slipping back, means depression—death. And the belief in personal immortality, with its accompanying threats has forced upon men the thought that this life is a failure—the world a desert drear. When your attention is taken from this world and directed to another, the sense of success vanishes, the body droops; exhilaration gives way to depression and animation either disappears or resolves itself into a feverish hysteria. Correct thinking is largely a matter of bodily condition. And the summing up is that we will never produce a great magnificent race of men and women until we cease all thought of another world and devote our-selves to this.

Emerson, who never preached personal immortality, in his *Over-Soul* had something to say very much to the point. The passage is this:

"Revelation is the disclosure of the soul. The popular notion of a revelation, is, that it is a telling of fortunes. In past oracles of the soul, the understanding seeks to find answers to sensual questions and undertakes to tell from God how long men shall exist, what their hands shall do, and who shall be their company, adding even names, and dates, and places. But we must pick no locks. We must check this low curiosity. An answer in words is delusive; it is really no answer to the questions you ask. Do not demand a description of the countries toward which you sail.

"Men ask for the immortality of the soul, and the employments of heaven, and the state of the sinner, and so forth. They even dream that Jesus has left replies to precisely these interrogatories. Never a moment did that sublime spirit speak in their *patois*. To truth, justice, love, and the attributes of the soul, the idea of immutableness is essentially associated, Jesus, living in these moral sentiments, heedless of sensual fortunes, heeding only the manifestations of these, never made the separation of the idea of duration from the essence of these attributes; never uttered a syllable concerning the duration of the soul. It was left to his disciples to sever duration from the moral elements, and to teach the immortality of the soul as a doctrine, and maintain it by evidences ✷ ✷

"The moment the doctrine of the immortality of the soul is separately taught, man is already fallen. In the flowing of love, in the adoration of humility, there is no question of continuance.

No inspired man ever asks this question, or condescends to these evidences. For the soul is true to itself, and the man in whom it is shed abroad, can not wander from the present, which is infinite, to a future, which would be finite.

"These questions which we lust to ask about the future, are a confession of sin. God has no answer for them. No answer in words can reply to a question of things. It is not in an arbitrary " decree of God," but in the nature of man that a veil shuts down on the facts of tomorrow: for the soul will not have us read any other cipher but cause and effect. By this veil, which curtains events, it instructs the children of men to live in today. The only mode of obtaining an answer to these questions of the senses, is to forego all low curiosity, and accepting the tide of being which floats us into the secret of nature, work and live, and all unawares, the advancing soul has built and forged for itself a new condition, and the question and the answer are one."

Marilla also quotes Dr. J. H. Tilden who says:"There is n't any thing immortal except the elements, and they are in such a constant state of change that type succeeds type, world succeeds world, and necessity succeeds necessity. There is no such thing as immortality of form except to ignorance—and that is optional—a reward offered for being good—and being good, according to the general and accepted standard, is to mummify the intellect and refuse to evolve—become immortal in type. " In everything there is constant strife to force change—get rid of the old and take on the new.

" The growing man is the best proof that immortality is not what the world needs. The curse of existence is the belief in immortality. The Catholic church is immortal; orthodoxy of all kinds means of opinion; the ignoramus is an immortal man; those who have no time to read nor think and those who have no inclination for anything except to struggle for money, are immortal beings. Everything that makes no growth is immortal, and continues immortal until evolution rolls it into forgetfulness. Mortality is what we need most; and the quicker we get rid of the present individuality, the sooner we will come into possession of a better. Today is the best of all days; yesterday is gone, and no one but an idler cares to have it return—perpetuated—immortalized."

¶ It is sometimes said that woman is the worst enemy of her sex. But no one has ever said this with Marilla in mind. Her life has been devoted to the defense of women. Most of her clients have been women, and much of her business has been to collect debts due to working women by rogues in high places who sought to defraud them.

She has argued for equal rights for half a century. She was an abolitionist with John Brown and Wendell Phillips and stood side by side with Fred Douglass, when to do so was to invite insult and ignominy. She has raised her voice in behalf of the children in mills, mines and factories, and wherever she has found man, woman or child standing alone, accused by society or law, by their side she has taken her stand. She has known every president since Lincoln, and all who have lifted their voice for a wide horizon for humanity she has upheld by tongue, pen and pocketbook. She was an evolutionist before *The Origin of Species* was published and had abolished the devil from her own estate before Bishop Bob did as much for orthodoxy.

Marshall P. Wilder

OME folks feel sorry for Marshall Wilder—
I don't.

It is the heart and brains that count, not body.
When you weigh Marshall, he will not be found
wanting anything that belongs to you.

And, if you please, weigh him Troy, not Avoir-
dupois ❧ ❧

The first time Marshall arrived here, he came up to me and said
in a James-Whitcomb-Riley voice, " Pa could n't come, and so
he sent me!" No visitor in the Roycroft Shop ever captured the
hearts of our girls and boys like Marshall. Love just flows to
that rogue.

I use the word rogue advisedly. A woman from Buffalo came to
see us with a fat friend, and as they walked through the bookbindery they spied Marshall perched on a high stool, intently
at work tooling a book.

The Buffalo lady looked at him, had another look, and turning
to her friend whispered in a stage voice, " I always heard they
hired a lot of disreputable people here—just look at that face—
there is crime written all over it."

One visitor, with a turn for economics, going through the place
with a straight-edge and note-book, stepped up to Marsh and
asked him what wages he got. "A dollar a month and board—
such as it is!" was the lugubrious reply. Then he got the man's
large furry ear and poured into it the worst call-down the Shop
ever got. Marsh told the man that I had kidnapped him from his
parents and kept him and many others in peonage. In fact that
as a kidnapper I beat Col. Crowe of Omaha, and those Turkish
patrols who captured Ellen Stone and regretted it when it was
daylight, were not in it with me. He declared that I corralled
hoboes, scrubbed them with sapolio and threatened to kill them

if they did not make beautiful jimcracks roycroftie—in fact I had everybody scared stiff, so that they just had to get busy, and if a fellow did not take the proper amount of joy in his work I would kick him all over the place.

The worst of it was the man took Marsh's tale of woe seriously, and went away and printed it.

I was justly put out and had a very plain talk with the little man in the wood-shed. And all he would say was, " Migod! how about you and Paul Bartlett taking me into a dining car, tying a napkin under my chin, lifting me up in a high chair and ordering the waiter to give me a bowl of bread and milk, while you two sat opposite and ordered fried chicken and everything on the bill of fare for yourselves! "

That was the time I took the little man to New York with me on a half-rate ticket.

Marsh and I are the same age.

The conductor came around and I handed him the tickets. He looked at me and looked at Marsh and then said, " How old is your son, Col. Littlejourneys? "

" He 's seven all right! " I answered and gazed out of the window indifferently, settling myself for a nap.

" He needs a shave," said the conductor as he punched the ticket and started on.

When we got nearly to New York I stopped the conductor as he walked through and asked, " If you thought the little fellow was over-age why did n't you ask me to pay full fare for him ? "

" Well," he said, " it was like this,—I thought that any one who had as much assurance as you two have, should be rewarded."

Marshall is worth, oh, something over a hundred thousand dollars—all made out of honest, innocent laughs. The man has intellect, sympathy, affection—wit. He has simply cashed in his disabilities and worked his woes up into fun. Had he belonged to the court of Philip the IV, he would have been companion and brother of Velasquez. He is the biggest little man and the littlest big man in the world today.

If you are liable to introspection, and given to grouch, ask your bookseller for a copy of *The Sunny Side of the Street,* by Marshall P. Wilder.

Marshall P. Wilder is dead.

He died as he should have died, and as he hoped to die—on the job! ❧ ❧

Happily, the world has passed forever from the time when we felt a sorrow for the dead. The dead are at rest, their work is done, their hands are folded—just so.

Marshall P. Wilder lived all his life in the shadow of the wing of Death ❧ ❧

He was a walking refutation of that dogmatic statement, *Mens sana in corpore sano.* His was a sound mind in an unsound body. He proved the eternal paradox of things. He cashed in on his disabilities. He picked up the lemons that Fate had sent him and started a lemonade-stand.

And he never asked for pity. In fact, he scorned it, and if any one ever got his ill-will, it was because the party was too profuse in endeavors to help him.

If Marshall was ever cast down in spirit he concealed the mood. He laughed his way into our hearts.

" I am the only man who ever deliberately walked into the office of a life-insurance company and demanded a policy," he used to say ❧ ❧

Many of his stories turned on himself. For instance, one quip that never failed to get a laugh was this: " The other day I was walking down the street with Jim Corbett. Two ladies came along, and one said to the other as we passed, ' Why, there goes Jim Corbett,' and the other asked, ' Which one? ' "

Marshall Wilder made money, and saved it. For a good many

years his income was around twenty-five thousand dollars a year.
¶ He always played the headliner and was the big man on the bill.
After the week's engagement he would go 'round and shake hands
with all the stagehands, the members of the orchestra as well,
and the stage-manager—just as every good vaudevillian does—
and he always left a generous coin in the palm of each.

He was a thrifty little Marshall, who knew the joy of giving and
of saving.

I have seen him stand in the wings speaking words of approval
under his breath to the party out before the " foots." His habit
was to encourage everybody, to give everybody a lift, and in his
jokes and quips and quillets there was no bitterness.

We can not mourn for dear little Marshall, because we do not
mourn our own losses.

Rather would we think of the joys that the little man supplied us,
for this world is a bigger, brighter and more beautiful place
because of the fact that little Marshall, America's court jester,
lived and joked and laughed.

If he could speak now, he would say that his only regret was that
he could n't finish the week.

Also, he might express a little protest with Fate on account of the
fact that he died on Friday.

For months he knew that the end was not far away. Yet he worked
just the same, and with his last breath he might have said as did
Mercutio, " It 's a grave subject."

He met the big men of the world on an equality. Henry Irving
had for Marshall a great and abiding affection. Gladstone took
him under his protecting wing when he was in England.

King Edward the Seventh wrote him many personal letters, and
when he attended a court reception at Windsor Castle and the
footman cried aloud as he entered, "Marshall Wilder!" he was
put in line with the marshals of England, next to the peers and
alongside of the lords, and as the six-foot guardsmen made way

no one smiled, and Marshall, solemn as an owl, clad in court suit, did sartorial goosestep.

The next day he wrote a letter to the editor of *The Times* complaining bcause his name had been left out of *Burke's Peerage*. Thus did the little man get his advertising, and supply a laugh to the elect.

Marshall was a lover of books and a very good critic of things literary and artistic. He had a grasp on big questions as well, but essentially he was always and forever the mime, subdued to the work of the stage like the dyer's hand.

The stage was his salvation. No man ever got more fun out of his work than he. This, of course, was also the secret of his success. His fun was spontaneous, and when he told the old jokes over he always hypnotized himself into the belief that it was a brand-new audience ❧ ❧

He gave big value and he grew rich by giving.

Hail! dear little Marshall! Hail and Farewell! We are the poorer for your passing.

We miss your name in life's vaudeville, but congratulate Valhalla on the added attraction.

Mangasarian

LIKE I. Zangwill, he has no Christian name. He is simply Mr. Mangasarian, Lecturer for the Independent Religious Society, Rationalist, of Chicago ✣ ✣

Moreover, he is the excuse for the Society, the raison d' etre—and he is reason enough.

He has no title in front of his name and no degrees behind it. Nature made only one Mangasarian, and then did n't have to break the mold, for men of this stamp are not made from molds, they are pounded out of sheet silver, like Gorham loving cups. Mangasarian has touched life at more strange points than any man I can name. He was born in Constantinople, within the shadow of a mosque and the sound of tolling bells on tower and kiosk calling men to prayer. The cries of the faithful Mohammedan fell with familiar sound upon his childish ears. His mother was a Jewess; his father an Armenian—a Christian missionary—descended from Greek stock, and a man who thought to make Byron King of Greece and revive the grandeur of long ago ✣ ✣

And as Cupid stands small show with theology, and women in the East are not supposed to have opinions anyway, the gentle Jewess found it easy to blend Isaiah and Numbers with John and the Acts. Mangasarian is a rationalist by prenatal tendency.

He knows all religions, and believes in all religions, yet has implicit faith in none.

If he were shipwrecked in the South Seas, and would swim to an island peopled with savages, as he came dripping from the brine he would at once ask, " Have you any religion here ? "

And the savages would answer, " Yes."

Then would Mr. Mangasarian say, " Teach it to me, for I came to learn—not to teach."

In the veins of Mangasarian flow all bloods but that of the Celt. I have often wished that he had in him a dash of the Irish—it would add one touch more to the bouquet, but alas! might purchase poetry at the expense of reason. The next thing omitted was his failure to be born at sea; but the next best thing is to have him die at sea. His body should be given back to the Great White Mother, the restless, tossing, moving Sea, just as he now gives his spirit to the thinking world.

The Independent Religious Society, Rationalist, meets every Sunday morning at Orchestra Hall, Michigan Avenue, Chicago. Orchestra Hall was built for the Theodore Thomas Orchestra. It is one of the finest auditoriums in the world. It seats about three thousand people. The place is always comfortably filled when Mr. Mangasarian speaks, and I have seen it crowded.

These people do not come out of curiosity, just to hear the lion roar—they have been listening to Mangasarian for ten years. They have been educated by him. He feeds their minds.

It is well that Mr. Mangasarian should be the Lecturer for the Independent Religious Society, Rationalist, for the man is independent, he is religious, and he is rationalistic.

Very few religious folks are independent, and most men who call themselves independent, only think they are. As for being rational, in the sense of accepting Reason as a counselor and guide, what other public man, besides Mangasarian does!

It is but a truism to say that the avowed " Liberal Denominations" are quite as dogmatic in their liberalism, as our orthodox friends are with their orthodoxy.

The liberalism that scouted and flouted Ralph Waldo Emerson, finds Mangasarian unpardonable. These are the people who rallied 'round the *Christian Register* when the *Fireside Companion* became obsolete. They believe, at the last, in a steam-heated hell. The timidity of Unitarians and Universalists, when it comes to following a reason to its lair, reminds you of Bob

Acres when about to fight a duel. Yet the situation is not complex—these liberal denominations are social clubs, their highest aim is culture, their goal flawless character, and the one thing that they fear is not being in the fashion. Pride and exclusion are the principal planks in their platform. Tolstoy to them is a fanatic, Emma Goldman a lewd woman, Susan B. Anthony absurd, and Jesus Christ is only acceptable because they have no faith in the resurrection, and so have no fear of His coming back ❧ ❧

Ask Rev. Dr. Barrows of Boston!

An honest, simple, frank expression gives them goose-flesh; and an honest life they refuse to accept even on suspicion.

Their liberalism consists in pardoning everything but truth. It need not here be explained that all orthodoxy is now essentially Unitarian, with no change in name—the fight being over a matter of labels. In time the world will become rationalistic—that is, we will reverence Reason. But in the meantime how about all these stiff-necked and hide-bound " Liberals " who die in their sins! John Henry Newman was right—there is no place for an honest man to set his foot between Rome and Reason.

Rome frankly accepts the rule of the dead, and does not pretend to think. Therein is Rome honest.

But Protestantism pretending to think, not only shirks conclusions, but damns those who accept them. Note the unblushing side-steppers in ordinary, and makers of sexio-religio maniacs, to wit: Sunday, Chapman, Torrey, Beiderwolf, who hypnotize adolescence and ignorance into unseemliness in the name of sweet reasonableness. Oh, the shame of it!

The power of Mangasarian lies in the fact that he intellectually is without guile, and that he is a bigger man than he is an orator. He never gets drunk on words, nor woozy on ideas. The religious jag is not in his line. He has an intellectual conscience, just as the giants in art—say Michelangelo, Rembrandt, Turner—had artistic consciences. They would have scorned themselves to have produced less than their best. Mangasarian does not seek to please—he would rather be hissed, or left alone without an auditor than to ogle justice and juggle with truth. His is no theological shell-game. He passes you out no canned-thought. Truth is the one thing sacred to him—and Truth to him is his present view of Truth. He knows that Truth is no pillar of salt, like Lot's wife. She is a living, pulsing reality, and therefore a changing and changeable entity.

But that which Mangasarian sees he throws upon the screen. Combined with great intellect and a ripe scholarship, this fearless honesty, this sterling disinterestedness, this beautiful indifference to all but the divine rudder of his soul, place Mangasarian before the world as a unique figure. He is big enough to say, " I do not know." He never besmears commonsense with metaphysics, nor points you to a road that leads nowhere.

He really has no competition in his chosen line—he has a clear field—he is an unconscious monopolist.

" To own a slave is to be one," said Emerson. A slave becomes a tyrant when he has the power. You can always tell a free man by this token: He is willing to grant freedom to others. Mangasarian is so big and generous that he does n't ask you to agree with him. To belong to his church you do not have to declare your belief or make a promise. He assumes that you will always act according to your highest light. If he can lend light, he is happy. If he can make you think he is satisfied. He has gained freedom by giving it. In stature the man is small. His body is shapely, graceful, exquisite. His voice is very gentle, his manner modest. His reserve is complete, and he often wins a battle with the guns he never fires. He knows how to pack a pause with feeling—to wait for the right word, and always and forever he gets an atmosphere. By his presence he masters the situation, more than by what he says. He does not merely seem! He is.

To an audience accustomed to the bishop's voice, the loud ballyhoo, and the brazen bazoo of popular oratory he would make small appeal. His is an educated audience, and he has had to do most of the educating.

The auditor has a duty to perform as well as the speaker. Mangasarian's audiences bring much, and therefore they never go empty away ✒ ✒

Happy audience! Happy Mangasarian! Happy anybody who reverences the human Reason as the highest reflection of Divinity and who believes that we are all Sons of God, and it doth not yet appear what we shall be!

As a little sample of Mr. Mangasarian's quality I quote the following, entitled "Prayer." A True Story.

At the age of seventeen I had a thrilling experience with the Kurdish brigands in Turkey. I was traveling in Asia Minor, going from the Euphrates to the Bosphorus, accompanied by the driver of my horses, one of which I rode, the other carrying my luggage. We had not proceeded very far when we were overtaken by a young traveler on foot, who for reasons of safety, begged to join our little party. He was a Mohammedan, while my driver and I professed the Christian religion.

For three days we traveled together, going at a rapid pace in order to overtake the caravan. It need hardly be said that in that part of the world it is considered unsafe to travel even with a caravan, but to go on a long journey, as we were doing all by ourselves, was certainly taking a great risk.

Let me interpolate here to say that, though I was a firm believer in Divine Providence, namely, that nothing, not even a sparrow, fell to the ground without the merciful notice of God—though I believed professionally, and as I thought at the time, sincerely, that to have God with one was better than to be with the caravan —nevertheless, I was as anxious as my Mohammedan fellow-traveler to hail the caravan.

It seemed to me even then that my faith would be more secure traveling with the caravan than traveling with God alone. At any rate God and the caravan made, I thought, a very much stronger combination than God alone, against the predatory Kurds who at that time and in that region of the Ottoman Empire were viciously active.

I forgot to say that we carried a rifle—one of those flint fire-arms which frequently refuse to go off. My driver had also hanging from his girdle a long and crooked knife sheathed in a black canvas scabbard. Both the driver, who was a Christian, and the Mohammedan, who had placed himself under our protection were, I am sorry to say, much given to boasting. They would tell how on various occasions they had, single-handed, driven away the Kurdish brigands who outnumbered them ten to one; how that rusty knife had disemboweled one of the most renowned Kurdish chiefs, and how the silent and meek-looking flint-gun had held at bay a pack of those " curs " who go about scenting for human flesh. All this talk was reassuring to me—a lad of seventeen, and I began to think I was indebted to Providence for my brave escort.

On the morning of the Eighteenth of February, Eighteen Hundred and Seventy-seven, we came to the valley said to be a veritable thieves' den, and where many a traveler had lost his life as well as his goods. A great fear fell upon us when we saw on the wooden bridge which spanned the river at the base of the hills, two Kurds riding in our direction. I was at once undeceived as to the boasted bravery of my comrades, and felt that it was all braggadocio with which they had been entertaining me. As I was the one supposed to have money, I would naturally be the chief object of attack, which made my position the more perilous. But this sudden fear which seemed to paralyze me at first, was followed by a bracing resolve to cope with these " devils " mentally.

As I look back now upon the events of that day, I am puzzled to know how I got through it all without any serious harm to my person. I am surprised also that I, who had been brought up to pray and to trust in divine help, forgot in the hour of real peril, all about " other help " and bent all my energies upon helping myself ❧ ❧

But why did I not pray? Why did I not fall upon my knees to commit myself to God's keeping? Perhaps it was because I was too much preoccupied—too much in earnest to take the time to pray. Perhaps my better instincts would not let me take refuge in words when something stronger was wanted. We may ask the good Lord not to burn our house, but when the house is actually on fire, water is better than prayer. Perhaps, again, I did not pray because of an instinctive feeling that this was a case of self-help or no help at all. Perhaps, again, there was a feeling in me, that if all the prayers I had offered in my life for divine protection could not save me now, neither would any new prayer I might offer. Or, again, perhaps it was because I felt that if God really wanted to save me, He would not let me perish because I did not pray to Him just there and then. But the fact is that in the hour of positive and imminent peril—when face to face with death—I was too busy to pray.

My mother, before I started on this journey, had made a bag for my valuables—watch and chain, etc.—and sewed it on my under-flannels next to my body. But my money (all in gold coins) was in a snuff-box and that again in a long silk purse. I was, of course, the better dressed of the three—with long boots which reached higher than my knees, a warm English broadcloth cloak reaching down to my ankles, and an Angora collarette, soft and snow-white, about my neck.

My dear mother had also told me never to refuse anything to the brigands, should I be so unfortunate as to fall into their hands. But I was loathe to part with the money in my purse, without which I would be left to perish on the highway.

I rode ahead, and the others, with the baggage horse, followed me. When the two Kurdish riders who were advancing in our direction reached me, they saluted me very politely, saying, according to the custom of the country, " God be with you," to which I timidly returned the customary answer, " We are all in His Keeping." At the time it did not occur to me how absurd it was for both travelers and robbers to recommend each other to God while carrying fire-arms—the ones for attack, the others for defense.

Of course God never interfered to save an unarmed traveler from brigands—I say never, for if He ever did, and could, He would do it always. But as we know, alas, too well, that hundreds and thousands have been robbed and cut in pieces by these Kurds, it would be reasonable to infer that God is indifferent. Of course, the strongly-armed travelers, as a rule, escape, thanks to their own courage and fire-arms. For, we ask again, if the Lord can save one, why not all? And if He can save all, but will not, does He not become as dangerous as the robbers? But really if God could do anything in the matter, He would reform the Kurds out of the land, or—out of the thieving business. If God is the unfailing police force in Christian lands, He is no police force in Mohammedan countries, at any rate.

But think! throughout the Turkish realms, the phrase " God be with you" is repeated daily, a million times, if it is repeated once. And yet there is not a single case of demonstrable Divine protection extended to a wayfarer. The strong escape; the weak suffer. The whole land is like a den of thieves, and murders are as numerous as daily orisons. I am of the opinion that in countries where there is more security, there is less praying, and conversely, in the most prayerful country in the world there is the least security to life and property.

Good reader, I speak plainly, not to offend you, but to replace your belief in " other help " by self-help. To explain the foolish beliefs which an ignorant and indolent clergy imposed upon our

intelligence when we were too young or too weak to defend ourselves, is not a crime—it is a duty. We have no right to be reverent
except toward what is true and just. Superstition is stupid, and
only cowards revere it.

But let me go on with the story.

As the two mounted Kurds passed me by, they scanned me very
closely—my costume, boots, furs, cap and so on. Then I heard
them making inquiries of my driver about me—who I was, where
was I going, and why I was going at all. My driver answered
these inquiries as honestly as the circumstances permitted. Wishing us all again the protection of Allah, the Kurds spurred their
horses and galloped away.

For a moment we began to breathe freely—but only for a moment,
for as our horses neared the bridge we saw the Kurds following us.
And before we reached the middle of the bridge over the river,
one of the Kurds galloping up close to me laid his hand on my
shoulders and unceremoniously pulled me out of the saddle. At
the same time he dismounted himself, while his partner remained
on horseback with his gun pointed squarely in my face, and
threatening to kill me if I did not give him my money immediately ஒ ஒ

As soon as I could pick myself up from the ground I walked
straight to the Kurd who sat in the saddle with his gun in my face,
and patting his leg gently, told him that no one was more willing
to part with his goods than I, and to prove it I dipped my hand
into my pockets one by one, bringing out their contents and
offering them to him. I saw at once that I had succeeded in
persuading the Kurds that I was the most accommodating traveler
they had ever captured. Expecting no resistance from me, the
Kurd put away his gun. When the other Kurd had relieved my
companions of all their belongings, he approached me. Immediately I turned to him and told him that my mother, whose only
son I was, had given me orders never to oppose the brave Kurds,

or to refuse them anything in my possession. Thus saying, I began to unbutton my vest.

" If you will only spare my life, for my mother's sake," I said, " for the news of my death will surely kill her—I will gladly let you take all that I have."

Of course, from a theoretical point of view, I was not honest with the thieves. But I shall discuss that point later on.

The Kurds, finding that I had no objection to being robbed, allowed me to search myself for them. What I wanted was to prevent them from putting their hands into my pockets, and this point I had gained by my apparent willingness to do it for them. I offered them every article I took out, explaining carefully the uses to which they could be put, but what the Kurds wanted was money and valuables—which I could not let them have.

The robbers were now growing impatient. They were morally certain I carried a purse, and yet they had not been able to locate it. Turning upon me fiercely, the Kurd who was doing the robbing let out a long string of oaths, in which the name of the Diety played the principal part. In all countries the name of God figures as prominently in the curses as in the prayers of the people. With a mouthful of oaths, the Kurd who had dismounted accused me of hiding my money, warning me at the same time with a blow on my back, of the consequences if I did not immediately hand over my purse to him.

Then the Kurd seized me violently and began a minute search of my person, pinching and thumping me all over.

I can never forget his savage grin when at last he found my purse, and grabbing it, with another oath, pulled it out of its hiding place. I have already described that my coins were all in a snuff-box hid away in my purse, hence, as soon as the robber had loosened the strings he took out the box, held it in his left hand, while with his right he searched in the inner folds of the long purse. While he was running his fingers through the tortuous purse, I slipped mine into his left hand and, taking hold of the box, I told him that I would not part with that little memento, as it was the dearest present I had received from my mother. So saying I carried the box into my pocket, emptied its contents in the twinkling of an eye, and then re-producing it, and still holding on to it as firmly as before, I declared with a touch of anger in my voice that he should at least leave me in possession of this little trinket. The Kurd, incensed at finding nothing in the purse which he kept shaking and fingering, snatched the box from my hand, opened it, and finding it as empty as the purse, flung it, with another oath, in the direction of the river. But it only fell on the edge of the water, which gave me a good excuse to run after it for a moment's relief from the fearful strain.

When I returned I found the Kurd who had done the searching in the saddle again. Of course I hastened to say, " God be with you," to them. But it seemed they had not finished with us as yet. "Are you Moslems, or Christians? " inquired one of the Kurds, to my companions.

" We are all Moslems, by Allah," they said.

In Turkey you are not supposed to speak the truth unless you say " by Allah," which means " by God."

At that time Turkey was at war with Russia, and the lawless Kurds made no ado about killing a Christian or two, to help the cause of the Sultan.

Of course it was not true that I was a follower of Mahomet. My companions told the Kurds a falsehood about me, which I did not correct. When I reached my destination many of my co-religionists declared that I had denied Christ by allowing the Kurds to think I was a Moslem.

To this day my conscience has never troubled me for helping, by my silence, to deceive the Kurds about my religion. In withholding the truth from these would-be assassins I was doing them no evil, but protecting the most sacred rights of man, the Kurds included. Here was an instance in which silence was golden. But I would not hesitate, any moment, to mislead a thief or a murderer, by speech as well as by silence. If it is right to kill the murderer in self-defense, it is right to deny him also the truth. He who resorts to brute force forfeits his claims to moral considerations ❧ ❧

"You should have told the truth and left the rest to God," said a Philadelphia Quaker to me, to whom I had related my adventure with the brigands.

Oh, dear! If I had, there would not have been anything left of me to leave to God!

I have told this story to show that dependence upon the supernatural makes weaklings of men. There would have been no civilization in the world if people had not stopped praying and begun thinking. Why create safeguards, provide means of defense—why build bridges, invent machinery, discover steam, and learn to control the forces of nature, if all that is necessary is to pray to God, and He will divide the waters for us, send us quails from the sea and manna from the skies?

Not until we learn that the only bread we can eat is the bread produced by human labor, and that without labor there will be positively no bread to eat, even if there were a thousand Gods to pray to, shall we learn that Human Labor is the only Providence. Can prayer take us across the ocean without sail or steam? Can we tunnel a mountain or span a stream or raise a crop with prayer alone? I know prayer and a boat will take us across the sea, but is it not true that while a boat can cross a sea without prayer, prayer can not without a boat?

If we all prayed very hard could we dispense with schools and colleges, or get our education without labor or study?

Will prayer take the place of physical exercise and fresh air? Will it protect a house against lightning? Then why are churches struck by lightning? If our questions appear absurd, is it our fault, or the fault of the proposition so pompously paraded that "whatever we ask of God in prayer, it will be given unto us?" Do we get our daily bread because we beg for it? Then why is there any poverty in the world? When it rains is it in answer to prayer? Then why does it rain on the sands of Sahara or the watery wilderness of unbeaten seas? And when it does not rain, is that too in answer to prayer? I know how present-day orthodoxy, honey-combed with heresy, protests against praying for material ends. But the Bible is close at hand, and let us quote just one passage from it:

" Now Elias was a man of like passions as we are: and he prayed that it might not rain, and it rained not for a period of three years and six months, and the earth gave not forth its fruits."

We congratulate ourselves that the race of Eliases is extinct. " To pray for private ends is meanness and theft," wrote Emerson. But take away private ends, and who would pray? Is it not more religious to abstain from suggesting to God what He should do and what He should not do?

How can God tell what kind of weather or harvests to give, if the prayers of the churches can change His plans? And if they can not, why pray? How can God tell whether the Japanese or the Russian will win, if it all depends on which side will pray the hardest? But if it does not, why pray?

Was it not Kant who said that to ask God to do right was superfluous; to ask Him to do wrong was an impertinence? If this is so, then think of the amount of time which could be put to better use than in urging God to do this or not to do that.

But if prayer can not do the impossible, what is it good for? We can attend to the possible ourselves.

Is not independence better than humility?

But all this goes to prove that fetich worship is still with us. What did the savage do when he was in peril? He kissed his amulet or repeated the charmed words taught him by his priests.

What does the Christian do today when he wants a favor? He falls on his knees, and repeats a string of phrases Aves and Pater-Nosters, et cetera. To say the six-syllabled charm three hundred thousand times in the course of one's lifetime was the highest aspiration of the Buddhist. Om Mani Padme Houm—the most glorious jewel of the lotus—Amen. In China and Japan we meet with a shorter form of this invocation—Amitabha Buddha—Save us, O Buddha. In the streets of the cities, in the crowded mart, in the country lanes, at the windows of the houses—everywhere, the traveler finds the lips of the people forever moving and murmuring "Amitabha Buddha"—Save us, O Buddha. On the shores of the Bosphorus, as in all Mohammedan countries, the prayer la Illa Allah is repeated from the housetops and the minarets, in the mosques, in the bazaars, in the kiosks—wherever there is a bended knee on a rug or a face turned toward Mecca. It is one unbroken murmur girdling the Mohammedan world—la Illa Allah—" There is but one God."

For the same purpose they have invented in the Orient what is known as the " prayer barrel," or " prayer wheel." At the doors of the houses in the Orient you will find these revolving caskets to which everybody as he enters or as he leaves is expected to give a twirl. While you are sleeping the winds keep shaking the barrel for you. We know, also, that the Jews carry out literally the words of the Bible which says, " Thou shalt write them upon the posts of thy house and on thy gates." Accordingly these people have a hollow reed or pipe in which there is a parchment bearing inscriptions from the Bible, among others Shaddai, one of the names of God. This is introduced in the wall to the right of the door, and as the Jew goes out or comes in, he touches this spot with his finger, and then kisses it, whispering at the same time the words, " Preserve me," which, of course, helps to keep him in a prayerful mood all day. The Turks pray formally five times a day. The mosque is never closed, and the name of Allah is ever on the wing. Catholics pray oftener and more fervently than Protestants. More prayers ascend to heaven from Ireland than from Scotland—from Spain than from Switzerland.

Is there, then, more morality, more humanity, more culture and prosperity, more happiness, where there is more praying?

Do the nations who depend most upon other help have better harvests, better homes, better schools, better governments? Was the printing press, the steam engine, the mariner's compass, given to man in answer to prayer? Was liberty, political and religious, handed down to us from heaven? Was it the priest's prayers which secured for us freedom of conscience?

In the countries of Europe, prayer has not prevented, though it certainly has postponed, the development of our own manhood because we have virtually renounced our trust in " other help " by giving our consent to the dictum that, " God only helps those who help themselves," which, if it means anything, means that man makes his own destiny.

" Prayer," said Emerson, again, " is a disease of the intellect." Nay, dear teacher! it is more: it is the paralysis of hand and head, making it impossible for the mind to originate, or for the will to do and dare!

Do not pray. Think!

Do not beg. Labor!

Socrates

IN Grecian history the time between the years Four Hundred Sixty-one and Four Hundred Twenty-nine Before Christ is known as the Age of Pericles.

It is known as the Age of Pericles because in twenty years of that time he adorned the city of Athens, and so beautified it that it has been the despair of builders of cities to this day.

This present age resembles the Age of Pericles, in that it is a time of great unrest, a time of great activity, a time when people are working, a time of great enlightenment.

Pericles had for his supervisor of public works, Phidias, a sculptor to whom the ages have not given a rival.

Phidias was a great teacher. The people of Athens appreciated art. He taught by example; his work was ever before the people. He set thousands of men to work with mallet and chisel, carving out wonderful marble ideals which their minds created.

One of the men who worked for Phidias was Sophroniscus. He married Phaenarete, a woman who had much skill in taking care of the sick, who knew something of the laws of life. Phaenarete's son was Socrates.

Socrates learned the trade of Sophroniscus and became a sculptor of some renown. He worked with hand, heart and brain until he had made a statue that fulfilled his ideal, when he said, " I have learned what I can from sculpture."

Then he set himself to another task. He made his brain think to a purpose. Everything that Socrates did had a purpose. Even his marriage with Xantippe seems to have served him even better perhaps than it served Xantippe. She could not understand his logic, and, clever as was Socrates, he never understood the needs of his wife.

If you will turn to the *Century Encyclopedia,* to the name of Pericles, you will find a little account of the wonderful power of this great man.

The biography is well written. It closes with an imperative sentence of two words, very forceful, very suggestive. Unless you are a stubborn person and not a lawful descendant of Pandora you will obey the command, "See Aspasia!" I obeyed, and read what this writer—who evidently believes in equal rights—had to say about a great woman. And, by the way, I noticed that it was a humorist by the name of Hermippus who accused Aspasia, which caused her to be placed under indictment and required the utmost skill of Pericles to keep her from persecution.

However, the biographers say that Socrates found much solace and satisfaction, as well as profit, in his breakfasting, dining and supping at Aspasia's house. There, Pericles, Aspasia and Socrates, these three, great in history, evolved a philosophy which is not worked out in our lives even yet.

Socrates lived more than two thousand three hundred years ago. We have not yet caught up with the teachings of Socrates.

Our word "school" comes from a Greek word, the meaning of which we have changed. Originally the word meant leisure, spare time. It is the spare time that every one has, when walking, after supper, in the evening, on the way to the theater, a concert. Such occasions to Socrates were leisure.

And Socrates thought, and always came to a conclusion in his thinking ๑ ๑

" What is its use ? " was the Socratic question.

Socrates had many pupils who have been world teachers. Plato and Aristotle are the two whom we know best.

There came to Socrates one day a rich man's son named Alcibiades. He asked the way to eternal life. For, to the mind of Socrates, a searcher after knowledge was a searcher after virtue. Said Alcibiades, " Socrates, how shall I become educated? "

Socrates said: " What can you do? Can you drive a mule to the top of the Acropolis, carrying one of those shining blocks of marble to be put in the top of the Parthenon? "

" Oh no, the muleteer does that."

" Can you drive a chariot? "

" Oh no, the charioteer does that."

" Alcibiades, can you carve a statue? "

" Oh no, we hire our statues carved."

" Can you cook your dinner? "

" Oh no, we have cooks to do this."

" Is it not strange, Alcibiades, that your father should give to his humblest servant a better education than he does to his son? " And Alcibiades went away sorrowful, for he loved ease and was slothful ⋗ ⋗

Socrates' idea of an educated man was the idea which is dawning upon the people today—that in order to be educated we must be useful, we must do useful work, and we must love to do useful work. Why is it that more than two thousand three hundred years have come and gone since Socrates knew these facts which are being understood a little by many people today? Possibly because work until today has had much drudgery connected with it. In order to accomplish a little, much toil was involved. All this before the age of machinery, before the time when man invented machines that would toil for humanity. Work has been a punishment and a curse, so denominated in Bible legends.

We are just learning, however, to illumine work and to understand that work can be lightened and brightened by love, art, joy, machinery, electricity and steam.

Best of all, we are learning to illumine work for children, so that to them it is play and pleasure.

Jean Paul

EAN PAUL, inspired by Jean Jacques, was the inspirer of the whole brood of young writers of his time. To him they looked as to a Deliverer. Jean Paul, the Only! The largest, gentlest, most generous heart in all literature! The peculiar mark of Richter's style is analogy and comparison. Everything he saw reminded him of something else, and then he tells you of the things that both remind him of. He leads and lures you on, and takes you far from home, but always brings you safely back. Yet comparison proves us false when we deal with Richter himself. He stands alone, like Adam's recollection of his fall, which, according to Jean Paul, was the one sweet, unforgetable thing in all the life of the First Citizen of his time.

Jean Paul seems to have combined in that mighty brain all feminine as well as masculine attributes. The soul in which the feminine does not mingle is ripe for wrong, strife and unreason. " It was mother-love carried one step farther, that caused the Savior to embrace a world," says Richter.

The sweep of tender emotion that murmurs and rustles through the writings of Jean Paul is like the echo of a lullaby heard in a dream ❧ ❧

Perhaps it came from that long partnership when mother and son held the siege against poverty, and the kitchen table served him as a writing desk, and the patient old mother was his sole reviewer, critic, reader and public. He called her, " My Gentle Reader"— he had but one.

For shame, hypocrisy and pretence Jean Paul had a cyclone of sarcasm, and the blows he struck were such as only a son of Anak could give; but in his heart there was no hate. He could despise a man's bad habits and still love the man behind the veneer of folly. So his arms seem ever extended, welcoming the wanderer home.

Jean Paul used to cry at his work when he wrote well, and I do, too. I always know when I write particularly well, for at such times I mop furiously—however, I seldom mop.

Dear Jean Paul, big and homely, what an insight you had into the heart of things, and what a flying machine your imagination was! Room for many passengers? Yes, and children especially, for these you loved most of all, because you were ever only just a big over-grown boy yourself. You cried your eyes out before your hair grew white, and then a child or a woman led you about, and thus did you supply Victor Hugo a saying that can never die: " To be blind and to be loved—what happier fate! "

Robert Louis Stevenson

OD! If this were enough,
That I see things bare to the buff
And up to the buttocks in mire.
That I ask nor hope nor hire,
Not in the husk,
Nor dawn beyond the dusk,
Nor life beyond death:
God—if this were faith!

Having felt Thy wind in my face
Spit sorrow and disgrace,
Having seen Thy evil doom
In Golgotha and Khartoum,
And the brutes, the work of Thine hands,
Fill with injustice lands
And stain with blood the sea.
If still in my veins the glee
Of the black night and the sun
And the lost battle run;
If, an adept,
The iniquitous lists I still accept
With joy, and joy to endure and be withstood,
And still to battle and perish for a dream of good:
God—if that were enough!

If to feel in the ink of the slough
And the sink of the mire
Veins of glory and fire
Run through and transpierce and transpire,
And a secret purpose of glory fill each part,
And the answering glory of battle fill my heart;

To thrill with the joy of girded men,
To go on forever and fail, and go on again,
And be mauled to the earth and arise,
And contend for the shade of a word and a thing not seen with
    the eyes,
With the half of a broken hope for a pillow at night
That somehow the right is the right,
And the smooth shall bloom from the rough:
Lord—if that were enough!

                    —Robert Louis Stevenson

We strut across the earth and then go into it.

En passant, we wrangle and pray.

Our wranglings are petty, and our prayers bear the stamp of cowardice. It is all of a piece with life, with the mewling existence begotten of the fears that make the days a procession of pallid shapes ✸ ✸

The bogey man is everywhere, thanks to orthodoxy. In the street, in the marketplace, in the pulpit, in the heavens, there is the shape that forbodes and forbids. There are no men. What seem so are fragments. If you pieced together the noblest qualities of a million human beings, the net result would not be a Lincoln, a Stevenson, a Whitman.

Most men are like the Farnese torso—a fragment. Mankind has in all ages reverenced the brave man because it deifies the qualities that it lacks.

Read all the litanies and prayer-books ever written; after you have finished, you feel the stifling oppression that settles on one in the steam-room of a Turkish bath.

These prayers whine, dodge, are hang-dog, round-shouldered and knee-worn.

Our attitude toward the Supreme Being is essentially barbaric. There is no difference in spirit between the savage's petition to his god and a Thanksgiving Day proclamation by the Governor of New York. The official " Thank you " begs the question, lacks directness, is the product of a skulking beggary.

Great souls never cringe. And in the measure that a man is brave, in that measure is he great. In so far as he puts off alien supports and substitutes a sense of interdependence for dependence is he strong. He will recognize his helplessness when standing out of relation to his fellowmen, but not for that will he sell himself. So much for the world; the rest I keep. And you shall not have the kernel of myself that I keep for myself, though you should slay me. I will be brother and friend, but not slave.

Of such stuff is the stentorian spirit. In the same manner that he fronts the frowning world will he front the Supreme Power. There shall be no fawning, no knee-quaking in His Presence. The strong soul will not be a subaltern in life's battle, no mere aide-de-camp to the General.

God shall be my Camerado.

Such was Stevenson's attitude toward life and God; and his great poem is his confession of faith. He will not palter with wrongs, nor blench at evil. Clear-eyed and strong-souled, he faces the Eternal and says: " I see things bare to the buff," and they are " up to the buttocks in mire." The fair things of the world are arranged like the fruit on a street-vendor's stand: the speck is carefully concealed; and if the speck is not there, there is a worm at the core. It is this vision of the world which Stevenson conjures up in his lines.

The world is fair and ever young.

Pan is born anew every day. The waters run, the stars shine, the sun gushes over the land like a divine benediction.

But this is not all. These are the meretricious coverings of things. The mind of the thinker can not be balked by appearances. It is licentious, and burrows. If the heavens proclaim the glory of God, what shall we say of the cancer hospital?

And the Vice and Want and Care that, gaunt and frowsy, stalk through our great cities—vices not willed into being by a race dwelling in a " sinless state," but vices that silently grow into being—the product of human relations, the outgrowth of legitimate wants, good instincts turned awry in the collisions of personality, vices woven of universal greed, craft begotten of inherent weaknesses?

It is thus things are in the mire. Mankind is a stunted aspiration. The palace which the soul of youth is given as a birthright is turned into a marketplace, where his strength is peddled to the highest bidder; at thirty he already hears the measured, noiseless drip, drip, drip of the days that wear the echoing hollows in the granite purposes of twenty. " I ask nor hope nor hire." We are always asking God for something. Our souls are mendicant; we are that beggar who stands hat in hand imploring a Divine Providence to drop a penny into it. The strong soul, who believes it less culpable to steal than to beg, does not wish to be paid for what he has done.

Pour into our souls the wine of truth, O God, and keep your crusts! Moisten our lips turned papyri with thirst! Keep your houris for lower intelligences! We care naught about " dawn beyond the dusk." We want the Light now, in the Eternal Present ꙮ ꙮ

" Adepts," we are indeed. From all eternity we have been waging war. Each atom that composes our bodies is a center of contending forces; each cell is an embryonic individual, menacing the stability of a million other cells. And before they were welded into the agglomeration that is styled James or John they fought elsewhere. They struggled in the parturitions of the primordial nebulæ and they participated in the sack of Rome.

But it is trite to say that life is a battle. To call the lists " iniquitous " is not only not trite, but it is decidedly bold. This is almost a judgment on the constitution of things. But it

does not whine. Stevenson accepts things with " joy to endure
and be withstood, and still to battle and perish for a dream of
good." " I was ever a fighter," says Browning defiantly in
Prospice another brave man's prayer. To both these poets
it is the fight that makes life worth the living. They prefer a place
in the " iniquitous lists " of Go;d they will take their places
on the firing-line of human endeavor, rather than rust and rot
in the ennui of a complacent optimism that stays at home and
mumbles in drowsy meditation of that "far-off divine event"—
to which the whole creation does not move.

In Stevenson's eye, all is not ill. In the murk of things he discerns
veins of glory that cross and transpire. A secret grace peeps out
at times. Men and women are beautiful in perspective. The
pageant of souls across the earth attracts. Love's ordinances are
imperative. The social impulse is a golden thread that girdles the
world. If pain fills the universe it is because of the discordancy
between the internal and the external. And all discordancy
breathes a promise. The world of willing is segmental. Action is
but an arc in the circumference of the soul's possibilities. The life
of the renunciant strikes the diapason below which the minor
chords dwindle and subside. It is on these heights that we " thrill
with the joy of girded men." The renunciant is panoplied 'gainst
fate. Like Socrates and Epicurus, the triumphant soul will
discourse of itself though death be creeping through its mortal
members. The fustian of circumstances can not balk its gaze. It
will go on "forever, and fail, and go on again "—words that
project the soul toward infinite spaces where upswirling
thought is dispersed in the glow of an exalted intuition!

Paradise as well as hell lies beneath the shadow of a hair. Everything is decisive. Each thought is an Atlas that supports a world
of thought. The fighter will contend for the shade of a word and
a " thing not seen with the eyes." The things that are tangible
are not real. They are but phantasms. Behind the fact visible

stands the spirit invisible, and this alone matters. This or that shall not hold the poet's attention. He looks beyond and still beyond. He will swim nowhere but in the infinite, soundless sea of tendencies. He is not concerned with you, but with your relations. Under his gaze you can not stand in limits.

You are the hub round which the multi-spoked universe revolves. You are playfellow to the stars, and the minutes are but hooded eternities ⁂ ⁂

What pathos in the closing lines of this greatest of all prayers:
" With the half of a broken hope for a pillow at night
That somehow the right is the right,
And the smooth shall bloom from the rough."

Misgivings again assail him here. Suppose right should not be the Right? Suppose our lights are bog-lights?

Every vice was once a virtue.

Shall every virtue become a vice? We can not go backward. What meaning has backward or forward in its relations to eternal duration? Life is evolving, but never evolves. We can never say, " Here we rest." All forward motion presupposes a goal—and who has with certainty named the goal of evolving life? In the circumvolutions of time, how stand we who have battled for the right, if " right" be but a euphemism—a gaudy word to cover a naked necessity? The ages wear a leer, and mock. Yet the spirit of man, indomitable and unafraid, believes the " smooth shall bloom from the rough!"

" Lord! If that were enough!"

Horace Mann

I HAVE been down to Antioch College, where I liberated a few rhetorical vibes.

Antioch College is at Yellow Springs, Ohio, a place where you wade knee-deep in tradition, and history hits you at every turn.

Yellow Springs derives its name from a chalybeate spring that gushes from a great cliff of limestone. This spring flows a hundred gallons of water a minute, and has, since the memory of the Oldest Inhabitant. The quantity of water never varies: in season and out, it flows its steady, big, busy, sparkling stream, coming from the Everywhere, going to the Nowhere.

The water running down the hillside and over the flat rocks below, leaves a marked trace of yellow iron—hence the name.

The first white man to locate Yellow Springs was Daniel Boone, who was led here by an Indian guide, that the great pioneer might drink of the waters and be cured of rheumatism. The Indians were not much on sanitation and prophylaxis, but they were heavy on dope.

They had a scheme here that has Mudlavia skun a mile. Daniel Boone describes it.

The Red Brothers heated stones and placed them in a little tent made of hides fastened to the ground with pickets, within which the candidate was safely enclosed.

They gave him a sweat beyond the dreams of Battle Creek. When the patient was about smothered with the heat, they cut a hole in the tent so he could stick his head out. Then they gave him advice and spring-water, and usually he drank a gallon or more. Also hot stones were pushed under the tent to increase the sum of caloric and the world's stock of harmless pleasure.

In the meantime the Big Medicine Man walked round and round

the patient and sang a Billy Muldoon melody to a Bernarr Macfadden two-step.

For a day and a night the candidate was kept in hoc signo Vincennes, Indiana. The plan really had much to commend it. All those who did n't die, got well. Daniel Boone got well, but he only stayed in the bath for six hours, giving up a squirrel-rifle, eight feet long, to get out. Evidently the Big Medicine Man who had charge of the case was on to his job, and the traditions still survive in ethical medical circles.

In Eighteen Hundred Thirty-two, there was a tavern here, built of logs, and in front of the tavern was a pile of crutches that would shame the Lady of Lourdes and put Doctor Munyon far to the bad.

About Eighteen Hundred Forty-one, the man who owned the Spring had a big idea. He must have been a mentally fecund person, gifted in the art of advertising, and a true Adscripter by prenatal tendency. This most enterprising gentleman warned all married ladies who did not wish to influence vital statistics, to keep away from Yellow Springs, as the waters had a quick Malthusian effect on man and beast.

The result was a great influx of Has-Wases, male and female. Ladies of discreet age dared the Spirits of the Spring to do their worst. It became bruited abroad that here, if anywhere, were the waters of Perpetual Youth.

Two big hotels were erected: the Yellow Springs Tavern and the Neff House

The latter was built by a Company, headed by Henry Clay. This hotel had four hundred rooms, and stables that accommodated a thousand horses. The colored quarters, where the servants lived, took care of five hundred negroes. These colored brethren proved all the admen claimed.

To run a hotel then was to have your work cut out for you. There was no calling up Cincinnati by telephone, ordering fifty cases of this or that. The Neff House had a farm which produced every-thing to feed and irrigate the throng, even to a distillery.

Yellow Springs is nine miles Southwest from Springfield, fifty miles from Columbus, twenty miles from Xenia, and one hundred miles from Cincinnati. It was on the direct stagecoach road between Columbus and the West and South.

Travelers all stopped off a day or so for rest and recreation, and women old and young, with a recklessness worthy of a better cause, flung caution to the winds and guzzled, gulped or sipped, as mood inclined.

The place prospered exceedingly, and there were rooms where the money stacked on tables by industrious gem'men with pasteboard proclivities made the colored waiters who carried trays in and out, turn white with astonishment.

But evil days were to come.

The Neff House had been built in three months with a penalty clause in the contract. Guests were living in tents waiting to move in. The hardwood timbers were green, and, according to the custom of the time, mortised and pinned.

Such a frame is built for the centuries. An earthquake could not shake it down; no blizzard could blow it over.

It had but one drawback. The green wood would warp. In time, the floors of this hotel looked like the ground-swell of the ocean after a storm. The Colonels swore that in places the floor flew up and hit them. To dance in the dining-room, you had to skate up hill and slide down. Beds were tilted by the right oblique. At night there were loud R. G. Dun reports of cracking, creaking timbers " letting go." No table stood on four legs. The colored folks gave it out that the house was haunted. And the Yellow Springs Tavern people whispered industriously that the Neff House was unsafe. About the year Eighteen Hundred Fifty there was no resort West of the Atlantic as popular as Yellow Springs, save the Mammoth Cave, alone.

At the Mammoth Cave there was a hotel very much like the Neff House, and no doubt Henry Clay and his colleagues stole a deal of adcraft thunder from Mammoth Cave. Both places were advertised in many ingenious ways.

A reasonable amount of humbug is always allowable, and, in fact, is in demand where idle people much do congregate. Ice was stored up at Mammoth Cave, where visitors were shown it hidden away in a cavern.

The temperature in the Cave never falls below fifty, and how the ice could form there was a question which long puzzled scientists, and caused much hot and angry debate among the Solons, until a nigger testified that he carried it in from the icehouse every morning ⚮ ⚮

Ice was also carried into a cave dug out under the gushing waters at Yellow Springs, and long gave a thrill of awe and breathless ohs! and ahs! to bridal couples and such.

Here came Ralph Waldo Emerson to lecture in Eighteen Hundred Forty-nine; for culture and cards, suh, were the happy possession, suh, of the Best Society of the South and West.

Emerson carried back to New England tidings of the growing metropolis ⚮ ⚮

Next came Theodore Parker.

At that time the Transcendental Movement was at its height George Ripley, Henry Thoreau, Horace Greeley, George William Curtis, Wendell Phillips, Horace Mann and the Alcotts were firing their shots heard round the world.

Brook Farm had failed for want of a business head, but a big crop of ideas had been produced and sent out for seed purposes. Horace Mann was quite the most level-headed and consistently safe man in the group.

He was a graduate of Harvard, a lawyer who turned schoolteacher and became principal of one of Boston's public schools. He had read Froebel and studied the methods of Arnold of Rugby. His ideas of education had been tinted by the Brook Farmers until his faith in the Classics had about departed.

He would bring men and women up to be useful, not ornamental. Also, he stood for co-education, at a time when to do so was to be regarded as eccentric—I use the mildest word that was applied at that time to those who dared advocate the education of young men and women together.

" I want a school where a brother and sister can go and graduate from the same platform."

This remark doubtless cost Horace Mann the Presidency of Harvard ✦ ✦

However, as a consolation-prize, his friends got together and elected him to the State Legislature—or General Court. He was chosen Speaker of the House, and served with distinction. The following year he was nominated for Governor of Massachusetts.

The nomination was equal to an election, but Horace Mann declined it. He had other ambitions. He was quietly raising money to found his Ideal College.

Horace Greeley, Peter Cooper, George Peabody, Ralph Waldo Emerson and Edward Everett Hale were on the Board of Directors ✦ ✦

A hundred thousand dollars in cash was raised as a " nucleus."

This college was to be the Harvard of the West—only it was to be an improved Harvard, a Harvard with all Harvard's flummery omitted, and all her virtues conserved.

Yellow Springs, Ohio, was chosen for the place. The fact that the wealth and fashion of the West and South converged at Yellow Springs was the casting vote.

A college must have a constituency—it must be braced by Society.

Yellow Springs—yes, certainly.

And Yellow Springs it was.

The hundred thousand dollars were invested in buildings, with as little delay as possible. The style of these buildings was worthy and right. They were built to last. In every appointment they were complete.

Brickkilns were erected, and the brick for the buildings was made on the spot. This brick-making was to become a part of the regular College work, and a planing mill was installed with similar intent ᔆ᷁ ᔆ᷁

The school opened with a thousand applications for entrance. Only half of this number could be accommodated.

But matters went swimmingly.

The faculty was made up of Harvard men, disciples of the " New School of Thought."

Many of President Mann's old friends came out to see him, including Emerson, who on one visit remained a week and gave lectures every day to the students, and to the people from the hotels who packed the hall.

Emerson was n't in very good repute at that time—even fair Harvard had disclaimed him.

He had given a goodly part of his library to the College. Theodore Parker had made similar gifts. These books are now in the library, and are spoken of by some of the townsmen as " that Infidel Library." ᔆ᷁ ᔆ᷁

Curiously enough—or not—the patrons of the hotels, the folks who came to drink the waters, were orthodox—very orthodox. Instead of helping the College they criticized it.

Horace Mann was an Abolitionist—all his friends were Abolitionists. It was rumored that the place was simply a station of the underground railroad.

Then the idea of setting people to work and of education for human service was beyond the Colonels.

" We don't want our son worked, we want him learned," wrote a fond Mamma to President Mann.

The good old idea of education for show and as a means of evading hard work was strong ever in the minds of many who intellectually assented to the new regime.

At first, the name of the school was to be simply The Horace Mann Institute, this on the suggestion of Peter Cooper.

Horace Mann, however, objected to having his name used so prominently, and insisted on the title, "Antioch College." Success of a product, no matter how good, turns often on the name you choose. It was declared that Horace Mann was not a Christian, and now as a sort of disclaimer he stuck to the word Antioch. "And the disciples were called Christians first in Antioch," says the Bible. The name was a subtle form of defense, and a mistake all around. Horace Mann was truly great, but like that good man mentioned by Carlyle he had his limitations. He should have let the world come to him, as it would have done. In order to put his college in first-class shape, he accepted a loan of forty thousand dollars, at five years, from the orthodox local nabobs; for nabobs who run horses, fight cocks and manipulate the pasteboards, when they are religious are very religious. It's a sad story—a story of the shipwreck of all the high hopes of as noble a man as the world ever saw.

The world was not ready for the New Education. And certainly it was not ready for the New Religion.

The student body dwindled away, debts piled up, the mortgage became due, for that is a way mortgages have.

And Antioch College was sold under the auctioneer's hammer. Peter Cooper and several other men of means came to the rescue and bought in the property, turning it over to a self-perpetuating board of trustees, and arranging a new charter that the place should never again be mortgaged.

Horace Mann continued the work with shortened sail. The stigma of failure was upon the enterprise.

Work, worry, debt, unkind criticism undermined the health of the brave founder. He knew his days were few. On a certain day all the students, a bare hundred, came to the President's house at his request. They filed by the bedside of the stricken man, and each one pressed his hand. He called each by name, gave all his blessing, and closed his eyes to open them no more.

So died Horace Mann.

His worn-out body was buried on the College Campus, and there a monument to his memory now stands.

A few years later, his bones were exhumed and taken by kinsmen to Rhode Island, where the good man and great was born.

It was the last sordid blow at Antioch, given by the cheap and unthinking. They would n't let the College which the man founded and for which he died, have even his dust.

And yet Antioch College still lives—and lives, too, the unselfish soul of Horace Mann.

The country around Yellow Springs is of rare beauty. Surely God has smiled upon the place. Such diversity of landscape one seldom sees. Gentle, undulating pastures, studded with noble, solitary oaks; fertile fields that laugh a harvest on sight of an Oliver Plow; woods as wild as Nature made them, lining the bluffs of the Little Miami River—woods that house a hundred kinds of birds, and hillsides that form a herbarium which would have delighted the soul of Linnæus.

These bluffs reveal the strata, touched by the tooth of time, of great masses of limestone, from which run in steady streams inexhaustible springs of pure and sparkling water.

No wonder that the Indians called it a Sacred Place where the Great Spirit made his home.

There is everything here that might appeal to the savage heart, the soul of a poet, or the heart of a lover.

Also, there are ruins here—and has not the taunt been thrown at America by blase Englishmen that we have neither a leisure class nor ruins?

But, suh, I 'd have you know, suh, that we have both!

John Bryan of Ohio, King of Cranks, recently bought the property where once stood the Yellow Springs Tavern, in order to preserve it, as Kenilworth Castle is preserved, just for the ruins. I think it cost him fully five hundred dollars.

The Tavern was destroyed by the devouring element, as the village editor would say, about forty years ago. Many of the bricks have been carted away by the colored brothers, who here constitute a true leisure class. But the remains of wide fireplaces yet stand, and toppling chimneys, which refuse to fall, wring from us our pity for the days agone.

In these old chimneys, thousands of swallows make their homes. Where the kitchen once stood is a cellar so well built of stones that it affords a refuge for skunks who drove out a family of foxes, and now rule by right of squatter sovereignty. On the spacious lawn, or what was once a lawn, groundhogs gambol and defy the colored population. There are the long strings of whitewashed cottages, and the remains of what was once the great barn, most of the wood having been carted away for fuel.

Down in the valley are the jutting ruins of a beautiful stone wall where the spring was dammed to make an artificial lake. The size of the lake can be safely gauged by stone steps, with big rusty iron rings where rowboats were moored and tied.

The great stone steps worn deep by the feet of travelers as they entered the Tavern are there, but there is no tavern.

The fountains are filled with watercress, fresh and crisp, over which the spring-waters flow, and where frogs and turtles sun themselves on the low wall and laugh softly in derision at the pomp and pride of men.

Verily the tumult and the shouting have died away, and the captains and the kings have departed.

There is a dance-hall across the creek, once reached by a picturesque suspension-bridge, and over which lovers lingered late in the moonlight.

The dance-hall is now a cow-shed. The ruins of the distillery still
stand, but no still is there, although through the place dance the
waters that gush from the hill. Evidently there will be water here,
even when whisky is no longer in demand.

In Yellow Springs there is now no hotel or inn for the tired traveler
but I was directed to a boarding-house kept by " a widow-
woman," who offered to house and feed me for four dollars and
fifty cents a week, being as how I was a college professor.

But while the hotels which once were mints of money are all gone,
done into dissolution by the devouring hunger of moth, rust, and
the death of the advertising man, the Antioch College buildings
are in good repair.

This speaks well for the trustees.

They have not made a great success of the college, but they have
held the plant intact over against the day when a strong man
would come and pick up the work of Horace Mann where the
great teacher left it.

And so the Messianic instinct never dies.

And surely Antioch College will be redeemed. Its buildings are
noble; its site is lovely beyond compare; its traditions are splendid
and inspiring. Here we tread the boards where have stood Tom
Corwin, Ralph Waldo Emerson, James Russell Lowell, Wendell
Phillips, Horace Greeley and Peter Cooper. All these men had
a great and loving solicitude for the place, because they loved
Horace Mann.

Antioch College and Horace Mann stood for the New Education,
the education for usefulness; and for the New Religion which is
the religion of the Now and Here.

These things worked the downfall of the Institution. But now
the world is catching up with Horace Mann. Every great college
is in degree patterning its work after the philosophy which he
expressed. And the orthodox theology of our day is the Unitarian-
ism of Eighteen Hundred Fifty-six.

Horace Mann, the abolitionist, died the year that John Brown was hanged, and the year when Darwin issued his *Origin of Species*. The next year died Theodore Parker, in far-off Italy, an indictment hanging over his head for treason and conspiracy. There was none to seize the standard as it fell from the dying hand of Horace Mann. It fell, and was trampled over by the hurrying rush of armed men.

During the War the place was used for a hospital for returned Union Soldiers, and as a storehouse for the Sanitary Commission. Since the War, several denominations have tried to maintain it, and all with a degree of success. Surely an Alumnus of Antioch College should be proud of his Alma Mater!

There are forty colleges in Ohio which come within the scope of the Carnegie Foundation. In truth, no State in the Union has been so blest and benefited by the small college, where every professor knows every student and the personal touch is not a theory. Doctor S. D. Fess, the present President of Antioch College, left a position that paid him five thousand a year to work here for one thousand dollars a year. He is a strong, earnest and tireless worker—a man of brains, all ballasted with commonsense. He is a teacher and a teacher of teachers.

Other teachers who could command two or three thousand dollars a year struggle on here for six or seven hundred. They love the place, and eventually they hope to tow the barque into the fairway of popular favor, where her sails will catch the breeze.

Just now they need help. But poor little Antioch, so rich in memories, so noble in traditions, is without the pale for lack of a paltry two hundred thousand dollars' endowment.

When Horace Mann had passed beyond the reach of praise or blame, as a sort of tardy recognition of the ideas for which he battled, his successor, Thomas Hill, was called from Yellow Springs and made President of Harvard. Hill was the predecessor of Charles W. Eliot.

What a pity that some Harvard man—aye! or some Ohio man—
does not think to render himself immortal by stepping into the
breach, writing his check for two hundred thousand, thus putting
this splendid old place on its pedagogic pedals!

There is just one thing wrong with Antioch College—just one and
no more—and that is its name. It should be The Horace Mann
Memorial ◆◆ ◆◆

The trustees have the legal power to change the name, and I
believe that if this were done it would give the place a new lease
of life.

Antioch was a city in Asia Minor. Long ago it crumbled to dust.
There is only one thing that can consecrate a place and that is
man. We are all hero-worshipers. But we only reverence places
because great men once lived there. The word "Antioch" has a
significance that grows dimmer as the days pass, but the name of
Horace Mann is a coming quantity.

In Yellow Springs, Ohio, lived and passed out a great and noble
and unselfish soul—one of the world's great teachers. From this
on let the school born of his hope and love bear the name of The
Horace Mann Memorial.

Alfred Nobel

HEN Mitchell Kennerly publishes a book, you can safely buy it—and also read it.

Publishers who issue books at the author's expense print a deal of Class B. Also, the publishers who strive for pelf and popularity do the same.

Mitchell Kennerly prints only that which he personally enjoys. Kennerly issues the books of Edgar Saltus, and Edgar Saltus is one of the half-dozen or less great living masters of English. ❡ Literature is a confession, and for the reader it is an excursion into the mind of the author, and his own. Life is a little journey of discovery. The book that reflects your own ideas you like. Kennerly is a connoisseur of letters. He delights in the subtle, the delicate, the witty, the wise, the incisive, the divine nuances. The only book I ever read through from " kiver to kiver" in a year is *The New Word* by Allen Upward, issued by Brother Kennerly. And I read it with such chuckles of joy, and gurgles of glee, that the Pullman car porter called in the conductor, and they put me under surveillance until I lifted the embargo with a dollar tip.

The New Word is a volume of three hundred pages, written to explain a certain word used by Alfred Nobel in his will.

In this will the testator sets aside a large sum of money, the interest upon which is to be divided into five parts. Each of these parts is to constitute a prize to be given to some special candidate who has done most in his particular line for the human race, in the preceding year. The only clause that interests Allen Upward is the following: " One share to the person who shall have produced in the field of literature the most distinguished work of an idealist tendency." And the only word in this clause that interests Upward is the word " Idealist."

This one word is the subject of the book. What is the meaning of the word—what is an Idealist tendency?

Just here let me say that I do not know who this man Upward is. I make a guess, however, that he is Mitchell Kennerly.

The name "Upward" is a nom de plume that casts a purple shadow. And the words that Upward uses are the suggestive, airy, fairy, floating figments of fact and fancy.

Of course, the book does not lead anywhere, and there is no moral to it except the one you, yourself, supply.

It merely shows you the vanity of words, and how no word can ever have a permanent meaning to all men. Then it makes you think, and this is well.

It is, of course, a fact that God devised a Plan of Salvation for a world doomed to death. But when He came to explain His glad tidings of great joy in print, hardly any two persons understood the scheme alike. Evidently, in the rush of going to press, the fact was overlooked that inspired writing demands inspired readers. This was a sad lapse. So we have over two million men hotly explaining the language of the Lord: with murders, strife and wars without end, all turning on the meaning of words used by the Prince of Peace.

This being so, how could a meek and lowly maker of dynamite in Sweden ever expect to write a will that would be understood! So here comes, astride of Pegasus a-gallop, Allen Upward, with fountain-pen in rest, to clear up the cosmic fog, and reduce philosophic chaos to cosmos.

So what did Alfred Nobel mean by the word Idealist?

Upward explains that the meaning of any word turns on who the man is who uses it.

With most delicate sarcasm Upward reveals Nobel as not only the inventor of the most destructive agent known to science, but as a seer and a prophet, as well.

Upward gets down all the dictionaries and encyclopedias to show

what the word " Idealist " means to the educated mind; then he
tells us what Noble meant by it. Nobel never told any one what
he meant, but the truth was divined to Upward, and to Upward
alone *** ***

The simple fact is, Nobel was a millionaire. And most millionaires
belong to the rudderless rich. They are the victims of their
dolodocci. When you own too much of anything, the thing owns
you *** ***

Doubtless millionaires have spasms of good-will, when there flits
through their minds a suggestion of the good their money might
do. But the work of warding off the idealists who would grab the
gold and use the millions for human benefit and the good of the
poor—themselves in mind—causes the man to clutch, as a habit.
But stricken with the wing of Death, and realizing that he could
not take the money with him—there being no pockets in a shroud
—Nobel accepted a great scheme for the good of mankind.

This scheme was devised by certain good men who thought
themselves Idealists. They were connected with the Swedish
Academy at Stockholm, and having no millions to trouble them,
and possessing all the time there was, they told Nobel how he
could send his name clattering down the corridors of time.
⊄ Thus was the plan perfected to give five prizes of between thirty
and forty thousand dollars each, every year, to as many different
persons who achieved certain big things. These prizes were to be
awarded by the Swedish Academy. This naturally compels us to
consider what the Swedish Academy, or any academician, would
mean by the word " Idealist."

An academician is a man who has arrived. And to arrive you have
to win the applause of the many.

Now, an ideal thing to the many—and to an academician—is
something which in the past has been done so well that it affords
a standard of perfection.

An academician is a man who knows the past and focuses on the things that were. He has learned from books and men. And while men can explain the past, if he pierces the future, he has to do it alone ﺣﻤ ﺣﻤ

In order to get into the Academy he must know Greek, Roman and Sanskrit. If he can speak and write a bit of Egyptian, Maya and Gallic, it tends to exalt him above his fellows.

He recites from Herodotus, Cicero, Iamblichus, and knows the times of the Thirteenth Dynasty when Memphis was supreme.

❡ The flight of the Children of Israel from Egypt and their wanderings in the wilderness are to him of more importance than anything happening now. It is a fact that many academicians believe chaos is soon to come to the world, and chaos is certainly not idealistic. The academician believes in an Ideal Man, an Ideal Book, an Ideal Government, an Ideal Education, an Ideal Religion, and an Ideal God.

All these things are things that were. And so when he bestows a prize for a book of an " Idealist Tendency " he gives it only to a book that fulfils his ideal—that is to say, a book which he himself might have written. This is natural, and it is the only thing that could be expected.

But the question still remains, Does the Ideal lie behind, or is it in the future?

A few years ago this Swedish Academy awarded one of the Nobel prizes—the Peace Prize—to an American.

The man they selected as most worthy of the honor—the one man who had done more for peace than any other man in the world— was a man who is a fighter by nature and a disturber of the peace by occupation.

This man who won the plaudits of the trustees of the Nobel prize rushed in and stopped a fight, which was all over save one final wallop that was due the bully in the case.

The strong man who rushes in and separates the combatants in a street scrimmage does not stand for peace. He is merely showing that he is bigger than the scrimmagers. Soon he will lick them both.

The only person in the world who ever told this Stone Age Strong Man to sit still and quit waving his hand at the populace was Hoxsey the Aviator. For thus advising the world's self-appointed advisor, Hoxsey should be awarded a Nobel prize—or a Carnegie Medal, at least.

Nobel having made his money out of the manufacture of dynamite, it is only poetic justice that a Nobel prize should be awarded to the most explosive man of the century.

The award was a comment on the mental processes of the Swedish Academy ✺ ✺

The case is typical—the opposites of things are alike—and no book of an " Idealist Tendency " will ever get a Nobel prize—this because an ideal book will require ideal judges.

So we will have to consider further what Nobel meant when he wrote that word " Idealist."

To the seer, the prophet, and the man of imagination, the Ideal lies in the future, not behind.

And while the dictionary will tell you that " the ideal is the fulfilment of the idea—the perfected thing—that which can not be improved upon," the prophet knows better. When the man of imagination is shown the ideal, it merely suggests something better—something beyond.

That is to say, an ideal realized has already ceased to be the ideal, save to a man who wears his mental haberdashery reversed, and has the soul of an academician.

Ideals can never be static unless they are dead. " To shoot a bird is to lose it," said Thoreau.

Words are the airy, fairy humming-birds of the imagination. A philologist is a man who catches words, fills them with sawdust and fastens them to the wall.

Now, the average man, the mediocre mudsill, the proletariat

playing in the gutter of gossip, studying languages that are deceased, and diving into history that is dead, prides himself on his prowess.

And what he strives for is to make everything static. To improve on his religion, his politics, his system of education, is to invite his wrath.

However, the prophet does not blame him. Spinoza, the Jew, having incurred the hatred of both Jews and Catholics, when a stone whizzed by his head smiled and said, " The man who threw that stone is expressing his nature, just as I express mine. Luckily, his aim was bad—so I have cause for gratitude."

It is the primal law of Nature that all living things are trying to create in their own image.

Everything in life is at work reproducing itself.

From the tumblebug to the bishop, it is reproduction.

The preacher is laboring to make everybody think as he does, the businessman the same. Salesmanship is the endeavor to make the buyer see the thing in the same light that you do. Courtship is an effort to make desire mutual. Love is contagion.

We are all creating in our own image.

Every man is blinded by self-interest, and every man believes he is right. And these things being so, he is logically bound to bring the world around to his point of view.

Doctors are intent on vaccinating you with the virus of their ignorance. Theologians all try to inoculate you with the microbe of Superstition. Individuality can only be preserved by cultivating a virginal indignation.

Naturally, a resort to the thumbscrew as an instrument of logic is looked upon as eminently justifiable. If that is against the law, then snub him socially, and buy your boots elsewhere. Starve him to it! &• &•

Chapman, Torrey and Alexander are organized to pour their limitations on mankind.

Safety for humanity lies in a balance of power. We are all in process, wiggling toward the light. Go it, ye mollusks!

Most individuals deem themselves ideal. At least they regard their opinions as such. Otherwise they would not try to spread these opinions and make proselytes between the soup and the fish ❧ ❧

How many men do you know who will sit quietly and smile while the hirsute crank makes the ether vocal with false doctrines! " Just stop right there a moment while I put you straight—" That is what you hear.

The wise man knows that nothing is final. To think at all is the beautiful thing: whether you think rightly, or not, matters little. We all are right—we all are wrong. We are red ants on the tongue of an armadillo.

Creeds are metaphors with ankylosis—figures of speech frozen stiff with fright. Hence all creeds are dead creeds. To slough them is the right and natural thing to do.

Explain this to the first orthodox preacher you meet and see what he says to you!

Teachers mark the pupil's lesson-papers, not on the individual pupil's ability to think, but on his ability to reflect the teacher. Orthodoxy is spiritual goose-step. The pupil must absorb the textbook, and the explanation of the textbook as given by the preacher is the right one and the only one—so he says.

The old maid is reproducing in her own image. Hers is a hot desire to make the town just like her—in word, act and thought. When a man looks in the glass he beholds his ideal.

And once having espoused a cause, no matter how silly or how base, we regard it as ideal, and would perpetuate it if we could by vitalizing the think-cells of all others with the germs of our fallacies ❧ ❧

Hence the remark of Maurice Maeterlinck, " All things die in the act of reproduction, just as does the drone-bee."

An idealist book to an academician would be a book that reflects the ideals of the Academy. But those are only ideal in name, since they are the limitations of the past—the gallstones of existence. ℭ And if the ideal is the unrealized idea of the seer, then how perfectly plain that no Nobel prize will ever go to a book that is genuinely Ideal.

This, indeed, must be so, since the virtue of true Idealism is that it outruns human sympathy, and depicts something which the many can not even imagine.

And the many, being busily engaged in creating in their own image, naturally destroy any attempt to create an ideal that is to supersede their own.

The following will give a taste of the Upward quality:

" There are two kinds of human outcasts. Man, in his march upward out of the deep into the light, throws out a vanguard and a rear-guard, and both are out of step with the main body. Humanity condemns equally those who are too good for it, and those who are too bad. On its Procrustean bed the stunted members of the race are racked; the giants are cut down. It puts to death with the same ruthless equality the prophet and the atavist. The poet and the drunkard starve side by side.

" Of these two classes of victims the stragglers are not more in need than the forlorn hope; but the ambulance has always waited in the rear. It would seem as though the vanity of benevolence were soothed by the sight of degradation, but affronted by that of genius. Even the loafer and the criminal have found friends. The thinker and the discoverer have been left to the struggle for existence. For them are no asylums; for them no societies stand ready to offer help. Millions have been spent in providing libraries for the populace; the founder of German literature was refused a librarian's place. And so philanthropy has cast its vote to this day for Barabbas.

" Nobel alone has had the courage not to be afraid of genius, and the wisdom to see that whatever is conferred on it really is conferred on all mankind.

" The third of these bequests may serve to illustrate the superiority of Nobel's method. Many benefactors have desired to relieve bodily suffering. But they have discerned no way of doing this except by building a hospital for the advantage of a limited class. Nobel's aim has been at once wider and higher. He has sought to relieve all suffering. He has demanded worldwide remedies; he has offered rewards for the abolition of disease.

" And in doing so he has at the same time remedied a great injustice, by endowing medical discovery. The mechanical inventor has long had it in his power to acquire wealth by the sale of his idea. Nobel's own fortune owed its rise to a patented invention. But the noble etiquette of the healer's calling voluntarily renounces an advantage that would hinder the relief of human pain. In medicine every advance made by one is placed freely at the service of all. For such saviors of humanity there has been hitherto no material recompense, and humanity has been content that it should be so. Neither parliaments nor emperors have ever wished that the healers of men should take rank with their destroyers, and that a Pasteur should receive the rewards of a Krupp. Nobel willed otherwise.

" The fifth bequest contains a yet more striking instance of that refined and beautiful inspiration which distinguishes the Testament of Nobel.

" This is a bequest for practical work on behalf of peace, disarmament and the fraternity of nations. At the time when Nobel Prew up his will these aspirations seemed to have no more active enemies than the Norwegian people. Norway was seeking separation from Sweden, and seeking it in that temper of hatred which, unhappily, accompanies such movements almost everywhere. The Norwegian Storthing was building fortresses on the Swedish frontier, and providing battleships. Every Norwegian boy was being trained with a view to an armed struggle with the Swedes, and taught to regard them with revengeful feelings, as American children were long taught to regard the English. Nobel was a Swede who loved his country, and he has placed the administration of his other bequests in Swedish hands. He entrusted the endowment of peace and brotherhood to the Norwegian Storthing.

" Surely no more magnanimous appeal than this has ever been addressed by a man to men. The directions of such a Testator ought not to be regarded lightly. They begin to assume the character of a sacred text.

" What was the wish of Nobel's mind when, in language destined to immortality, he drew up the Fourth Bequest: ' One share to the person who shall have produced in the field of Literature the most remarkable work of an idealistic tendency?'

" There is hardly any class which gives so much to humanity, and receives so little in return, as the class of men of letters. There is hardly any class whose sufferings are greater, and there is none which philanthropy has done so little to relieve.

" The works of Homer have been an unfailing spring of noble pleasure for three thousand years, and during all that time humanity has repeated with more complacency than shame the story of the poet begging his bread, and has warned its children to shun the literary career. The dreadful death of Chatterton seems never to have roused a momentary pity in any philanthropist. Had that boy been blind, or dumb, or idiotic, or incurably diseased, how many benevolent hearts would have yearned over him! How many luxurious homes, standing in stately gardens amid glorious scenery, would have opened their doors to take him in! On his behalf the preachers would have preached, and the purse-proud would have loosed their purse-strings. But because, instead of being blind, he saw too well, saw the beauty and the wonders of the world, and would have told of them, philanthropy

turned its back on him, and humanity would not suffer him to
live ❧ ❧

" Poe, himself the most gifted and the most wretched of his kind,
has declared that the laudation of the unworthy is to the worthy
the bitterest of all wrong. But what, then, of the rewards of the
unworthy? and the rewards of literature are too often in inverse
ratio to its worth. The author of a successful farce destined to
three or four years' life could afford to look down on the Nobel
prize. The writer who faithfully reflects every prejudice in the
public mind can never stand in need of charity. But what of Bok,
Hearst & Co., of Dante and Milton, of Villon and Verlaine?
" The man of genius—above all the men of original genius—must
generally look for bread to some other pursuit than his own. The
exceptions are those whom robust health, or some strong talent
auxiliary to their inspiration has enabled to overcome the public
prejudice of their own day. And too often the victory has been won
at some cost to the abiding value of their work. Happy is he who,
like Spinoza, has been able to make out a livelihood by grinding
lenses, instead of demeaning himself to the tasks that humanity
offers him through its agents, the booksellers and editors.
Unhappy, who must echo the mournful cry of Shakespeare:

' My nature is subdued
To what it works in, like the dyer's hand.'

" And yet the title of genius to protection and relief is hardly
other than that of the idiot, the epileptic and the paralytic.
Science has told us that the lunatic, the poet and the criminal are
compact of one clay. The lives of the poets reveal them as sufferers
from strange infirmities often beyond the reach of medical lore.
The most precious possessions of literature are verily pearls, the
glorious disguisement of some inward sore.

" Literature is the chief ornament of humanity; and perhaps
humanity never shows itself uglier than when it stands with the

pearl shining on its forehead, and the pearl-maker crushed beneath its heel.

" There is in England a thing called a Royal Literary Fund, for the pretended purpose of showing charity to men of letters. By the published rules of this institution its alms are only to be bestowed in those whose lives and writings are alike free from reproach on the score of religion and morality. What a clause for the charter of a hospital! It is evident that those responsible for this public insult to literature are inspired, not by compassion for genius, but by fear and hatred of genius. They know well that it is as hard for a great poet to be a regular churchgoer and a respectable father of a family, as it is for themselves to write a great poem. Their true object is to give alms in the name of literature to the enemies of literature. And so they have built an asylum for well-behaved dunces, and have written over the door: ' No admittance for Shakespeare and Goethe.'

" If Nobel had only made a bequest to literature, he would have done a brave thing. As it is, he has done a far braver.

" The word Literature is not an exact term, because literature is not an exact art. It is a term wide enough to cover every kind of communication by means of words, from the *Song of Songs* to the least newspaper advertisement. Nobel has manifestly used the word in a broad sense. He was not thinking of literature from the literary standpoint, nor has he laid the stress upon artistic merit. Instead of offering this prize for the best work of literature, he has offered it for the best work of idealism, coming within the field of literature.

" That such is his intention seems to be fully recognized by a provision in the statutes drawn up since the Testator's death to govern his Trustees:

" The term ' literature,' used in the Will, shall be understood to embrace not only works falling under the category of Polite Literature, but also other writings which may claim to possess

literary merit by reason of their form or their mode of exposition.
" The spirit which breathes in this bequest is the same as that which breathes in the others. The Testator has kept one end steadily in sight: the increase of human happiness. His method is to encourage those whose work is, in his opinion, the most beneficial to mankind—the work of the inventor, the work of the idealist, the work of the peacemaker.

" In this bequest the word idealist is mightier than the word literature, and must prevail over it. This is not an endowment of the author, but of some one greater than the author.

" Nobel died, and the publication of his Will brought about a significant discovery. No one could tell the meaning of the word ' idealist,' or ' idealistic.'

" The history of the world is glanced at in the following inquiry. Here it will be enough to say that while it was in use in all the leading languages of Europe in the Testator's lifetime, his Will revealed it as a riddle.

" In what astonishing senses the Testator's word was understood appears from the list of the explanations given me by educated men in various walks of life, soon after I had launched in this investigation. Here they are: 'something to do with the imaginative powers;' ' fanatical;' ' altruistic;' ' not practical;' ' exact;' ' poetical;' ' intangible;' ' sentimental;' ' that which can not be proved;' ' the opposite to materialistic.'

" The mood of humanity towards the poet is that of the schoolboy towards the butterfly—without pity, but without malice. Towards the prophet it is that of the spoiled child towards the physician—one of angry resistance.

" There is no more pitiful sight than this; mankind suffers under no such curse; it is the tragedy of the world, the stoning of the messenger of good tidings. ' Ye build the sepulchers of the prophets, and your fathers killed them.' Alas! it is in sacrifice to the dead prophet that the living prophet is offered up.

There is no instinct much more deeply rooted in the heart of man than this old cannibal one that the suffering of the best man is for the benefit of mankind. ' I exiled Dante,' exults proud Florence, ' and lo! the *Divine Comedy.*' ' I hounded forth Mohammed,' boasts Mecca, ' and here is Islam.' It needs a Diagoras to ask where are the votive offerings of those who were wrecked. It takes a Nobel to discern the difference to mankind between the labors of Hercules and the agony of the Moriah. The instinct of hatred is stronger than reason. It is not to be baffled by etymologies. Whatever the uncertainty belonging to the Testator's language, his fourth bequest was taken very differently from the remainder of the Will. It drew to itself the prompt hostility of the two great schools of thought which divide between them the intellectual government of the world. Pharisee and Sadducee both scented danger in the unknown word. Both felt themselves threatened by something more formidable than a literary competition.

" The antagonism of both was summed up in the scornful criticism that Nobel had offered a prize for a new religion. Nobel himself was branded as a dreamer. There were those ready to insinuate that he had not been in his right mind.

" In the present age, more than a hundred millions are paid every year for the repetition of old texts; in England alone, there are several custodians of prophecy who receive each year a sum greater than that here proposed as the life's wage of the prophet. Nobel wished to give eight thousand pounds a year among the writers of new texts. That was his dream. His madness lay there. Humanity is not mad to spend one hundred millions a year on phonographs. Nobel was mad to offer these few thousands for a living voice.

" On the whole the feeling aroused most by this bequest was incredulity. It was regarded as a challenge to materialism, a word not really better understood than idealism, but taken to signify the spirit of modern science, triumphant in so many departments of life. And in these days material science is very great, so that the very word idealist is in some discredit. There is an opinion abroad that while Idealism has been talking, Materialism has been doing. Materialist science has conferred endless benefits on mankind. It has given us new medicines and tools and carriages, and all manner of useful and pleasant things. It has opened up the history of the world and man, and bidden him recast all his beliefs and habits. Inch by inch it has invaded every province of human knowledge; and now it is carrying the war into the very citadel of Idealism, and beginning to measure nerves and brain-cells instead of arguing about mind.

" Now this bequest does indeed come as a challenge, but not to those very materialists to whom the Testator has given the chief place among his legatees. The challenge is a challenge to the idealists, to show that they also are contributing to benefit mankind

" Because of that it marks an era in the history of philosophy. Three hundred years ago a challenge was addressed by Bacon to the physical sciences, under the name of natural philosophy. His famous substitution of inductive for deductive reasoning amounted to no more than this advice: Learn from the things themselves, instead of from the words about the things. But in asking for fruits he proposed to the philosopher the same end that Nobel has proposed—the benefit of mankind.

" It is since that date that the physical sciences have arisen out of their sleep and marched to victory. Height after height has been scaled, and all the glory of creation has burst on our eyes. But still our eyes remain dim eyes. The march of reason has not kept pace with that of knowledge. Men stand before the wonders of the scientific revelation as they formerly stood before the sculptured stones of Egypt, unable to decipher them, and half afraid to try.

" Nobel, it seems, has hoped for a Champollion. He has asked for interpretations. Like the Babylonian king of old, he has sent for the magicians and the astrologers, the Chaldeans and the sooth-sayers, and has bidden them expound anew the meaning of that dream which is called Life.

" For thousands of years the metaphysicians and moral philoso-phers, the theologians and logicians, have been muttering the words of their mystery in corners; now at last a brave man has flung down this bag of gold in the midst of them, and has said: Let us see what it all really comes to. Let us see if you can help men to live.

" In the field of Literature the academy and the idealist meet as natural foes. The academy is, by its constitution, the judge of literature, and not of truth. The idealist is only a man of letters by accident—there are no accidents!—by necessity. Of the very greatest teachers of mankind, only two are known to have written anything, and only of Mohammed can it be said that his book affords any measure of himself. To the perfect Idealist, Lao, is attributed the saying: ' Those who know do not tell; those who tell do not know.'

" When the Idealist enters the field of Literature he does so from the opposite side to that of the academy. For him the spirit is everything; for the academy the form is everything. It would seem easier for the rich man to enter the kingdom of heaven than for the idealist to find grace with the academy. Yet the Testator has placed this endowment in the hands of the illustrious body styled the Swedish Academy.

" In doing so he has shown himself not less inspired than in the rest of the Will. For he is not concerned with idealism as an end, but as a means. The end is still the benefit of mankind. To this end the idealist is called upon to choose speech rather than silence. When he speaks, he is to be judged by his words.

" Had the Testator done otherwise, had he directed that the

idealist was to be judged by his ideals, he would have done what he has been ignorantly accused of doing: he would have founded a new Catholic Church. As it is, he has founded a Forum. By giving the prize to eloquence and not to truth, he has done what is best for the idealist, best for mankind, and in the long run best for truth. He has secured the freedom of thought by the bondage of expression. This golden fetter is placed on the right foot.

" At the same time he has given back to literature by the word 'marklig' all that is taken from it by the words 'idealist tendency.' ✺ ✺

"I can not render it by the official translator's word 'distinguished' because that has now become cant. By a distinguished man, we mean a man who has distinguished himself in a frock coat and tall hat and kid gloves; by a distinguished writer one who has daintily picked his words out of a dictionary of synonyms, and made a delicate mosaic, rather than one in whose mind strong emotion has melted the element of language and cast down the diamond of literature.

" What the Testator has asked for is the most glorious work. Nobel was an idealist, and not a man of letters. The great subtlety with which his Will was drawn is not that of the grammarian or the lawyer, but that of a sincere mind thoroughly possessed of its purpose and wresting words to that purpose. Has he not given this very legacy to the idealists who shall contribute most 'materially' to benefit mankind?

" The words of such a Testator must be approached in the spirit in which lawyers pretend to approach all testaments. The object must be not to explain the words by themselves, but to gather from them what the Testator wished to be done.

" It is in that spirit that I have tried to shape the following inquiry. The question I have asked myself is not, what is the meaning of the word Idealist, but—what did the Testator mean by it ? ✺ ✺

" How I was tempted to undertake the task is here beside the question. I need only say that I began it just after the official publication of the Will, in the year Nineteen Hundred One, and when it was the subject of discussion as a matter of public interest. It is as a member of the public, of that great Public designated by the Testator, under the name of mankind, as his ultimate heirs, that I am interested in this Will, and that, no one else coming forward, I have been bold to vindicate it.

" The years that have elapsed since that time have not materially changed the situation. Striking works of an idealist tendency are not being written at the rate of one every year, or if they are, they have not been brought to the notice of the Trustees of this bequest. In the dearth of such works the Trustees have done doubtless what the Testator might have consented to, if not what he has directed, in awarding this prize as a testimonial to distinguished men of letters, at the close of their careers. But inasmuch as they have framed no authoritative interpretation of the governing word in the bequest, they seem to be in the position of a Court which has not yet delivered judgment, and therefore may be addressed without impertinence by any counsel interested in the case ❧ ❧

" I lay these imperfect suggestions before the public in the hope that they may be found of some interest, apart from their exciting cause; and in the further hope that, if they do not increase, at any rate they can not lessen, the public gratitude for a high and unique example of benevolence.

" For addressing them more directly to the illustrious body charged with the execution of the Trust, I have no real excuse except that there would have been a certain affectation in doing otherwise ❧ ❧

" I make no claim to speak as an idealist. I am a scientist, and my science is ontology, commonly called truth. Now, this bequest is not in favor of works of a true tendency, nor even of the truest works of an idealist tendency. Nevertheless, I think, perhaps, that Nobel might have pardoned what I do, and let me lay this little essay in interpretation as a wreath upon his tomb."

Ambassador Bryce

IF his countryman, Andrew Carnegie, wishes to do a particularly gracious act at this time, let him pension Ambassador Bryce with a stipend of, say, a hundred thousand dollars a year for life and give him the title of Ex-Officio Ambassador Emeritus, with an official residence in New York City

There let the Ambassador Emeritus consider all questions in international dispute, and put in a minority report as his good judgment may decree.

We have been told that republics are ungrateful, but the same remark can be applied to monarchies, granting the hypothesis that the British Nation is a monarchy.

No man of recent times has been more pecked at by young ducks and hissed at by ganders than has Ambassador Bryce. The Tory press of England have united in making silly, absurd accusations about him. The standard of stupidity was set when one of the leading London papers declared that Ambassador Bryce, although in the employ of the British Nation, was really an American at heart, and placed the interests of the United States before those of Great Britain.

That great and good man, Orange John, of Cambridge, Massachusetts, was once asked to give the English translation of the Latin motto to be seen over the gates of fair Harvard. And Orange John replied, " What them words mean is this, ' To Hell with Yale! ' "

In spite of Doctor Johnson's dictum that " patriotism is the last refuge of a scoundrel," many people in England, and alas, in America also, think that patriotism is a matter of hate toward every nation but your own. And as some of our natives are still fighting the War of the Revolution, and boastfully referring to Jackson's defeat of the British at New Orleans, so there are

Englishmen who never use the word "Yankee" without the classic prefix prescribed by the Solid South.

Bryce has had a long and varied career, and he has gathered strength and increased personality with the years. But his frame is light, strong, agile, and his mind is keen and crystalline. Great Britain should take a great and pardonable pride in this man's achievements. He will live in history.

His book, *The American Commonwealth,* is the best picture of the United States that has ever been presented. It is a book that no American could have written. It has the value of perspective. It told us some unpleasant truths—truths we should have known, and that we did know, but which we tried to conceal.

When James Bryce said that municipal government in America was the weakest point in our entire fabric, he put his thumb on a very sore spot. But this weak point we have been and are strengthening ๑ ๑

The English papers have criticized Mr. Bryce severely on account of his friendly attitude toward commercial reciprocity between the United States and Canada.

This is something that, officially, was none of Ambassador Bryce's concern. Canada enjoys fiscal freedom, and it was for her to decide whether she wished commercial reciprocity with the United States.

England had no right to interfere, and Mr. Bryce, as England's representative, would have been very much out of place in interjecting himself into the argument.

That an ambassador should not be allowed to hold private opinions on any subject is a rather strange proposition to bring up at this day and date.

Bryce has done the United States great good in disillusioning us in reference to some of our fallacies concerning the British nation. Bryce is essentially a democrat in his mode of thinking and in his habit of life. He is get-at-able, approachable, kindly, generous, friendly. He toadies to no man. As a public speaker he is frank, witty, appreciative, unresentful. He does not wear his prejudices pompadour.

He is essentially an economist and a worthy successor to Adam Smith ✤ ✤

He mixes in no idle gossip. He is above all petty scrimmages and scrambles for place and power.

He has dignity without ankylosis, and decided opinions without dogmatism ✤ ✤

Essentially, he represents the new time. He is a businessman. He believes in creation, evolution, development, transportation, distribution. Nothing that is human is alien to him.

To part with this man seems like losing an old-time friend. The English newspapers are certainly right: he is an American by habit of thought. Better still, he is a universal citizen. And while he is eminently loyal and true to England, at the same time he is friendly toward America.

He realizes that we are practically one people, that England's Shakespeare is our Shakespeare, and that our history merges off and becomes English history. Largely, our interests, our hopes, and our destinies are one.

Our hearts are with the Honorable James Bryce. Let Carnegie do his duty!

Max Stirner

N Ralph Waldo Emerson's revolutionary essay, *Self Reliance*—a passionate call to arms from a mighty soul on fire with the glorified vision of its own individualized destiny—occur, among other memorable sentences, these words: " Society is everywhere in conspiracy against the manhood of each one of its members. The only right is what is after my constitution; the only wrong what is against it." ❡ Walt Whitman and Henry David Thoreau uttered equally radical words. But neither of these men was an anarchist. They were too sane to take themselves literally. What they believed in was the spiritual evolution of the individual, a self-overcoming, a throttling of the ghosts in one's own soul—the ghosts of fear and ignorance, the ghosts that within ourselves stand at the crossroads of every crisis that invites to action, demanding toll of our self-reliance.

Self-emancipation must precede social emancipation. If you want to abolish a mass you must begin by reconstructing the units of that mass. Of course you can blow the mass up with gunpowder, but you blow up the units with it.

If society everywhere conspires against the individual it is because the individual has not yet freed his mind of the fixed idea that he can do without a State. The fault comes back to each one of us. The State is not a thing; it is an organized instinct; one of the skins of evolution not yet sloughed off; a tool that has not yet completed its work in the hands of the World-Ego.

The weaknesses of " society" are the shadows of our individual weaknesses. Its transgressions are the sum of all individual transgressions. Society is no better than the average between the best and the worst individuals living within its pale.

Its crimes against the individual are in exact ratio to the crimes of individuals against one another. Organized society will exist so long as there is an instinct to organize among individuals. Emerson says, let each one of us fit ourselves to do without society—just as we have outgrown the old monstrous theologies. The State will then be sloughed. "Physician, heal thyself!" Social workers and anarchists today are fighting what they call " general ills." There are no such things.

There are only individual ills. Be yourself, emancipate yourself, abolish the State by learning to do without it—that is the message of Emerson, Whitman, Thoreau, Ibsen.

The latter cried, "Away with the State!" and, clairvoyant thinker that he was, he added as an afterthought—" of course, I mean by spiritual means."

Nietzsche wrenched man out of his social socket and made him a beatified Cain. He was the poet of the Ego. Had he ever heard of Max Stirner, the War-Lord of the Ego?

Stirner's book, *The Ego and His Own* is the last word in egoism—the last word in revolt. It is not the most dangerous book ever written, because its philosophy is hopelessly impracticable. Ibsen and Emerson and Whitman are more dangerous in their teachings than Stirner. The latter has given us one of the most stimulating books ever written, a book that thrills, invites a man to himself; a book that lays all the sacred spooks and ultimately brings the reader 'round.

Egoism makes strange bedfellows!

You shall leave all; the Kingdom of God is within you. Max Stirner makes the Ego of man God, and to serve it you shall leave the State, the home, the family, religion and everything that battens on the aspiring soul of man, though after he has gotten rid of all these " earthly spooks," just what you should aspire toward is not clear, unless it be what Stirner calls man's " Ownness"—a word that Kipling makes comprehensible in his famous injunction, " What you want go and take."

The individualism of Stirner is thus founded on the most rational idea in the world—the idea that only the individual is glorified, that only I matter—with the most irrational implications. Away with State, Church and family!—they prevent my Ego from realizing itself. Crime is my business. Citizenship is slavery. Parents maim their children from the cradle. Society tickets me. Laws prevent me from getting my " own." What I can do, that is right. Evil is failure. Success is the only righteousness. All regulation is emasculation. Only I, myself, am holy. The thing I can use is good; the thing that uses me is bad. Altruism is merely sickness of the will.

All this is not as dangerous as it sounds, for as a matter of fact all strong men—all men who do anything in life at all, all those who differentiate themselves from the mass—act on these principles in one degree or another, generally unconsciously.

Men never like to have their motives to action formulated. They hate even to formulate the matter secretly to themselves.

And Max Stirner's boldness merely consisted in putting what he thought into print. The Albany and Harrisburg legislatures are reeking with men who would no doubt suppress Stirner's book if they ever heard of it—men would long ago have known the book if it had been titled, " Cash; or Grab Your Own." Stirner's anarchy is purely analytic and idealistic. But at Albany and Harrisburg the brand of anarchy is intensely practical.

⁅ And to Stirner's individualism there is a rational, majestic, sublime side. His Ego is the hungry animal inside of us all, an animal that has intelligence and imagination, it is true, but an animal nevertheless in that every movement of its psychic, physical and emotional nature is toward its own. Men will only marry and procreate, they will only pay taxes and support churches, as long as they can be made to believe that they are getting something out of these things; they are good so long as the good gives them pleasure—that is, swells their own Ego.

They are good and altruistic for the same reasons that they are bad and egoistic: they believe that there is a gain somewhere to them. For at bottom when you tear away the rags and tatters of hypocrisy and the moldy crusts of convention that cover the real palpitating core of a man, what will you find? A being that adores itself and loves and worships only where it believes it is loved and benefited by that worship in return. Stirner asks, "What is good?" And he answers, "What I can use."

Man is a warrior. No matter how subtle and complex life becomes, as in New York City today, no matter how highly "civilized" we boast of being, it is our own—our "Ownness," Stirner calls it— that we are battling for. We each of us, whether in a "state of nature" or a state of society, are fighting for the conservation of the Ego. Some of us believe that the marriage institution, children, the State, help us to conserve that Ego; others believe that these adjuncts suppress it. It depends on the Ego. A business man, generally speaking, finds it aids him to subscribe to the common plan of life. A thinker like Herbert Spencer or Schopenhauer finds it does not. But both classes of men worship at the shrine of the same god—the Ego. Self was the first law; today, as ever, it is the first virtue.

The Ego is a blood-smeared fact. Man once lived in a perpetual state of war; he brutally struck down whatever stood in his way— if he was not struck down first. Today we are still in a state of war, but for the same reason that we found it necessary to kill in the old time we find it necessary now to preserve. The Ego seeks its own through destruction and construction. There was a time when kindness and goodness and charity would have destroyed the race. Use was God; Use is still God. We, the men and women of today, with top-hats and lorgnettes and tin pails and steam-shovels, are not different in our aims from the caveman and shaggy brute that peered out of the forest brambles. Scratch us and the old ghost walks again. We are still the victims of egomania.

Our methods are different—that's all. This warrior instinct can not die. It is our virtue. It is our sap and our virility. We are becoming masters now of the death-dealing forces in us and around us; we have disciplined the things that disciplined us. It is another mask for Ego. It is on these unquestionable truths that Max Stirner has reared his doctrine of the Ego.

Hence it follows that this announcer of Ego does not admit the idea of self-sacrifice into his scheme of life. And here again Stirner thinks boldly and clairvoyantly. For no doctrine has had more adherents and fewer sincere believers than the doctrine of self-sacrifice. Ego will not be sacrificed. It will lend, but it will not vanish. Self-sacrifice should be the prerogative of power; as it is, it is most often the excuse that weakness makes for its inability to live for itself alone. Suppose the doctrine of self-sacrifice became universal! We should have the absurd spectacle of each person living for the good of some other person. That, of course, is unthinkable. Self-sacrifice must, in the very nature of things, be subterranean egoism. Stirner speaks of the " egoism of the stars." It is a good example. Each star shines for itself; as an incidence of power it throws its radiance into space, giving light to the darkness, shedding warmth. But its giving is incidental. It exists first of all for itself. The good it causes comes out of its surplus. And self-sacrifice should be self-glorification. All gifts should be gifts of power, not a hand-out from Duty. " Everything is for me! " cries Stirner.

Even what he gives is still his. And there can be nothing to give unless one has cultivated his Ego before conferring the gift. Unless the gardener has given his time to raising the most beautiful plants, how can his gift be worthy? Strangle your instincts, throttle your inner nature, stifle the soul's cry for joy and power and its hunger for its " ownness"—and Nature will brand you a sloven in your very gait and secrete the venom of your secret spite in all your " gifts."

Stirner's doctrine of the Ego leaves no room for the Socialistic state. He deals sledge-hammer blows at that fallacy. Socialism is to him, as it appeared to Herbert Spencer and Gustave Le Bon, another form of slavery.

Socialism is only that old enemy, the State, popularized. The mantle has fallen from the shoulders of the old gods onto a newer being—the People. The Socialist believes that the State can do what the individual can not do, forgetting that the State is no other thing than the people. As Stirner truly says, there is no such thing as a body; there are only bodies—that is, the State, like all abstractions, is a myth; there are only individuals with Ego. The Socialist believes there are individuals and a State. He makes a thing out of a word, galvanizes it into a semblance of life, sticks a crown on its head, puts a gilded wand in its hand, sits it on a throne of theories, and cries, " Behold the Deliverer of Man—the State, the People! "

Always the slave of words—this poor bewildered Man!

Always there is a New Jerusalem—a lazy man's Utopia! Once it was Paradise—now it is Socialism. It is only the latest illusion. There is no short cut to happiness. There is no backstairs to the House of Life. What the individual can not do for himself the State can not do for him. Nothing degrades like dependence; nothing undermines a man like the certain guarantee of a living. The Ego must fight and bleed for its " own "—that makes the Ego godlike.

Stirner foresaw this great Socialistic propaganda that is on us. He foresaw a slavery more terrible than that which ever prevailed in ancient times following the erection of the Socialistic State. By destroying the competitive system, the principle of individuality, the profoundest principle in Nature, would be sapped at the core. Men, always certain of life and the necessities, would lose the one supreme characteristic of their manhood—the ability to struggle and to conquer.

Under Socialism we should be ruled by a gigantic Trust called the State or the People—all names for one thing. The Ego would be regulated as in medieval times, and on the same theory, the theory of all tyrants—" public improvement." Instead of a few politicians we would have a world of 'em.

What should a man be helped to do, then? To make a better fight, to give a deadlier blow, to strike surer, to battle for the preservation of Ego. But he should be guaranteed nothing except death if he fails. What is injustice? The equal distribution of goods— guaranteeing to those who can not fight; preserving the weak at the expense of the strong. All men are born unequal. Socialism— the Social State, Stirner calls it—is confiscation of Ego. It is popular with those who have nothing.

Whatever of great things has been done in the world has been done by the individual.

The individual—not the State or the family—is Nature's unit value ॐ ॐ

All that makes for material or mental development has sprung from individual initiative, lashed by the thongs of Pride and Necessity—lured by the lust for Power. And wherever the State or the Church has attempted to regulate the individual and the activity of the Ego, decay has followed. The Dark Ages were dark because the Ego was dead. The Ego awakened with Dante, Gutenberg, Michelangelo and Martin Luther.

The old autocracy reigned on the theory that one man should rule all men.

The new autocracy is called Socialism; it merely reverses the scheme ॐ ॐ

It believes that all men should rule each man.

Socialism abolishes the fear of danger in the Ego of the individual. She smashes his mainsprings, fear and courage. No man is born with the right to a living, or to anything else. Man's only right is a competitive right. The State is always evil, asserts Stirner—

and Socialism is merely another gag for our tongues and fetters for our feet.

Max Stirner's dream of an emancipated Ego is futile, but his reasons for dreaming it were sublime. The direction his thought takes is right, but he had visions beyond the reaches of our souls. He imposes on our brains a sublime ideal of human development. It is like the North Star, a great light to steer by, but he who tries to reach it is mad, mad, mad, my lords.

Charles W. Eliot

THERE was put forth on July Twenty-first at Cambridge, Massachusetts, the most important announcement made since Lincoln issued his Emancipation Proclamation.

I refer to the address of Dr. Charles W. Eliot, given before the Harvard Summer School of Divinity ❧ ❧

The importance of Lincoln's Emancipation Proclamation was on account of the man who put it forth, and the time at which it was issued. John Brown issued a like Proclamation, and got himself quickly hanged for his pains.

Brown's act was inopportune, and his name did not have sufficient gravity, anyway. The value of a thing depends quite as much upon who says it, as on the words themselves.

Henry Ward Beecher proclaimed the divine right of negroes to freedom, again and again.

The business of Wendell Phillips was to do the same, and although he sounded his tocsin, only a few heard him on account of the noise ❧ ❧

Theodore Parker proclaimed freedom to the men in bonds. His voice carried clear to Virginia, where he was indicted and a price was placed upon his head. He fled to Italy and died there in Eighteen Hundred Sixty.

Lincoln listened not to Greeley's advice, but waited many weary months for the psychologic moment to arrive before he gave forth his Proclamation. He waited until the North had achieved a victory. After the reek and the riot, after the tumult and the shouting, there came a calm and then it was that he spoke. He spoke like the practised orator that he was: he did not speak until his audience had exhausted itself and was ready to listen.

Dr. Eliot, President Emeritus of Harvard, is the most conspicuous intellectual figure before the American people today. His position is one of singular dignity.

He resigned his office as active President of Harvard, not on suggestion, request or demand, but of his own free will. No word of reproach has ever been brought against him.

In his presence the quibbler has been quiet and the carper dumb. Dr. Eliot has ever been alive and alert to the best interests of Society, but in expression he is the prince of diplomats. He has never laid himself open to the charge of being a crank. He is not erratic nor verbose. His appearances are as studied and as carefully timed as were those of Pericles. His utterances are thought out before they are delivered, not afterward.

Dr. Eliot represents high and sane conservatism in pedagogy, finance and the whole social order. He, of all men, knows that organization should precede dissolution. Upon his official toga is no smirch nor stain, nor upon his personal and private 'scutcheon is there a blot.

A million intellectuals in America look to him for guidance. For them he keys the Cosmic Symphony.

Dr. Eliot has always been a conservative in the sense that he has conserved everything which is valuable, never tearing down the scaffolding as long as it was needed. He represents the established order. He keeps step with the procession—in the front rank—but never ahead of it. He is a mouthpiece, not for the bourgeois or the proletariat, but for the many thousand who are teaching the young bourgeois close markmanship.

He is a teacher of teachers.

His social and intellectual position is secure and unassailable. The Trustees of Harvard University refused to accept Dr. Eliot's resignation, excepting as working manager, so he is now President Emeritus by official appointment.

The President of the United States desired to send Dr. Eliot to the Court of St. James, feeling that no man in America could so well honor the position, but Dr. Eliot declined, giving his poverty as one of the reasons why he could not accept.

Then come forward alumni of Harvard and make up a purse of five hundred thousand dollars and present this money to their beloved President.

Dr. Eliot is seventy-five years old, and declares he has no use for so much money. Finally, however, he is prevailed upon to accept it in order that he may be free to teach as the spirit moves, without thought of food, clothing and shelter.

And this is the man that now speaks.

Dr. Eliot has always had a " genius for conduct," to use the phrase of Phillips Brooks. He has loyalty, devotion, personal disinterestedness, high emprise and a conscience as true as the magnetic needle. He has had the handling of millions for two score of years, yet you find him in his old age practically without funds, and living in a house to which he does not hold the deed.

That such unflinching purity of purpose is a paying policy is shown by the gift of half a million dollars made to Dr. Eliot within a few weeks. I admit that the argument could be made that virtue is not sure to bring its own reward, since no one in America but Dr. Eliot has ever tried it on so high a plane, and his case might prove exceptional.

This much, though, can be said: his experience need not discourage us. The position of Dr. Eliot is commanding. He is popular—he is respected—and by those who have the good fortune to know him closely, he is beloved.

So much for the man.

As for the audience to whom he delivered his pronunciamento, it was, please bear in mind, a Divinity School made up of preachers, old and young, representing various Protestant denominations—that is, a school conducted for the study of Theology.

This school was founded in Sixteen Hundred Thirty-six, and its business and intent has always been to prepare men to go out into the world and explain the Supernatural. The students of a Divinity School are supposed to know the plans and purposes of Deity, and to make these plans and purposes plain to the people is their profession. To this end they have " a call."

And now comes a man who has been at the head of Harvard College for just forty years, and explains to the students of this Divinity School that its teaching of the Supernatural has been founded on a fallacy, and that God is the Great Unconscious working toward the Conscious, with man as His chiefest instrument. Moreover, man, should be the highest object of man's solicitude, and not God; since, if anything is divine, it is man. God does not so much need man, as man needs man.

The value of Dr. Eliot's Proclamation means this, that from now on you can be intellectually free if you choose to be, and yet be acceptable in the Best Society. Heretofore, the free-thinker has been tabu. He has been pigeon-holed with the Ebrew Jew, as one who deliberately rejected " the Savior."

Charles Bradlaugh fought the House of Commons for nine years, and was forcibly ejected from that body, because he refused to take the prescribed oath of office and swear by things which have no existence outside of the brain of one who believes in witches and the benign influence of black cats.

Now, however, the affirmation of a man who does not believe in the " Holy Evangel " is just as valuable as the oath of one who does. Also, since Dr. Eliot's Edict we can invite such a one to our Four-o'Clock without being socially smirched.

So here then is printed the principal points in the Proclamation by Dr. Eliot. The title of the address is " The New Religion."

" The New Religion will not be based upon authority. The future generation is ready to be led, not driven.

" In the New Religion there will be no personification of natural objects, there will be no deification of remarkable human beings, and the faith will not be racial or tribal.

"The New Religion will not teach that character can be changed quickly; it will admit neither a sudden conversion in this world nor a sudden paradise in the next.

"The Christian Church has substituted for human sacrifices the burning of incense. The New Religion will get rid of these things, for they give a wrong conception of God.

"The New Religion will not think of God as a large and glorified man, or a king, or a patriarch. It will not deal chiefly with sorrow and death, but with joy and life. It will believe in no malignant powers ☙ ☙

"God will be so imminent that no intermediary will be needed. For every man, God will be a multiplication of infinities. This religion rejects the idea that man is an alien or fallen being who is hopelessly wicked.

"It will be a religion of 'All Saints.' It will respect all lovely human beings. It will have no place for obscure dogmas or mystery. It will include and comprehend all persons of good will, for, after all, they alone are civilized.

"In past times, to the sick and downtrodden, death has been held out as compensation. The New Religion will not make such promises. In the New Religion there will be no supernatural element; it will place no reliance on anything but the laws of nature ☙ ☙

"It will accept no sacraments, except natural, hallowed customs, and it will deal with natural interpretations of such rites. Its priests will strive to improve social and industrial conditions. The New Religion will not attempt to reconcile people to present ills by the promise of future compensations. The advent of just freedom for mankind has been delayed for centuries by such promises ☙

"Prevention will be the watchword for the New Religion. It can not supply consolation as offered by old religions, but it will reduce the need of consolation.

"Pain formerly was considered a just punishment, but human suffering will now be attacked surely and quickly. The New Religion will not even imagine the justice of God.

"Based on the two great commandments of loving God and one's neighbor, the New Religion will teach that he is best who loves best and serves best, and the greatest service will be to increase the stock of good will.

"One of the greatest evils of today is that people work with hearts full of ill will to the work and the employer.

"The New Religion will foster the new virtue—the love of truth. The true end of all religions and philosophy is to teach man to serve his fellowman, and this religion will do this increasingly. It will not be bound by dogmas or creeds; its workings will be simple, but its field limitless. Its discipline will be the training in the development of co-operation, kindness and good will."

In Eighteen Hundred Forty, Ralph Waldo Emerson, an alumnus of Harvard Divinity School, gave an address before this same institution, in which he very mildly expressed a few of the thoughts now so frankly put forth by Dr. Eliot. For his temerity, all Harvard visited upon Emerson its indignation.

Twenty-eight years went by before the author of *Self-Reliance* was again invited to enter Harvard Yard.

The thoughts expressed by President Eliot are those of avowed and open Rationalism. And his prophecy that the religion of the future must be a religion of this world is fast coming true.

Dr. Eliot is not a prophet, he merely announces that which is at hand. He issues to his student body, to his teachers and professors, and to the vast Harvard Alumni, a Proclamation to the effect that henceforth they may be mentally free.

This does not make them free, because freedom is not a gift, it is an achievement.

Dr. Eliot merely supplies the opportunity to be rational and yet be respectable.

Robert Ingersoll once said to the Rev. Minot Savage, "You should be grateful to me, for my radicalism has made yours respectable." ❧ ❧

Every item in the creed of what Dr. Eliot calls "The New Religion," I have been proclaiming for twenty-five years. Many of the people who now accept Dr. Eliot's New Religion have dented my shield, and on my corduroys are the stains of their rheum. Across my nose is the mark of Torrigiano's hammer. I have been a scout of civilization—and I have been on the picket-line. The main army has often mistaken me for the enemy. But now the main column has come up, Dr. Eliot riding ten paces to the front. And at the head of his Legion he reads the address which I have been twenty-five years in preparing.

Do I then say that Dr. Eliot has been taught at the feet of a farmer in East Aurora?

Not at all, although he reads the Warm Stuff. He probably believed twenty years ago all that he now states. The truths that Dr. Eliot now expresses, and which I have been trying to express by my pen, on the public platform, and in my life, were first uttered by Pythagoras six hundred years before Christ; by Socrates; by Jesus of Nazareth; by Seneca the Aristocrat; by Epictetus the Slave; by Marcus Aurelius the Roman Emperor; by Hypatia the first Martyr to the New Thought—torn limb from limb in a Christian Church; in degree by Cassiodorus, by St. Benedict, and Francis of Assisi; by Bruno and Galileo; by David Hume; by Thomas Paine, Benjamin Franklin and Thomas Jefferson; by Voltaire and Jean Jacques Rousseau; by that courier of civilization, Robert G. Ingersoll.

All these stood for the grandeur of the human intellect, and the sweet reasonableness of allowing men to use their brains. And against them, the Church, the Army, and the State were in league. For them the hemlock was brewed, the cross erected, the scaffold built; dungeons, fetters, gyves, hunger, disgrace, were their portion, and for them the fagot-fires lighted the heavens. The few who escaped torture did so only by veiling their thoughts and saying things in a language which the many could not understand. All this down to the days of Robert Ingersoll, who sacrificed nothing but the Governorship of Illinois.

So to conclude: The marvel is not in what Dr. Eliot says, but in the fact that he says it, and that the people listen without resentment—millions of them having themselves come to the same conclusions ﾟﾟ ﾟﾟ

As for the rest, if they still hug to their hearts a savage fetich, a legacy from the brutal and bloody past, they have the privilege, but they can not longer apply to us the cheerful thumb-screw if we fail to do goose-step when their theological bagpipe plays. When Lincoln issued his Emancipation Proclamation, only one per cent of the colored population could read or write. Now, fifty-eight per cent can read and write. But not all colored people are yet free. Many are in bonds to ignorance, superstition, laziness, brute appetites and incompetence.

In these respects the colored contingent is just like the white population. In other words, the colored brother is a black, yellow or liver-colored imitation of a white man.

Dr. Eliot's Proclamation is a right brave and manly document. The time was ripe for its issuance; for freedom stands a-tiptoe, like jocund day, upon the mountain-top. Will we as a people receive her?

Children, like adults, are not alike, but infinitely different; the object of education, as of life, is to bring out the innate powers, and develop to the highest possible degree the natural and acquired capacities of the individual.
—*Charles W. Eliot.*

WHEN Charles William Eliot was born March Twentieth, Eighteen Hundred Thirty-four, his father was mayor of Boston. This office of the father then gave to the family honors which that distinction does not now give.

All that refinement, culture, schools and travel could give were
bestowed upon or achieved by this child of fortune, who is now
President Emeritus of Harvard College.

We are fond of tracing greatness to surroundings of poverty and
ignorance, because we know it is the exercise, the struggle, the
effort, that develops the individual, and such a beginning gives
hope to the many. Yet we know that better conditions should not
be a disadvantage, or why are we striving to change the environment of the poor and unfortunate?

It seems that inherent within the child are, or are not, the
possibilities of development. Whistler said of Art, " No hovel is
safe from it;" and we add, no palace is safe from it either. When
we ask why one person is capable of greatness and another is not,
what environment will produce a great man, we are asking about
the Unknowable. Certain conditions make for better living, we
believe, but no man has yet been wise enough to know how surely
to secure that divine fire in the soul of man.

No one can tell why Charles W. Eliot was not content with the
pleasures and luxuries that might have been his; why he was not
blended into the opinions, customs and ideas of the scholars and
cultured men of his time. Why was he not content—this gentle
man of peace—to keep to himself the conclusions of his learning
and wisdom? He has been a student all his life. He knows all that
books have stored. He knows all that teachers can tell. He knows
the value of all modern culture. He has received all the benefits
of travel and the intercourse with the most talented and the wisest
of all countries. He has been justly named, " America's first
citizen." All the honors that our country could show to the most
honored President of its most elaborate and largest institution of
learning were bestowed upon President Eliot. Why was not that
enough to satisfy one man? Why does the Divine Energy in
Doctor Eliot insist upon his making plain to any who can read,
that the modern race is fast passing from its childhood and

adolescence into its maturity? Doctor Eliot tells us that we are passing out of the age where brute force rules, into the age where brain is the power. America is demonstrating this fact to civilization. He says that, in one hundred and seven years, " the United States has been a party to forty-seven arbitrations —being more than half of all that have taken place in the modern world."

War disregards all the rights of the individual.

The welfare of the individual has become dear to us, and we protect him. Man has the right to think and to act for himself, to live his own life and to be happy.

Individualism was never so dear to the race as now. The race was never so dear to the individual as now.

The tendency of the times is to give equal opportunity to each man and to all men.

Doctor Eliot knows the history of humanity, what race has evolved and declined, its infancy, its childhood, its manhood, its old age and death; how one civilization differs from another; and that this present, modern race shows that we, as we are entering upon our maturity, " are heirs to all the ages " in that which makes for a perfect and permanent civilization.

❡ Knowing these things, Doctor Eliot sees that necessarily we shall have a new religion, and it will be a religion that shall appeal to the intellect, to the brain of man. Hitherto, religion has had emotion in excess. Religious wars are proof of this statement.

❡ Reason, pure brain action, has taken the lives of very few men or animals ◦◦ ◦◦

It is the heat of passion, the unguided emotions, which kill.

❡ Doctor Eliot knows that with the evolution of humanity everything has changed, and that this will continue to be a world of change, for life is motion.

There is a current that has forever moved us on, until we need different surroundings, different customs, different laws, different government. Now at last, we dream of a time when each shall be a law unto himself and do the right without pressure or persuasion—that cause of quarrels, of wars, of the bloodshed of the world.

Man is developing all the powers of the brain. Ultimately, man will think before he acts, and his actions will be controlled by brain and not by passion.

Brain must be fired by feeling, but brain must not be consumed by feeling.

The race is reaching a period in its development where it is becoming rational. The mental attributes will be developed and be active in proportions that will give sanity.

The time is coming when the idea of sacrifice, the shedding of blood, will be abhorrent to us, and we shall no longer ascribe to an All-Wise Power a taste or desire for anything of that nature. When man emerges from the childishness of wanting to be cared for, of desiring gifts without giving an equivalent in value, he will make a new religion, save himself, and so cease to sin through ignorance of common knowledge.

If man needs an ideal, a hero, he will take for his example a natural man, one who, like Bjornson, has developed to its best every muscle and nerve of his body, every cell of his brain.

℄ The appellation of " Chief Citizen " is a title which belongs to Doctor Eliot. The United States is in name a country for the individual, a universal House of Lords, with no King, no House of Commons.

Some one said of Whitman, " He is Democracy." He did talk and write gloriously of democracy, of the divinity of the individual and of his divine rights and privileges. But Whitman's poetry and life have the lilt and meter of iconoclasm, not of construction.

℄ Doctor Eliot is " democracy " in a truer and greater sense than was Whitman. Doctor Eliot's life and teaching are positive and constructive throughout.

Build! Build! is the overtone that you detect in all he says. "How Build?" Build for individual development, for life, liberty and the pursuit of happiness. This can be done only through universal brotherhood—treat others as you would be treated ❧ ❧

In Doctor Eliot's teaching there is no lack of sentiment; he suggests as much as does Whitman; but Doctor Eliot adds intellect. He gives a ratio of mental attributes that is more stable, possibly more safe to build upon.

Doctor Eliot says, "Self-sacrifice is not a good or a merit in itself; it must be intelligent and loving to be meritorious, and the object in view must be worth its price."

This introduces the qualities of wisdom and judgment. A man recently risked and lost human life to save the life of a dog.

In the fighting of duels, one life must be the price of that elusive something called a man's honor. If one man said that another had lied, a challenge, a fight, a death was the consequence. Doctor Eliot says, count the cost, use your brain.

Truth-telling has not yet become an established custom in the world, nor can all the bloodshed of all time make it so.

Only the love of truth, the desire for truth, can do this. This love and desire can come only when we understand that truth is best for each individual. Mythology can not save us, nor fairy-stories.

℃ The world has not been saved by brute force, nor by will-power, nor by emotionalism, though all three have been tried singly and together. Nor can intellect save us alone. But just now we do need to use more intellect, wisdom, in the power that we are using to save the world.

Doctor Eliot's teaching is that of self-reliance. Develop yourself so that you do not need to ask another to pay your debts, wash away your sins, or give you a passport into Paradise. People have been promised mansions afar off, salvation hereafter. But only a narcotic has been administered; the disease remained.

Doctor Eliot teaches that " repentance wipes out nothing in the past, and is only the first step towards reformation, and a sign of a better future."

He does not wish to have " men and women reconciled to present ills by promises of future blessedness, either for themselves or others. Such promises have done infinite mischief in the world by inducing men to be patient under the sufferings of deprivations against which they should incessantly have struggled. The advent of a just freedom for the mass of mankind has been delayed for centuries by its effect of compensatory promises issued by the churches."

The sharpest and hardest criticisms that have been made on Doctor Eliot's "New Religion" are about what he has said concerning that of which man knows nothing—the unknowable, as Herbert Spencer calls it.

Doctor Eliot says, " In the new religion there will be no super-natural element. In all its theory and in all its practice it will be completely natural. In the new religion there will be no deification of remarkable human beings! It will admit no sacraments, except those which are the visible, spiritual grace, or of a natural, hallowed custom."

Doctor Eliot prophesies that the human race will evolve a natural, rational religion.

Then both Catholic and Protestant say, " This is not Christian and this idea of a new religion is not that of a Christian religion." They speak of it as a "PROPOSED" new religion, and call it " Atheism or Pantheism."

In rejecting the supernatural, they say that he has rejected God who is thoroughly supernatural, and they add, " Without a belief in the supernatural there is no possibility of true worship, and without worship there is no religion."

It had not seemed that Doctor Eliot was "proposing" a new religion. Doctor Eliot is a seer, and simply gives expression to what he sees inevitably coming to us. He has prescience—a longer view than most people.

We are all travelers going into an unknown country. Our eyes are of different focus. *America* (Roman Catholic) sees its own diocese, and so does *Zion's Herald, The Christian Advocate* and others. They are deep in the primeval forests of their ancestors' thought and can not see beyond. Doctor Eliot is on a mountain-top looking out upon a beautiful future of light. To those in the forest, what he sees is not in existence, and it seems impossible, undesirable, that any one should see these things.

❡ There is a story that when Cleopatra's messengers, sent out to bring her tidings of Mark Antony, brought back news she did not want to hear, she had them killed. But their tidings were true. A few people before Doctor Eliot's time have affirmed what he has. They have become prominent because of these statements. But the popular religion tried to dispose of them quickly by putting upon them the labels, " Infidel " and "Atheist," and the greater number of them were killed. Oblivion and opprobrium were theirs, so far as their being taken as authority by the many.

❡ Doctor Eliot had become authority as a leader of thought among men, " the most eminent teacher and scholar in America," before he gave the memorable address before the Harvard Summer School of Theology, in Nineteen Hundred Nine. The effect of the address was profound. So far as I know, no one has dared call Doctor Eliot names, but his statements have caused a little reclassification of people and ideas.

It has been a year since the address was made, and that year has seen a wonderful advance in freedom for thinking men and women. The timid have taken courage. The bold have become confident that freedom is even at the door. Doctor Eliot is a scholar and a gentleman. His language is the language of culture, so that orthodox parents are not too startled to send their boys to Harvard where the influence of the great man still lives.

When Doctor Eliot says, " The modern man would hardly feel any appreciable loss of motive power toward good, or away from evil, if Heaven were burned and Hell quenched," he speaks the truth that all thinking men and women recognize. The next generation will speak of these unpleasant myths as the nightmares of adolescence.

Even now, people who are able to analyze motives of action and influences that cause or restrain conduct of life, know as Macbeth says, " We 'd jump the life to come. But in these cases we still have judgment here."

It has long been, and is today, the immediate consequence of an act that men consider—from what their neighbors say to what is the extreme penalty of the law for a misdeed. Humanity as a whole works for reward and to avoid punishment. The threat and the promise are still potent and will be for some time to come. But our myths, legends, literature and traditions have, for so many ages, assigned one cause for action—whether good or bad— that it is with difficulty that men can think in any but the ancient terms.

The sweet sentiments of the lullaby are enmeshed in our mind with the folk-lore concerning angels and the good, devils and the evil ✍ ✍

The love of truth which science fosters is affirmative, positive and beautiful for the generations to come. The beauty, the poetry, the food for the imagination are all in truth, scientific truth, and can be had for the looking, provided one has eyes that can see.

❧ The child-mind finds joy in the fantastic pictures of Milton, of Virgil, of Homer. Children brought up with the ideas of Santa Claus are frightened to face the fact that there is no such fairy. But grown to manhood, away from the childhood where sweets, toys, things and pastimes fill the mind, Santa Claus is pronounced a foolish joke of very doubtful good even for young children. That the truth is better is the consensus of opinion.

Doctor Eliot's prophecy concerning the new religion was printed and criticized in the Summer of Nineteen Hundred Nine. It was read widely by students, scholars and thinkers then. It is of more interest today than it was a year ago. More people recognize the truth Doctor Eliot expressed in this address, and more people see the prophecy being fulfilled before their eyes.

The churches are giving their thought more to bettering the temporal conditions of people, and less to promises and threats. Churchmen are making their effort more to reconcile religion to science, than in repressing or warping the truth of science to the mythology in the Bible.

Doctor Eliot stands to us supremely as a teacher. He graduated from Harvard in Eighteen Hundred Fifty-three. Then he became tutor, assistant professor, studied for two years in Europe, then for four years was Professor of Chemistry in the Massachusetts Institute of Technology.

In Eighteen Hundred Sixty-nine, after Harvard was reorganized, Doctor Eliot was made President and continued in that office until May Nineteenth, Nineteen Hundred Nine.

At the beginning of his work as a teacher he saw the demands for changed conditions that the march of civilization makes. He was always a reformer. Harvard took the lead in making courses elective instead of prescribed. Then Doctor Eliot shortened the college course so that a young man might not be taken too long out of life before being put back into it, lest in the meantime he might have forgotten how to live. Doctor Eliot saw, too, that in youth is the time to learn by doing and not by contemplating. The young should be living, working, doing, and the old should go to college to see how life compares with theory and history. College is a place to contemplate, retrospect and speculate— activities which belong naturally to old age.

Doctor Eliot is a financier. He has had millions of dollars to take care of, to invest wisely and well.

He has added to literature an inestimable wealth. His thoughts, experiences, wisdom and learning are unique in their value. He tells only that which is truth, and his expression is accurate and exact. You quote his statements as authority, because you know they are authority.

He knows politics, government. He can compare the present with the past, and knows what progress we have made in this strange unit we call national life.

He has been at the head of a great institution for forty years, and knows humanity, collectively and singly.

The family extended gives an institution, the institution multiplied by many gives a government. The needs of the government or care of the institution are the needs in kind of the nation. ⁅ It is soul that leads and controls nations, just as it issoul that leads and controls institutions.

Doctor Eliot puts a premium on the simple virtue of developing yourself, body and brain, and his work and teaching is to show us that life more abundant is within our reach.

Alice Hubbard.

Clara Barton: A Symposium

NE of the greatest women of modern times—or, in fact, of any time—was Clara Barton.

She was a Human Being. Clara Barton possessed superb sympathy, great skill and rare breadth of vision. She had the world-vision. She was not a villager, not a provincial. She did not even belong to the United States. She was a citizen of the world. Also, she was a citizen of the Celestial City of Fine Minds.

In her composition, resentment, fear, prejudice, hate, existed, if at all, only as a chemical trace. She accepted slights, ingratitude contumely, stupidity, all quite as a matter of fact, realizing that these things are universal, and that it is our business not to imitate either the rogues or the fools.

Clara Barton passed away only a few months ago, aged ninety-one, sane, sensible, aspiring, interested in world problems to the last. If ever an individual realized the truth of General Sherman's famous remark in reference to war, it was Clara Barton. She knew only too well the difference between pageantry and war.

We have been told that women take no part in war.

Woman's part in war is to clean up the mess; to bear the resultant burdens, woes and sorrows; and to live, in spite of hell—bearing in mind the Shermanian Slogan. Woman's share in war is to live when her husband is in his grave, her children starving, her home in ashes—and the heroes crowned.

Men who go to war do not assume the responsibilities of war. Neither do they pay the debt of pain, anguish or money. These things are left to others.

Clara Barton was a woman, and she took care of one side of the business of official murder, the side that no man could have done. And in this she brought to bear a degree of patience, persistency, effectiveness and physical endurance unequaled by any man that can be named: She could go longer without food, be deprived of sleep more hours, march farther in burning heat or Winter wind and storm, than the best.

Clara Barton, a few years before she died, became possessed of a Big Idea.

And this idea was the utilization of the skill, talent, ability and experience of the physician, without compelling the man to get his meal-ticket through the perpetuity of misfortune, the misery, woe and ignorance of his patients.

The Bible says, " They who are well need no physician."

That is, we send for a doctor only when we are sick. He makes money out of us only when we are stricken. Consequently, his material interests lie in the direction of our being sick, and not well ❧ ❧

Doctors are men. They represent, not men of extraordinary capacity, but plain, simple, average, every-day men, seemingly lifted into social prominence—more or less. They are educated in the matter of medicine, of lessening pain, of ministering to the afflicted. Their training is all along the line of the abnormal, the peculiar, the unusual.

The ideal of perfect physical health is not in the mind of the average physician, simply because he does not deal with the healthy, the well, those with bounding enthusiasm and strength, plus. His associations are with the sick, the inefficient, the depressed. In degree, necessarily, he becomes subdued, like the dyer's hand, to the medium in which he works.

Businessmen thrive only as their customers thrive. Railroads prosper only as the people who live along their line prosper. But doctors thrive on pain and misery; lawyers thrive on misfortune; and preachers wax fat on ignorance and fear.

It is impossible to expect a physician to be any better, stronger, more heroic, or more unselfish than the average man. It is absurd to expect him to enter on a line of work which will destroy his own business, lessen his influence and sink his personality into nullity. It is very easy to say that the good doctor is working to destroy his business and show people how to get along without him. This is merely literature. No doctor does it, or could do it. Doctors have families dependent upon them. They have rent to to pay; interest to meet; food to purchase; raiment to secure. They occupy a prominent place in the social world, and gasoline costs money.

The practice of medicine is not only a profession—it is a business. These men are not endowed by the State, nor pensioned by Andrew Carnegie. The money they receive comes from the people to whom they minister; and the people to whom they minister are sick people—for again let it be stated that when we are well we do not send for a physician. All of his charges are based on the services rendered to sick people. " To call, medicine and prescription for self "—this is the regulation charge record in his day-book ◆◆ ◆◆

At long intervals, there may be instances of men drawing a check payable to a doctor who has shown them how to get along without him. But it is not probable that one doctor out of fifty, living a lifetime, has ever had one such experience come to him.

Even people who have been sick are apt to be very slow pay, when it comes to cashing up for the services of a physician. Doctors have to collect up close and sharp, otherwise there is great danger that they will never get their money at all.

Republics are ungrateful. So are monarchies. And the fact is, all humanity is ungrateful. To secure money by banking on gratitude is immoral.

Now, no individual can be named who ever had a wider experience with physicians and surgeons than did Clara Barton. For forty years she was intimately associated in work with them. She saw them on dress parade. She saw them on duty. She saw them when their hearts were laid bare and their faces unmasked. And her admiration for physicians was very great. And yet, the net result of her conclusions was this: that as long as doctors look to sick people for sustenance, the doctor, being but human, will be interested in perpetuating disease, and not in eradicating it. If he could eradicate disease, he would eradicate himself.

Medicine, as a science, is not going to deliberately wipe itself off the map. Doctors are not going to commit hara-kiri in the interests of society. Their " ethics " are all in the line of self-preservation ✺ ✺

All State boards of health, all medical associations, all national laws authorizing boards of health, are careful to see that the laws authorizing these institutions also authorize that their management shall be under the care and guidance of some certain school of medicine. Nominally, their object is to protect the public, but their actual reason for existence is to protect the medical profession. Medical societies are labor-unions, intent on the self-preservation of their members. And self-preservation is the first law of life. No man is going to destroy the business in which he is engaged. Doctors will make people sick in order to cure them, just as long as they thrive thereby. As long as a doctor thrives by injecting into a healthy body a virus will this practice be continued. And the men who uphold the plan and custom of giving an individual a disease in order to keep him from catching one are honest and sincere. They are self-deluded individuals. We are all prejudiced, and violently, too, in the direction of self-interest. All of which, Clara Barton, being a good psychologist, saw with unblinking eyes ✺ ✺

Her desire was to conserve the knowledge, the experience, the skill of the physician, and utilize these for the benefit of humanity, and make it the business of the physician to keep humanity well —in other words, to cure them before they got sick. Accidents may happen; but the number of accidents in life are gradually being reduced by many safety appliances and precautions which society at large is constantly inventing. Disease should be a disgrace. Most diseases begin with functional disorders, and these, continued, evolve into organic conditions, which we call " disease."

Disease, however, strictly speaking, as Doctor Weir Mitchell has so well said, is only the symptom of a condition.

Well did Doctor Oliver Wendell Holmes say that to educate a child you must begin with his great-grandmother. In order to cure humanity of its ailments, we must first change the conditions under which men live. We must destroy the germs of disease before it has evolved into this unkind tissue-destroying and function-killing state that we have honored with some specific name, say, " Bright's Disease."

A certain line of living will lead up to Bright's Disease. Any intelligent physician can give you a recipe whereby, in the course of time, if you are patient and persistent, you can have any one particular disease in the Materia Medica.

Physicians often produce disease at will, just to test out their theories ﮰ ﮰ

Physicians are naturally well fitted to protect society and the individual from sickness. But only in a very slight degree are they doing it. They are certainly not doing it to an extent that destroys their own well-being and their own position in society—this, not because they are selfish, or without conscience, but simply because they are men.

The business world has discovered that the way to make money is to tell the truth and bestow a benefit on the people with whom you deal. All transactions in which both sides do not make money are immoral.

This does not apply, however, to the three learned professions. Lawyers thrive on receiverships, bankruptcies, deaths, quarrels, misunderstandings, crimes and litigation.

And so most lawyers yet are parasites.

But there are a few lawyers who have discovered that by working for the best interests of the community and associating themselves with commerce, they keep the businessman out of trouble, instead of getting him in.

And as the big businessman is willing to pay for this service, the lawyers, instead of preying on the world, protect it.

But the clergy and the physicians lag behind. Clergymen thrive by perpetuating a fetish. Some of them have discovered that they can dilute the fetish, and still keep certain features of it, and thrive thereby to an extent which they could not, were they to stand for the whole line of orthodox, oriental, Asiatic superstition. But no clergyman is intent on redeeming his congregation from the demons of fear, which are bound to germinate and flourish where the so-called science of theology is taught. The whole fabric of theology is founded on untruth. Hypocrisy, pretense, untruth, are woven into a web of falsehood, in order to save the soul of a religious organization.

Preachers are fighting for victory, not truth. The thing that is vital to them is the perpetuity of the institution, not the freedom of the individual. " The truth will make you free," they say, but they are careful not to preach the truth.

These organizations take on human betterments from time to to time, in order to strengthen their position. You ask a clergyman now what he thinks of the Immaculate Conception and the Deity who had one Son, and sacrificed this Son for the good of the world, and this man will refer you to an orphan asylum, a hospital, a home for the erring, and say, " Look at the good we are doing!" The original lie still endures, and it is his business to gloss it, galvanize it and perpetuate it, simply because he is a man. That 's the way he gets his meal-ticket. That 's the way he is able to buy a shawl for his wife, a dress for his daughter, and a suit of clothes for his boy. Economic needs are upon him, and anything that redounds to his credit, that makes for his personal self-preservation, he is going to uphold. He is a man. He is educated in this particular line. That's all he can do. His needs demand that he shall be a falsifier; and he salves his conscience by saying, "If I do not teach them this, some one else will."

Henry Ward Beecher once said in confidence, "It pains me to the quick when I see a man with a first-class mind join my church, because I know from that moment forward this man will be enslaved just in the degree that he is true to this religious institution." ॐ ॐ

Henry Ward Beecher was big enough to realize that he was thriving on hypocrisy and untruth. And yet he was not big enough to break loose from it. He ministered to the weaknesses, the fears, the foibles of superstition in the minds of his people to the last. And this does not mean, for a moment, that he was really bad. He did the only thing he could do. He glossed the most gigantic lie that has been perpetuated from century to century—that is, the lie upon which the Christian religion is founded: the assumption that we are "lost."

All of which Clara Barton knew. Yet she was not an iconoclast. She was not bitter. Her heart was full of kindness; and her desire was to make both the clergy and the doctors free.

We must utilize the services of the clergy and the physicians, and this without injuring them.

Just how to make the clergy free, and still not destroy them, Clara Barton did not know. But she did have a definite program for freeing doctors. The knowledge and skill that some physicians possess should be preserved. And her plan was to make all doctors attachés of the State, not allowing them to receive fees from sick people.

Let their business consist in showing people how to keep well. Let them act as advisor, counselor and friend. People who are sick should have the privilege of going to a wise physician, and he could tell them the truth about themselves, and frankly inform them why they are sick, without any fear of losing his source of income thereby.

That is, Clara Barton wanted physicians to thrive through keeping people well. Self-interest must be on the side of health, and not on the side of disease, as far as the physician is concerned. The Chinese plan of killing the physician, when the patient died, was not wholly bad.

Clara Barton's desire was to formulate a system whereby it would be easy for a doctor to tell the truth, and a difficulty for him to do otherwise ♪ ♪

This is the entire intent now in business: to make it easy for every employee to do what is right, and difficult to do what is wrong. The right is the natural and the normal; the wrong is the wasteful, the extravagant, the silly, the absurd. And yet, so topsy-turvy have been things that, in the past, men have thriven through violence, through untruth, chicanery, pretense, deception, And this condition, in great degree, the Christian religion has fostered, by postponing the rewards of virtue until after the man is dead. Well does Charles W. Elliot say that truth is the new virtue. Truth is now recognized as an asset. Lawyers, in degree, are taking on truth.

But we have with us as yet the ambulance-chaser—the lawyer who makes money by getting somebody declared incompetent, and taking the care of the property out of their hands; the man who stirs up strife, hatred and discord, and starts groundless damage-suits. And the limit is reached when a New York lawyer has a client make a will, naming him as residuary legatee, and then takes this client out in a rowboat and comes back alone ♪

This last symbols the business in which about four out of five of all lawyers are yet engaged. The legal hold-up and the judicial frame-up are still with us. One-half of all damage-suits are founded on fraud, as every judge and every lawyer well knows. The damage-suit is simply an opportunity to grab into the strong-box of the man who happens to possess one. Individuals without property are free from the frame-up. No one else is. And this condition in the legal profession is well understood, and is undisputed even by the lawyers themselves.

The sad part about theology and medicine is that doctors and preachers will violently dispute the truth of statements herein made, claiming that they are doing a necessary service. Preachers preaching obsolete mythology, in the name of faith, telling us folk-lore, devised in the Orient twenty centuries or more ago, passing this out to us today as literal truth, and doing it honestly —this is the tragic part of the situation.

Doctors who look upon a man who keeps well and who gets along without him, with suspicion and contempt—these are the men who form a menace to mankind.

For their own good, we have got to reverse the proposition, and make it to the interest of a physician to show us how to get along without him. This can be done only by making him an attaché of the State, pensioning him, as it were, subsidizing him, and thus making him free.

Ewing Herbert says, " Any man who wants something and wants it bad, can be depended on to lie in order to get it."

———————

IN all the opposition that has been made to economic independence for women and to Woman Suffrage—and I believe I have heard and read the entire gamut of argument from the politician's " reasons " to the old villager's objections to " petticoat government "—the clincher to the whole round of talk is, " Beside, the final test of citizenship is ability to defend one's country. Women can not go to war and therefore they must not have the vote."

One man said, " How it would look to see a regiment of women making a charge! " and he was not a prinking bachelor either.

But what effect have all the objections in view of the fact that women do go to war and have been to war? Sometimes they have gone, as did the Boer women, to actually bear arms against the enemy, but more often to care for the wounded and sick—work far more fatiguing and requiring more endurance.

Clara Barton was telling us last summer a few of her war experiences.

We questioned her about the work of her long and most wonderful life, and found she had spent more time on the battlefield, more time in dealing with actual war, than many a general whose business is war.

"Women can't go to war?"

They have.

Clara Barton's mission on the battlefield, in the camp and in the hospitals was not to kill, but to save life. The enemies she fought were death and the grave. Her victory was not in subduing mankind by greater brute force, the sure aim of the deadly bullet, or superior death-dealing appliances, but by life-giving care, quick relief to the wounded, food to the starving. Clara Barton went to war to save life. It made no difference to her, or to the women who worked with her, on which side the wounded man had fought. He was suffering and sick: that was enough. To Clara Barton all were friends. There was only humanity on the field of battle.

This great woman's life has been a refutation of all the limitations men and tradition have placed upon women.

Without defiance, without premeditation, without special desire to have it so, the Power that makes for righteousness has made this woman's life to be revolutionary to a prescribed sphere. The Divine Spirit has played through Clara Barton and opened ways of eternal life to women and men for all time to come.

Clara Barton was the youngest child of Captain Stephen and Sally Stone Barton. The child nearest to her in age was Sally, and

she was twelve years old when on Christmas Day, Eighteen
Hundred Twenty-one, Clara was born.

The Baby was the object of the admiration, care and thought of
the family, grown-up sisters and brothers included. But she was
the special care and companion of David in anything that
pertained to life out-of-doors.

In her little book, *The Story of My Childhood*, she tells of
wild, fascinating rides bareback, on highbred colts, through
pastures, uphill, down dale, charging into a herd of colts to see
them scamper away. David was in a saddle by her side holding
his five-year-old sister by one foot as they did their roughriding.

❧ Was there a kind fate that arranged all these lessons in child's
play that the woman on the battlefield might be skilled to fly for
life in a trooper's saddle on a strange horse in the front of pursuit?
Surely there 's a Divinity that shaped the life of Clara Barton.

❧ All her experience was educative, and all her experiences were
needed to develop and train the potential power within her.

❧ The child was timid before people and suffered untold misery
from causes that the ordinary child would not notice. This
sensitiveness made deep impressions that developed skill of vital
value to many people years later.

The bashful child grew into a bashful girl. The father and mother
tried a boarding-school. The suffering was more pitiful, and the
teachers were powerless to bring the right remedy. So Clara
Barton went home, eager for work, but what? David fell sick—
the result of an accident—great, splendid David! Clara would
not leave him, and for two years she was his nurse, taking the
responsibility of his case. One good friend recommended larger
responsibilities, a few years later, as a cure for the form of introspection that tortured Clara Barton. Women were allowed to
teach school then, so she began to work with humanity. In her
thought for and of her pupils, she for the first time forgot herself
and in that found happiness and a new life.

A few years later, affairs in the Patent Office at Washington were in a tangle. To many people, even then, a Government position meant ease, graft, smuggling and much pay for little effort. " Serve the public? " It has seldom been served.

Somehow, some one thought of Clara Barton as a person who could untangle the threads of the unskilled, disloyal weavers and whose influence would put to shame dishonesty.

But this some one had thought of her as a person and not as woman. There were only men in the Patent Office. American men are especially gallant to women, tradition says, except where there is woman suffrage. Well, there was no woman suffrage in Washington in Eighteen Hundred Fifty-eight, and there is none now ॐ ॐ

Clara could not vote, but she could work, " excellent well." All the schoolboy annoyances that a bad boy could think out in a country school, these men—servants of the people—in the Patent Office used to torment this woman.

Are men superior to women? Only when they are.

These men were not.

Clara Barton won, then lost, then she won with honors in her work in the Patent Office in Washington.

At this time there were rumblings of war all along from the Atlantic to the Pacific, from the North to the South. The rumbling grew to a mighty thundering of discord and then came war, awful, awful, war.

At Baltimore there was bloodshed—there were wounded and dead ॐ ॐ

How this great woman's heart ached no one can know except those who see and feel as Clara Barton does.

A Massachusetts regiment she knew was being brought to Washington. Clara Barton did not stop to think whether a woman should go to war or not, or " how it would look " for her to go to the station to meet a regiment of soldiers. She just went because she must: she could not help it. Her heart was bleeding for those suffering and wounded men.

Miss Barton is an organizer, a systematizer.

There is an old story that the Creator had chaos to work with at the beginning, and out of it worlds were formed. Such creative power has Miss Barton. This chaos of sick, hungry, suffering humanity; and tons of food, stores of medicines, bandages, lint, clothing, people willing to help, room, were the materials she had to use. Her clear insight, strong will, ability to do and to direct work, made Miss Barton the natural leader and she created what was required. The hungry were fed in an orderly way, the suffering was relieved, the Nation was served.

This fighting at Baltimore was the beginning of a civil war that lasted four years. Miss Barton knew that awful chaotic conditions would ever be in the wake of battle. All her heart's desire was to help the poor boys who were marching, marching, marching into an agony they could not understand until they reached it, and from whence there was no return.

Did Clara Barton think of consequences, of her own welfare? No, nor did she think of that abstract something which we call patriotism. Her thought was for humanity, the comfort, the well-being of the people who make a nation, who are the State. She loves the State not less, but humanity more. Clara Barton's work has always been for people. Her desire is to add to the sum of human happiness, to save life and to give hope.

The quarrel? That sinks into oblivion when men and women are stretching out arms for help and you can save them. Rebel pain and Federal pain? Pain is pain. Jew or Gentile, bond or free, all are one. Pain creates a genuine democracy.

Napoleon, the ambitious, crossing the Alps, gave orders for his whole army to turn out for a peasant woman who was coming down the mountains with a great load of fagots. " Respect the burden! " was the little Corporal's command.

Primitive conditions bring us back to natural living and a pure heart if we are wholesome. Great is the mind that can see the fundamental truth in everything. Let others fight if they must; Miss Barton came to bring help to the sick and wounded.

Across the Potomac River went the Northern army. Across the Potomac River followed Miss Barton with her relief cargo. The army moved inland. Miss Barton followed.

Is it strange that President Lincoln, Cabinet members, high officials, listened to Miss Barton's requests? Thousands of dollars in goods and supplies were sent to her to distribute, and all in faith, knowing that it would reach those who needed help. Miss Barton never asked for means to help—she never needed to do so. She stated the situation of sickness and suffering to the right people and they gladly gave.

She used her own money. She gave herself.

At Antietam, Fredericksburg, Bull Run, in the swamps of the South, everywhere that there was suffering, there was Miss Barton. From battlefield to battlefield she went, the deadly bullets singing around her, in rain and sleet, under the scorching sun, in darkness and tempest. She was not attached to any regiment. She was under the command of no general but her own heart: so her work was never done, she had no rest or parole. Wherever there was suffering there was her duty.

Dying soldiers left their commissions of business, their last messages of love, with her to deliver. There was no end to the work which must be done.

Can women go to war? Ask Clara Barton, as she waded through mud enriched by the life-blood of the best youth of our country. She was not following the fife and drum for glory nor did her pulse run high with the excitement of the heroic cry of battle song. Nor did the pageantry nor hope of honors intoxicate her to forget for a moment that war is the most awful thing that can come to any country.

To Miss Barton were left only the horrors of war—the woman's portion—the dead, the dying, the suffering, the disorganized remnants ❧ ❧

She faced every horror. She worked for the love of humanity. Like Walt Whitman, she took nothing for her service from her country. And like him, too, she could say, " I do not feel as the dying soldier, I am that man! "

Do unto others as ye would have them do unto you! This is what Miss Barton has done all her life.

The Civil War closed. The army was disbanded.

The bivouacs were over, save only the bivouac of the dead on many a ghostly battlefield.

Back to home and constructive living went the remnant of the legions that left office, farm and factory four years before. ❡ The horrors of the battle were exchanged in many cases for the misery of ruined business, lost property, disorganized industries. The camp had changed the current of life for many men. There is enforced idleness, unprofitable mental habits and disintegrating inactivity. For a soldier there are few, very few, days of action compared with the long days and nights of waiting for the call to arms.

Of all the hardships resulting from war, possibly none is more difficult than the struggle in adjusting life to the new conditions. Things were not at home as they had been left four years before. Everything was new and strange. The soldiers were not physically fit for peaceful work, nor were they mentally fit. Many lives were lost in war—more lives were ruined.

And then there were the missing! Wives, mothers, sisters, many of them had no certain news of death. The armies of the North and South were disbanded, but their loved ones did not return. We had no organized bureau for finding the lost, and no provision was made by the government to do it. Eighty thousand were missing from its rolls.

Clara Barton's work was known to almost every woman of the North who had any one dear to her in the war. Naturally such inquiries as these were sent to Miss Barton: " Have you seen my boy? Can you find him for me if he is still living? Is he in the hospital sick unto death? If not living, let me know, I beg of you, where he lies buried! Where? When? How? "

The pitiful prayers of the agonized came pouring in to Miss Barton and she gave her heart to the work of searching for the lost, for the purpose of comforting the widows and fatherless—those whose hearts were bleeding for those who had gone, never to return.

Four more years Miss Barton gave of her life to organizing and carrying on the work of identifying the dead and taking care of the sick, delivering the messages of the dying.

Finally, this work was done.

Clara Barton must rest. She had supped with sorrow so many days and nights, she had been on such intimate terms with death for so long, that her strength gave way. Entire change of thought was insisted upon by friends. Across the sea Miss Barton could not be appealed to by the sad and suffering. She decided to go to Switzerland, where the blue of the sky, the crisp air, the peaceful life would steal into her veins, giving new life and strength.

Is there a divinity that shapes our ends? Clara Barton went to Geneva, but she did not get away from war nor from those who needed her help. The Franco-Prussian war came. All Europe was astir with interest.

Miss Barton was visited by a company of people who were going to the center of battle to help care for the sufferers.

These people were organized for work and had an organization behind them—it was the International Red Cross of Geneva.

◖ Would Clara Barton go with them to help with her splendidly trained mind and her practical experience?

Yes, gladly; she gave them Godspeed and joined them three days later ❧ ❧

What was this International Red Cross?

At Geneva, in August, Eighteen Hundred Sixty-four, there met in Convention men and women who organized there a society known as the Red Cross—their flag was a Greek Cross in red on a white field.

The object in forming the society was to have an organization that should be recognized and respected on any battlefield anywhere. The Red Cross was to be exempt from capture and to be protected under treaty. It undertook to care for wounded men where they fell, no matter to which belligerent armies they belonged ❧ ❧

Thirty-one governments had signed this treaty.

The United States had not. Clara Barton saw at once that wherever there was War, there must go hereafter the Red Cross—organized relief service. She had used the same methods the Red Cross Society used, but without the protection of the Red Cross. A degree of health came to Miss Barton and the pressing need for her help gave her more strength.

I have heard her tell the story in brief of the Franco-Prussian war—of wading in human blood as she climbed the hill to the wounded soldiers, to the dead and dying, lying in helpless heaps on the plague-stricken field.

Oh, awful war!

Clara Barton worked with the organized force of men and women; disentangled the dying from the dead; had tents erected where the surgeons could work to advantage. Tents were there, too, where patients were carried to a clean bed, and where nurses ministered to them.

There followed days, weeks, months of work for Miss Barton, organizing, directing and working with her own hands.

Again the war was over.

Again Miss Barton saw the attempts made to take up the broken and tangled threads of life by soldiers and by the wives and children of soldiers. And she saw that the Red Cross was pre-eminently a benefit to humanity.

Miss Barton came home for change of scene to recover from her work on the battlefields in Europe. She had gone to Europe for rest from war in America: she came back to America to rest from war in Europe.

Terrible as had been her experiences here, they were more terrible in France and Prussia.

There was one deep, strong purpose in her mind when she came back—the United States must sign this Convention, which thirty-one countries had already signed and from which such benefit had followed.

It was months, even years, before Miss Barton could take up this work—for work it was to get the attention of the officials and let the people know what the Red Cross would mean to us. The Red Cross is not a war measure, but as Miss Barton says: " The Red Cross shall teach war to make war upon itself.

" The Red Cross means, not national aid for the needs of the people. but the people's aid for the need of the nation."

Miss Barton told the officials in Washington why we should ally ourselves with this international, humane measure, even though we should never again be driven into war. She told them the history of the Red Cross.

At the Battle of Solferino, June Twenty-four, Eighteen Hundred Fifty-nine, a citizen of Switzerland, M. Jean Henri Durant, was present. The awful suffering that was caused there because of the lack of organization and sufficient help caused M. Durant to call the attention of the world to this particular horror of war and to suggest a remedy. He proposed that a society should be formed in every country in time of peace for training nurses, and collecting supplies so that when war came there should be this relief at hand. The plan was well received and resulted in an international conference at Geneva in October, Eighteen Hundred Sixty-three. This, in time, resulted in the diplomatic congress, where fourteen nations signed the Geneva Convention. This made no direct provisions for Red Cross societies, but made such possible.

This was an international peace measure, at heart, an entering wedge for peace.

Now, in the year Ninteen Hundred Ten, the Convention has been ratified by forty-three nations and is an international power.

❧ Miss Barton spoke to many large audiences, and finally educated the people so that they realized the value of what she was urging upon their attention.

She gave her own observations on the field—the futility of attempts made by charitable persons in the United States to relieve sufferings caused by the devastations of the Franco-Prussian war. She said: " Ships were sent over from the United States freighted with supplies, but when these things arrived no one was authorized to receive them, and they for the most part went to utter waste. Had they borne the stamp of the Red Cross they would have been forwarded, and through them a vast amount of misery might have been saved. It was indeed a pity that so much generous effort should have failed of its end. " In a moving army the elements of destruction, armed men and munitions of war, have the right of way; and the means of preserving and sustaining even their own lives are left to bring up the rear as best they can. Hence, when the shock and crash of battle is over, and troops are advancing or retreating and all roads are blocked, and the medical staff trying to force its way through with supplies, prompt and adequate relief can scarcely ever reach the wounded. The darkness of night comes down upon them like a funeral pall, as they lie in their blood, tortured with thirst and traumatic fever."

At last the President sent out a proclamation setting forth the necessity for the United States to ratify this convention, and in the year Eighteen Hundred Eighty-two it was done.

Miss Clara Barton was made the first president of the American National Red Cross Society.

Miss Barton proposed that the use of the Red Cross should be extended so that its relief should go wherever there was calamity, and this most valuable addition now has international sanction. It is known over the world as the "American Amendment."

¶ It did seem as though Miss Barton's lifework were done when she had served humanity as she had, and had caused her own nation to ratify this international measure.

But she has done several lifeworks since.

She is a great commander, is Miss Barton. She went, or sent her relief corps and provisions, to the Michigan Fire sufferers, to Florida, yellow-fever stricken, to the Johnstown Flood, Russian Famine, South Carolina tidal wave, Armenian Massacre, and to the Spanish-American War.

Miss Barton has commanded a battleship, but not for belligerent purposes. She took this ship with provisions into dangerous waters where the enemy was on every side. She was perpetually having to make decisions where our national interests were involved. Her every action and word must be diplomatic. The enemy was an enemy, and yet humanity must be served.

Miss Barton was the general always. She was diplomatic and just. She never offended her superiors in office, nor did she receive from them anything but the high respect due her.

She never asked for favors or aid because she was a woman. Her work has ever been done as by a human being for humanity. Miss Barton never has had a protector in any way since her childhood, nor has she ever needed one.

She has always had a clear and distinct purpose and work that filled her life full. No one has ever whispered that her work was inferior to any other—in public office, on the battlefield, or where calamity had been. She has done, magnificently well, deeds pronounced impossible for woman.

And she has done what no other American has done.

The head of the Frauenverein or Woman's Union of Baden, the Grand Duchess of Baden, gave to Clara Barton a Red Cross brooch. The Grand Duke decorated her with the Gold Cross of Remembrance ❧ ❧

Empress Augusta, with the Emperor of Germany, conferred upon her the Iron Cross of Merit, accompanied by the colors of Germany and the Red Cross, and the Iron Cross is given only to those who have earned it on the battlefield.

Miss Barton has lived with the great. All the honors that even the ambitious could desire have been bestowed upon her. Her own country loves her with a deep, abiding love and she has no living peer.

" She was born in Eighteen Hundred Twenty-one," do you say? " Then she must be a very old woman now? " Oh, no, she is not. I saw her last December and she was not old. She was animated with plans of work for humanity.

The aspiration of her heart was not dimmed nor was her vision of truth and the ideal in the least clouded. And in a letter from her, only a short time ago, there were unmistakable signs of the strength unquenched by the flight of years.

Oh, no, she is not old nor is she limited by traditions. She has proven to women and men for all time that any human being can do the work she desires to do when her desire is great and good.

Alice Hubbard.

ON the evening of May Fourteenth, Nineteen Hundred Twelve, just a month after Clara Barton had joined the Choir Invisible, there was a National Memorial Service held for her in the Garrick Theater, Philadelphia.

The Philadelphia School for Nurses made this the opportunity for their annual meeting. Miss Lilian Frazier, who is principal of this school, had much to do in arranging the Memorial, and great credit is due her for making this evening one long to be remembered ✒ ✒

Clara Barton had anticipated that there might be such a service, and had said to her friend of many years, Doctor Eugene Underhill: " If there should be such a meeting, Doctor, I want you to give the address. It is not at all necessary to have a memorial; but if my friends desire it, I want you to be the principal speaker. Do not make it a serious occasion. Let the people laugh if they want to, and tell stories. There is no reason why it should be solemn." ✒ ✒

To carry out the wishes of Clara Barton seemed to be every one's desire. It was not a solemn occasion, but it was an impressive one. The stage and the boxes of this beautiful theater were decorated with flags that had been presented to Clara Barton. Some of them were of heavy silk, rich and magnificent. Some of them were battle-stained and bullet-scarred. Some of them Clara Barton had carried on to the battlefield, holding the Red Cross high, that the sick, the wounded, the dying, might see, while she was yet a long way off, that help was coming.

There were flags from England, Germany, Belgium, Italy, France, Russia, Cuba, Prussia, Holland, Greece and Switzerland.

Even the unspeakable Turks knew of the loving ministrations of this woman, and had given her their flag.

Just to have seen this collection of flags from over the world, brought together through the mercy and loving-kindness of one woman, made us feel that a Peace Proclamation was not an impossible thing.

Clara Barton had seen several of these countries in the agonies of war. All these countries had received, through their wounded and dying, the ministrations of Clara Barton. Her heart had throbbed with theirs in the agony and horrors of war. And there was also the flag of the United States.

Doctor A. Monae Lesser, a war surgeon of renown, who had been on the battlefield with Clara Barton, told us a little of his experience as Surgeon-in-Chief of the American National Red Cross. He was with Clara Barton many days and weeks in the Spanish-American war. He said he never knew a human being to have such endurance as this little woman had.

Clara Barton was seventy-six years old when she worked in Cuba with Doctor Lesser. He had seen her on the battlefield, horrible as only a battlefield can be, slippery and awful with the lifeblood of our best American youths; the sun pouring its stifling heat upon the dead and dying, and the thermometer registering one hundred ten degrees in the shade. Men fainted from the fatigue and heat and nerve-strain. But Clara Barton carried life and hope to the suffering, days and nights, without rest or cessation from work. " Her endurance is unprecedented, and I have never known her equal."

Doctor Underhill, later in the evening, told us that Doctor Lesser, himself, after the battle of San Juan Hill, had worked at the operating-table for thirty hours without rest. And all that time, and for hours after, Clara Barton did not rest.

Among the ruins of the battlefield, Clara Barton organized a hospital corps; she constructed a temporary hospital and manned it. Her executive ability was so great that men in high standing in office, even in military service, gladly did her bidding, knowing they were responding to superior wisdom.

Mrs. John A. Logan, wife of General Logan, told us of the relief funds that were sent to Clara Barton in this Spanish-American war. The women in Revolutionary times seemed to have had a better understanding of what the sick and the wounded needed on the battlefield, and they sent materials which nurses and doctors could use.

But in later years we either get a mania or a panic when we are asked to look upon a serious condition. We act with as much reason as people who, when their buildings are afire, carry out the empty birdcage, leaving things of value.

We sent ball-dresses, dancing-slippers, remnants from the milliner's store after the season was passed, ribbons, cake, candy, bunting, and dress-suits out of fashion. These contributions were estimated of so much value in money. Then we smacked our philanthropic lips, like a Lord Mayor of London, as he tasted charity soup, and said, " Excellent food for the poor! "

No one but those equipped with commonsense, mechanical genius, and New England economy could have made something out of some of the boxes that were sent for the relief of the starving Cubans.

Clara Barton took this conglomeration, these hit-and-miss collections, and utilized them.

At that time our hearts were very much exercised over the starving Cubans, and we sent to Cuba the relief funds—some of which I have suggested. Of course, there were food and clothing of real value.

President McKinley gave Clara Barton command of the ship, *State of Texas,* and said to her, " Go to the starving Cubans, if you can, with your relief-ship, and distribute as only you know how." ❧ ❧

But the Spaniards were there before her. Clara Barton saw the flash and heard the terrible explosion which caused the battleship *Maine* to sink out of sight, carrying with it hundreds of American sailor-boys ❧ ❧

" I am with the wounded," she telegraphed. The navy under Sampson and Miss Barton with her ship assembled at Key West, and as Doctor Underhill said, " There met in this harbor two opposing, tremendous powers: Admiral Sampson, who came to kill; Clara Barton, who came to save."

These powers were sent by one nation, the Savior to follow the Destroyer ৶ ৶

Stupid, uncivilized people are we, not yet capable of using our reason and judgment to a purpose!

Clara Barton tried to get the right of way to carry out her commission, to get relief to the starving Cubans in the fastnesses of the Cuban jungle.

But Sampson said: " Not so. I go first! I am here to keep supplies out of Cuba."

And Clara Barton said: " When you make an opening, I will go in. I know my place is not to precede you. You will go and do the horrible deed. I will follow you, and out of the human wreckage, restore what I can."

Oh, the horrible, useless, tragic waste, which no Peace Congress has yet been able to avert!

O treacherous Fate! that made this great woman of peace, with a mother heart which enfolded the whole world as her children, wait and see men of blood go before her to kill, wound, devastate, before she might go and do what little she could to repair this ravage of war!

Doctor Underhill told us much of Clara Barton's experience in the Spanish-American war. He told us of the headquarters of the Red Cross over which Clara Barton presided.

There were tons of supplies sent to the starving Cubans; but Miss Barton, as I said, could not reach them. She must wait and do what merciful deeds she could.

And one day after the Battle of San Juan Hill the Colonel of a certain Rough Rider Regiment came to the Red Cross Headquarters with a blue bandanna around his neck, and asked to buy supplies to relieve the wretchedness of his sick and wounded. Doctor Gardner brought the message to his chief. Clara Barton said, " We have nothing to sell."

Doctor Gardner returned saying: " The Colonel says they must

have something to relieve his men. They are in very great need."
Clara Barton said, " Tell him to ask for it, then."
So Colonel Roosevelt asked for aid, and out of their supply they
filled a bag with things he wanted. And he, the vigorous, sturdy,
muscular power that he is, took it on his back and strode away,
carrying relief to his men who so urgently needed the help.
❡ A few years passed. Clara Barton had received honors from
almost every country of Europe. Decorations, recognitions,
priceless jewels, were bestowed upon her.

For more than twenty years Miss Barton alone and unassisted
was practically the Red Cross of this country. She gave her life
and her income to it.

She had given to the International Red Cross Society the ideas
which she had worked out here, and which was her own inaugura-
tion, known as the " American Amendment." This idea was not to
confine the Red Cross service to war. But the organized Red
Cross Society should go wherever there was human suffering
which came from fire, flood, earthquake, devastation—public
calamities of any kind where systematized relief was required.
❡ Then she organized what was known as " First-Aid Work." Her
purpose was to have in every city, town, village and hamlet
First-Aid Societies—that is, people trained to know what to do
in case of accident or calamity. It was their duty to go where
accidents or disasters occurred, just as firemen are required to go
when the call of fire comes.

Miss Barton was an organizer. She organized the Institution of
the American Amendment and First-Aid Work.

But in Nineteen Hundred Six it occurred to certain people that it
might be desirable to get control of the Red Cross in America.
As newspapers of April Twenty-third, Nineteen Hundred Twelve,
said, " This was a clique of Washington politicians and ambitious
society people." They were strong financially, socially and
politically ❧ ❧

They went before Congress and secured an amended charter for the Red Cross, which included none of Miss Barton's friends, but Miss Barton's name was still there. This was done without Miss Barton's knowledge or consent.

Because the name of Clara Barton headed the list in the amended law, the bill was passed. The Members of Congress supposed it was a bill that Miss Barton wanted, because her name headed the list. However, Miss Barton was ignored by the new organization. Her name has never been mentioned in their reports or publications. She was never invited to attend any meeting of the Society which she had created and established in this country.

I do not know who made the accusations against Clara Barton's methods of distributing supplies in times of war.

The term "Accusation" used in connection with Clara Barton is not only the blunder of boors, but it is crime and sacrilege. But an accusation was made that she had diverted the use of supplies sent to her.

That is to say, we sent supplies to the starving Cubans. Clara Barton could not reach them, but she could reach the sick, the dying, the sons, the brothers, the fathers, the lovers, of the people who has sent these supplies, and she did not withhold her hand. She gave to the children and to the relatives the supplies which American citizens had sent to her.

This was the diversion.

The great, beautiful, loving heart of Clara Barton was bowed in grief, different from any grief it had ever felt before.

She knew ingratitude. She had not expected gratitude. She worked for humanity, for whom she had a love unparalleled in history. Any wounded, sick or suffering human being she was friend to, and would minister to him. Then, when the people approved her for so diverting supplies, an investigation of her accounts was ordered without ceremony. They went to her headquarters and took her books from her. They said, " Clara

Barton has money; where did she get it? "—with eyebrows lifted. She must give an accounting of all moneys and all supplies. They asked Clara Barton for an accounting of those things she had given out on the battlefield, in the midst of shot and shell, among the groans of the sick, the wounded, the dying: food and medicine and bandages that she had distributed in the turmoil of battlefields, where had lain the wounded for many hours, and Clara Barton their first relief. They demanded of her an accounting of all supplies given out under these conditions.

General William H. Sears, who was Clara Barton's private secretary for many months, and Field Agent at Galveston, told us of opening many letters containing checks made out to Clara Barton—not as President of the Red Cross, not as President of the National First-Aid Association—but to Clara Barton, a woman, to use as she personally desired and as her best judgment saw fit. A large percentage of cash contributions came in this way. Many letters containing remittances stated, " For your own personal use."

Many and many checks were sent to her just in this way.

But an investigation was ordered.

It was not a Congressional, but a Red Cross investigation. On this committee were two or three Members of Congress.

" But where did Clara Barton get her money? " said the gossips. " We have investigated and we find that her father left her but five hundred dollars, and this she gave to her brother many years ago. She used eleven thousand dollars in identifying the dead in their shallow graves on the battlefield after the War. Where did she get that eleven thousand dollars? "

The usurpers must know.

General Sears said that he was one of the three attorneys selected by Miss Barton's friends to defend her in this investigation. I believe the glorious General would defend Clara Barton with the last drop of blood in his veins.

So one day when he and Clara Barton were discussing this sorrow, he said: " Miss Barton, where did you get your money? They are going to ask this, and I had better know. I want no surprises sprung." ৯ৡ ৯ৡ

" Surely," said Miss Barton; " it is right that they should know. I was brought up in New England, and I have the New England thrift ৯ৡ ৯ৡ

" I began teaching school when I was fourteen and taught for a number of years. I saved my money and invested it successfully.

" I had a Government position in Washington, being the first woman clerk. I saved my earnings and invested them well.

" I lectured for several years. The people wanted to hear what I had to say, and I received one hundred dollars for every lecture I could give, and this money I saved.

" This of course was no great sum as businessmen count money.

" In Eighteen Hundred Forty-nine one of my brothers and Another, went out to California to the gold-field. Two years later my brother returned. The Other did not. But he sent to me by my brother ten thousand dollars in gold—all his savings. I put this in the banks, but I felt that I could never use this gold nor even the interest on it. It was too sacred a fund. But after the War, when the lonely cries came from the mothers and wives and sweethearts to know where their beloved lay, and if their beloved were dead, I knew this fund was not too sacred for this use. I used eleven thousand dollars of that money for that purpose.

" As you know, the Government after a time returned to me not only eleven thousand dollars, but gave as a compensation four thousand more. And I had fifteen thousand dollars to put in the bank to hold for another sacred cause."

Beside that, while Miss Barton was in Europe, assisting the Red Cross in Paris, Edmund Dwight came to Miss Barton, stating that he had a shipload of supplies and about one hundred fifty thousand dollars in cash contributed by the people of Boston to the people of Paris. Mr. Dwight did not know how to dispense this money. He was sick and had to go back to America. He insisted that Clara Barton with her organization should distribute it. He endorsed a draft to her for the money not yet used. So she felt compelled to take this responsibility.

One of the principles of the Red Cross Society is not to pauperize, not to spend the people's money when it is not needed, not to help those who can help themselves. There were thirty thousand dollars left of this fund when the cause for charity was no more.

Clara Barton sent the money back to Mr. Dwight in Boston. By the first mail he returned it to her and said: " This money is yours; the people of Boston want you to keep it for what you have done for humanity. Take care of it and use it as you think best." ⮞ ⮞

Again Clara Barton returned it to him, having endorsed the draft for thirty thousand dollars to Edmund Dwight, and said, " This belongs to the people of Boston."

And Mr. Dwight, with authority, placed this amount in an endowment fund, in the Massachusetts General Hospital in Boston, with this provision: that Clara Barton was to have for her own use six per cent interest on thirty thousand dollars for so long as she lived. She drew it for forty years.

Clara Barton's New England thrift caused her to be able to do consummate work with the money and means which many waste. She has given us a constant lesson in thrift. There was not a woman in that great audience at the Memorial Service who did not feel the crime of waste. We realized the economies which Clara Barton lived and practised, that she might give life and aid to those who were in dire need. Her herculean work was done with means that most men would scorn as too trivial to begin a work with. What a paltry sum it was that Clara Barton had! And great business it was officially to investigate!

" Where did she get it? "

I wonder how the people felt when they had torn from her heart with their coarse fingers her sacred secret, that they might justify their course!

What a trifling sum it was! Women of fashion could dispose of that amount of money and never know they had spent it.

Clara Barton, who knew work and how to work, as even the great prophets of work do not know, lived so simply that at her desk, at work, a piece of bread and cheese and one apple was her dinner, a frugal supper, and the most abstemious breakfast. Few have chosen to live like this. Her dress was so simple that no one tried to follow her fashion.

And yet it was demanded of her that she give an accounting of goods and food distributed to dying and wounded on the battle-field ᵴ ᵴ

The unspeakable Turk never did anything so bad as this.

From Eighteen Hundred Sixty-nine to Eighteen Hundred Seventy-one, Clara Barton worked in the Red Cross service in Europe: in the Franco-German war and its hospitals, at Haggenau, Metz, Strassburg, Belfort, Woerth, Baden Hospitals, Sedan, Montebelard, Paris (Fall of the Commune). And she was appreciated by the European Powers.

Emperor William and Empress Augusta decorated her with the Iron Cross of Prussia, the only woman who has been so honored. The Gold Cross of Remembrance was given by the Grand Duke and Grand Duchess of Baden. The Medal of the International Committee of the Red Cross of Geneva, Switzerland, was given her. She was given the Red Cross by the Queen of Servia; a Silver Medal by Empress Augusta of Germany; a Flag was voted by the Congress of Berne, Switzerland; Jewels were given by the Grand Duchess of Baden; a Diploma of Honor by German war veterans; Jewels by the Queen of Prussia; Diploma of Honor from the Red Cross of Austria; Diploma and Decorations by the Sultan of Turkey; Diploma and Decorations by the Prince of

Armenia; Commended by President McKinley in a Message to
Congress; Diploma and Decorations by Spain; Vote of thanks by
the Cortes of Spain; Vote of thanks by the Portuguese Red Cross;
Decoration of the Order of the Red Cross by the Czar of Russia
in Nineteen Hundred Two.

She has represented our own Government at four International
Red Cross Conferences. During the Civil War, beginning with
meeting the Massachusetts Sixth Volunteers in Washington on
their arrival from the Baltimore attack, April Nineteenth,
Eighteen Hundred Sixty-one, she was on the battlefields and
personally administered relief at Cedar Mountain, Falmouth,
Fort Wagner, Deep Bottom, Chantilly, Fredericksburg, The
Wilderness, Petersburg, Second Bull Run, Charleston, Spottsyl-
vania, Richmond, Antietam, Morris Island, The Mine, Annapolis.
The Summer of Eighteen Hundred Sixty-five she spent at
Andersonville, identifying the dead, thirteen thousand.

Four years following the Civil War she spent searching for the
missing men of war—eighty thousand of them.

Seven years she worked in the United States to educate our
people to understand the benefit of organizing the Red Cross, and
taking part in International Red Cross Associations.

From Eighteen Hundred Eighty-one, when the Michigan Forest
Fires made the Red Cross aid necessary, to the year Nineteen
Hundred Four, through flood and fire and famine, hurricane and
tidal wave, Clara Barton ministered to our own people, and without remuneration.

Throughout the Cuban War she was on the battlefield.

Texas, Michigan, Illinois and Cuba have done her honor, and
have given recognition of her great work.

As a nation our recognition was to order an investigation of how
Miss Barton spent her funds.

But this is not the way the nation feels toward Clara Barton!
That was only an exigency, an excrescence, a malformation, a wart

on the nose, that assumed a prominence it does not deserve. The people of the United States reverence, admire, and devotedly love Clara Barton.

Doctor Hubbell said that Clara Barton was always young. Although she had lived more than ninety years, she never gave the impression to any of her most intimate friends that she was an old woman. " Her age knew no time."

She was a worker from infancy. She knew the value of time, of every material. She was an economist. From her early childhood she was economically free. She gave to the world nearly a century of work, Clara Barton's work, taking neither vacation nor recreation. Like Heine, she was refreshed by a great thought.

Her interests were world interests. The pettiness of provincialism was never hers. She had no time to hate; only time to serve, to love, to give.

Clara Barton is glorious today. She is not dead. I could not even say that she is away, for Doctor Underhill in his Memorial address told us this story:

Stephen E. Barton, nephew of Miss Barton, who was with her often on relief fields; Doctor Julien B. Hubbell for twenty-three years General Field Agent of the American Red Cross; and Doctor Eugene Underhill were with Clara Barton when she passed from sight. It was they who saw that her wishes were carried out to the letter; that there should be no solemn mourning; that they should make no event of her passing. She said that death was only one of the things incident to life, a part of life.

It was Miss Barton's wish that her ashes should be laid in the cemetery at Oxford, Massachusetts, near those of her father, mother, brothers and sisters.

These friends had engaged a car to take all that was mortal of Clara Barton to its last resting-place, and there was to be no transfer going from Glen Echo, Maryland, to Oxford, Massachusetts. The route was by way of Washington and New York.

From Jersey City the car is usually put on a ferry and sent across the Hudson.

Stephen E. Barton, Doctor Hubbell and Doctor Underhill had just retired on this car. It was near midnight.

When they reached the station for the ferry a brakeman came along and said: " There is such a fog covering the city, the river and the harbor, that it is impossible for us to use the ferry tonight to carry this car over. You will have to unload, cross the Hudson in the Tube, and an automobile will take you across the city to the Pennsylvania Station."

" What shall we do with the casket? "

" Put it in a baggage-car," said the brakeman, unconcernedly.

" We will see that it gets across. You 'll have to hurry."

The three men were concerned.

Clara Barton, no matter what the provocation, had never deserted the dead or the dying. She had never betrayed a trust. That casket could not go in a baggage-car. They could not entrust those precious ashes to stranger hands.

It was after midnight now. The cold, penetrating fog made them shiver. The city seemed desolate, and most unfriendly.

Two stood by the casket and one went in search of a vehicle to take them across the city. There was no time to lose if they made that train they had planned to take.

At last an express-wagon was found. An Irishman was the driver, and his old white horse was scarcely able to draw a load. However, the expressman was finally persuaded to undertake the task of making the transfer.

Doctor Hubbell and Stephen Barton stood, one on each side of the casket in the wagon. Doctor Underhill rode with the driver to inspire and urge him on.

The Irishman grumbled and growled, and met every request of Doctor Underhill's with a difficulty.

The cold deepened.

The desolation and the sadness of the whole situation was creeping into the hearts of the three men.

Finally the driver said: " We can never get up that Forty-fifth Street hill. It 's impossible. I say it can't be done. My old horse will never do it." Doctor Underhill had his doubts, too.

However, he said: " It has got to be done. We 'll push going up the hill and get along somehow. Urge your horse all you can." And the old horse pulled and tugged at its load.

How indifferent the old man was! How rough and wretched the pavement! How discordant the rumble and rattle of the wagon! It was so unlike what they wanted for this beautiful lady, this great Mother-Woman whom they longed to serve.

Finally the Irishman said, " Who is in that box back there you are making such a fuss about? "

" Who is in the casket? " said Doctor Underhill. " That is Clara Barton." ✒ ✒

" Clara Barton, you did n't say Clara Barton! "

" Yes, Clara Barton," said Doctor Underhill.

" Not THE Clara Barton? " gasped the Irishman.

" Yes, THE Clara Barton."

" My God! She saved my father's life. He was a Confederate soldier on the battlefield at Antietam. You don't mean that that is Clara Barton back there! He was bleeding to death and she saved him! " ✒ ✒

" Yes, that is The Great Clara Barton."

" I 'll get you to the station in time, stranger. I 'll get you to the station in time." And he laid the lash on the old horse.

" Why, you 're cold, stranger—you 're cold. I have got a horse-blanket here. It smells pretty bad, but it will keep you warm a bit." And with the tenderness of a woman he tucked that old horse-blanket around the Doctor and wrapped him up in it.

❦ And Doctor Underhill knew that Clara Barton was not dead. She lived again in the touch of a rough man's hand, made tender

by the mercy and loving-kindness of Clara Barton. They made
the Forty-fifth Street hill all right, and they reached the station
in time. The Irishman threw the reins over the old horse's
back, pulled off his hat in the chilly night, and said, " If you
will just allow me, sir," and with tears running down his face,
he took hold of the casket as with a trained and gentle hand, and
with Stephen Barton, Doctor Hubbell and Doctor Underhill,
carried the casket into a waiting car of the second section of the
Federal Express. This train had been divided by order of the
railroad authorities, one section waiting for the honor of carrying
to its last resting-place the greatest woman of all times.
And so has
Clara Barton joined the choir invisible
Of those immortal dead who live again
In minds made better by their presence; live
In pulses stirred to generosity,
In deeds of daring rectitude, in scorn
For miserable aims that end with self.
In thoughts sublime that pierce the night like stars,
And with their mild persistence urge man's search
To vaster issues.
So she has joined the choir invisible
Whose music is the gladness of the world.

Alice Hubbard.

————————

ONE day while visiting with Clara Barton at her home in
Glen Echo, I asked her to tell me what was the most terrible
experience she had ever had on a field.
She answered promptly, as though the event were well classified
in her mind:
" It was at the battle of Antietam. The poor boys were falling so
fast that I rushed up into the line of firing to save them from
bleeding to death, by temporarily binding up their wounds.

Bullets went through my clothing, but I did not think of danger. I loaded myself with canteens, went to a nearby spring and filled them with water. " I staggered under the load that I carried. The wounded were crying for water. I went to one poor boy who was wild with thirst. I stooped, lifted his head, and was giving him water from a canteen when a cannon-ball took his head off, covering me with blood and brains.

" I dropped the headless body and went to the next wounded soldier. And so all day I worked through this awful battle, and refused to retire, though officers and men tried to drive me back. " At night I assisted the surgeons at the rude tables at the farm-house under the apple-trees. They amputated limbs and dressed wounds all night long. The morning light revealed to us limbs that had been thrown to one side during the work of the night. It was like a great pile of wood. My dress and shoes were soaked with blood ❧ ❧

" That night the surgeons had no candles. I brought them my supplies, and soon there was a blaze of light about the operating table. They had no food, but from my wagons I brought them meal which we had used in packing the medicines and supplies. " I think I was in the greatest danger at Fredericksburg, where I crossed the pontoon-bridge under fire to reach the wounded on the other shore. There I worked all night long.

" The weather had changed during the night and turned bitter cold. When morning came I found many of the Confederates wounded and frozen into the mud. I took an axe and chopped their bodies loose from the ground and helped take them to deserted negro cabins. There we built roaring fires in the old fireplaces, washed and dressed their wounds and fed the men with gruel. We warmed them with heated bricks taken from the tops of the chimneys." ❧ ❧

After Miss Barton had told me these horrible stories, I asked her to tell me the most beautiful experience she had ever had on the field. Again without hesitation the story was on her mind. It was this:

" It was down in Virginia on Aquia Creek.

" I was walking along beside the long columns of infantry one day. We suddenly reached this stream, as wide as a street. " I was young and strong and loved to walk. I had four great wagons loaded with supplies for sick and wounded soldiers. These were coming in the rear. I decided I would not get my feet wet, but wait for my wagons and cross in one of them.

" The soldiers splashed into the stream in solid ranks, the water being about a foot deep.

" Suddenly the captain of a company in midstream called out: ' Company, Fours, Left, March! Halt! Right, Dress! Front! Now boys,' said the captain, ' I want you to kneel down in the water, on your right knees, and let Miss Barton walk across this stream on your left knees.'

" This order the soldiers instantly obeyed. I stepped from knee to knee, the soldiers reaching up and holding my hands. And thus I passed dry-shod to the other shore."

As Miss Barton related this incident the tears streamed down her cheeks and she said, " This was the most beautiful tribute of love and devotion ever offered to me in my life."

Some people have criticised Miss Barton's business methods. The following is one of my experiences with her. I leave it with the intelligent people who read to judge whether these criticisms are just or not. When the awful storm struck Galveston, Miss Barton invited me to accompany her to that field.

The night before we started I stayed at her home. After supper she came out on the porch of her beautiful home at Glen Echo, Maryland, and sitting down in front of me said, " General, what are we going to! "

" We are going to an awful scene of death and desolation."

" Yes, General, but what are we going to? "

" We are going to nothing, are n't we? " (Almost impatiently.)
" I suppose we are."

Then she continued very earnestly:

" Why, at Johnstown, I hunted half a day and could not find a thimble with which to do some necessary sewing. Here, General," she said, handing me a bunch of keys, " take these keys and go through my house. Wherever you can find anything that can be used where there is nothing, you pack it up."

Then I fully realized what she meant.

I suppose her critics would say, " How unbusinesslike! "

I took the keys and went through her great house with its thirty-two rooms and seventy-six closets. There I found carefully stored away, supplies of every description. There, too, I found packing-chests, trunks, valises, telescopes, all ready for use.

" I worked until nearly morning packing every thing I thought could be used where there was nothing. The next morning two great dray-loads of these goods were taken to the depot and shipped to Galveston. Everything I packed up that night was used at Galveston. When Miss Barton and her help reached the stricken city we went at once to the Tremont Hotel. Miss Barton was called in conference with Mayor Jones and the Relief Committee ৯ ৯

Mayor Jones offered to turn the whole field with all supplies and money over to Miss Barton for her administrations.

" No, Mr. Mayor," said Miss Barton; " I can not do this. I did not come here to take possession of the field. I came simply to help and to give you the benefit of such experience as I may have gained on the other fields for your assistance on this one. I would be glad to serve as a humble member of your committee."

Miss Barton was immediately made a member of the committee, and became its adviser and practically its head.

" Have ward committees been organized? " Miss Barton asked.

" No," answered the Mayor.

" How many wards are there in the city of Galveston? "

Mayor Jones replied that there were twelve.

" Do you go at once and organize strong committees in each ward. Provide ward headquarters, and a storeroom where each ward committee can take care of supplies furnished.

" Have your committees canvass each ward thoroughly and get the names and exact needs, which shall include, in the case of clothing, the exact sizes of the clothing needed.

" Have your committees make a requisition on the Red Cross for each person who is in need of clothing, and send all requisitions to my headquarters. My corps of helpers will see that these requisitions are promptly filled. The goods will be sent to the ward headquarters for distribution."

This did not sound unbusinesslike to me.

Mayor Jones and a committee proceeded at once to organize these ward committees.

Miss Barton immediately called her staff about her and said to us, " Now we must get to work! "

To Mr. Lewis she said, " Do you go at once and secure a good saddle-horse and direct the organization of Mayor Jones' Ward Committees ❧ ❧

" General Sears, go out into the city and secure a headquarters building for the Red Cross. It must be large, and suitable for the classification and storage of our supplies, just as a department-store is arranged, so that goods can be quickly issued.

" Mr. Talmage, you will go at once to Houston and stay there until every car of Red Cross supplies is forwarded to Galveston.

" General Sears, when you have secured a proper building, engage as many carts as are necessary to bring supplies from the steamer-docks and railroad-depots. Take with you a man with paste and brush, and have one of our big paper Red Crosses pasted on every package before it is put in any cart.

" Major McDowell, you will go to the headquarters secured by

General Sears, and take charge of the unpacking, classification and issuing of supplies.

" Mr. Ward, you will go with Major McDowell and open an office at headquarters. Keep a careful book-account of the receipt of all supplies and money received and issued.

" Mr. Marsh, you will go with Mr. Ward and be his assistant. Mrs. Ward, you will stay by me and take such directions as I may have to give you from time to time. Miss Coombs, you are to be my stenographer and typewriter; and I think I may be able to find enough work to keep you busy.

" Miss Spradlin, as soon as General Sears has secured his headquarters building, you will go to him and arrange for proper space for the opening up of an orphanage. Then proceed to gather up all homeless, uncared-for orphans in the city, and take care of them." ❧ ❧

After our headquarters was opened up and everything well organized, Miss Barton gave orders that a rooming and boarding house be established at our headquarters. From the wreck of an orphan asylum in the city were secured furniture, beds, cooking-utensils, and dining-room service. Soon the entire staff and corps of assistants were quartered in the headquarters building, and taking their meals there at very small expense.

" No more big hotel bills—the money must be saved for the flood-sufferers," said Miss Barton to me.

Very little had to be furnished aside from fresh vegetables and meats. We used from the supplies shipped to us, which was the most economical thing for the Red Cross to do. Not one out of ten of the Red Cross helpers received any pay for service. Miss Barton commissioned me to proceed at once to the coast towns of Texas and find out what the people needed. She had heard that these people were in great need. Her information was true ❧ ❧

I scoured the country, and made a list of the people in each place

with their exact needs. Every night, assisted by committees, I
prepared requisitions for each individual sufferer and telegraphed
them to Miss Barton. It was always midnight before these
telegrams were sent, but before noon the next day the great boxes
of supplies arrived; and the clothing for each individual was found
tied in a separate package, carefully labeled with the name of
each. In a few hours every destitute person was well supplied
with clothing that would fit.

The object of the Red Cross relief is to make the people self-
supporting. As soon as this is accomplished, all relief is withdrawn.

❡ Early in the Spring Miss Barton furnished the people of the
coast district millions of strawberry-plants. This she found would
be the quickest way of putting the people on a self-supporting
basis. And her judgment was good!

For years after, Miss Barton received at Glen Echo boxes of
strawberries grown from these plants which she had given to
these people in their time of need.

One little incident, out of many, which occurred in Galveston, is
an example of the dramatic events of Miss Barton's life. When
she and her staff arrived in Galveston from Texas City they
entered carriages and were driven to the Tremont Hotel.

As we were leaving the dock, an officer of the Texas National
Guard in the uniform of a Major of Cavalry, sprang from his
horse and ran alongside our carriage holding to it with one hand.
With the other he lifted his cap and smiled up to Miss Barton.
" Don't you know me, Miss Barton, don't you know me? "
Miss Barton who was seated at my side, leaned forward and said:
" No, I seem to have forgotten you. Tell me who you are."

" Miss Barton, I saw you at the Battle of Sedan in the Franco-
Prussian War. You nursed me there in the field hospital."
Miss Barton took his hand. She remembered him then and told
him to come and see her. This soldier was the son of an English
nobleman who had served with the French in this war.

Another incident I must give here: A Boston lady, the wife of a Massachussetts ex-Congressman, visiting in Washington recently, related the following incident about Miss Barton.

Shortly after the War I attended a reception in Boston given in honor of Miss Barton. It was a full-dress affair, and the elite of Boston were there. I stood beside General Butler and said to him, " What beautiful arms Miss Barton has!"

General Butler replied, " Yes, and I have seen those beautiful arms red with human blood to the elbows!"

Miss Barton will surely be accredited her true place in history. The memory of her great deeds is enshrined in the hearts of the people. We shall ever be grateful that such a woman has been among us on earth, blessing us with her presence for more than ninety years.

General William H. Sears.

TO the memory of the late departed Miss Clara Barton, formerly President of the American Society of the Red Cross, who during the war in the year Eighteen Hundred Seventy was in Karlsruhe, and afterward founded a comprehensive and blessed work in Strassburg. Her Royal Highness, the Grand Duchess Louise, has most graciously inscribed the following lines addressed to the General Secretary of our Society. (Translated by Hermann P. Riccius.)

The public press has within the last few days brought tidings from America of the death of Miss Clara Barton, a name well known there, and which recalls wonderful memories to many here. However, it is unknown to many in Germany, because her work was done here many years ago.

It is my task to express in these few lines in our publication of the Baden Women's Society, a commemoration of Miss Clara Barton, and to express the gratitude with which I think of her and will always think of her in looking back on the events of forty-two years, which have connected me with her in constant affection.

¶ When, in Eighteen Hundred Seventy, the war had thoroughly awakened us to the great relief-work under the Red Cross, and the neutral powers far and near willingly offered to co-operate and sign the covenant of the Red Cross, there came, in the middle of September, to Karlsruhe, the President of the American Red Cross. She was supplied with funds from America, and was accompanied by several representatives of her Society to offer us her assistance.

Miss Clara Barton was then entirely unknown to us.

In America she was not unknown. There she had, during the war between the North and the South in Eighteen Hundred Sixty-one to Eighteen Hundred Sixty-five, summoned forces for the care of the sick in the field, gathered them together, and organized them into a hospital corps.

She was the first American woman who, knowing the needs of the wounded, alone, unafraid, independent, went into the battlefield to care for the sick and the wounded. At each battle she worked with inimitable devotion, assisting the Doctors, never fearing the shower of bullets, in order to aid the wounded.

She opened the way for woman's care of the sick in war in her country. After she had worked long alone, her example inspired many assistants. The place which she made and won for herself then was unprecedented. The commanding general, General Grant, was thoroughly appreciative of her work. In the entire army she won honor, gratitude and admiration. This was true until the end of her life. In the heart of the nation she was held in great honor.

The Red Cross movement, which was then beginning, she grasped with her peculiar energy, clear understanding, and unselfish affection. She was chosen the first President of the Society of the Red Cross in America. In this capacity she came to Germany to us, filled with the desire to work and help us wherever it might be to our benefit. She had not been in a foreign country, she did not know the German language, yet she did not hesitate to go upon the battlefield in a foreign country wherever her help was needed. So she came to Karlsruhe. Other workers of the Red Cross accompanied her. They went to other places to work. But Clara Barton offered herself as near as possible to the frontier and to Strassburg, then still besieged.

She was at that time fifty years of age. She was quiet and unobstrusive in her bearing; indeed of such great modesty that it only rarely occurred that she could be induced to speak of her own experiences. When she came to us I learned to know her, and suggested to her that she inspect our hospitals. As she was unfamiliar with the German language, we could not ask her to go into the field at once.

After a comparatively short time she said that our auxiliary for the voluntary care of the sick was better organized than the American. She could offer no betterments for the temporary hospitals ❧ ❧

But she saw that the work in the immediate vicinity of the troops was not well carried on by our organization.

With clear insight as to what was to come, and with great self-sacrifice, she offered herself to us for work there when the fall of Strassburg came.

And she was of great use then. She was the first one who, as President of the Red Cross, immediately after the fall of Strassburg, appeared there in the midst of the frightful scene which had occurred, and at once sought and found a place with the other workers as a welcome neutral.

The French military hospitals were cared for by the French army nurses as well as by Deaconesses and Sisters of Mercy.

The German wounded were not brought into the city, but were transferred to German relief-stations as quickly as possible. The many victims among the inhabitants lay in the great municipal hospitals ✦ ✦

Miss Clara Barton, recognizing what a deep sympathy existed on the other side of the Rhine for the hard-pressed inhabitants of the fortress of Strassburg, perceived at once the way in which their sympathy might be brought into practical use.

In an embittered and defeated community, the wives and daughters especially were discouraged, and it was difficult to bring them back to their former work. Business and trade were completely disrupted, and the poverty and distress of the siege made them for a time entirely impossible.

Miss Clara Barton returned to Karlsruhe and proposed to us to establish a workroom for the women and girls, in which articles of clothing, laundry, etc., might be given to them to be worked on in their own homes and to be well paid for on their return. The articles themselves, however, should come from the municipal government for the relief of impoverished families in need.

This was her plan which, thank God, was carried on for several months ✦ ✦

For all of us this work would have been very difficult on account of the unfriendly attitude of the people. But Miss Clara Barton volunteered her co-operation as well as her mediation, and adjusted our relations with the city authorities. And so, in a few days, the work of reconcilement in the guise of charity began. And it was productive of great good.

Miss Hanna Zimmerman, daughter of the Zimmerman who was at that time pastor of the city and also chaplain of the House of Deaconesses, was the first of our women helpers that we were able to send to Strassburg.

Hanna Zimmerman had for several years had the supervision of the small classes of girls which I had formed in the castle for the instruction of my daughter. Her invaluable ability was shown in her work in Strassburg.

Since the work begun in Strassburg was not properly the care of
the sick in war, it was necessary that this work should be made
self-sustaining.

I shall never forget my visit to that work-room, where countless
women obtained work and went away well paid. They were also
taught to do better sewing by other sister-workers who had come
there ✍ ✍

The position of our ladies was not an easy one. Miss Clara Barton
was the helping and mediating power.

Standing out from the many horrible impressions of my second
visit to Strassburg, that work left with me a vision of quiet and
peace ✍ ✍

For many weeks, indeed months, this work was continued. The
American Red Cross even contributed liberal funds for it.

How much more Miss Clara Barton worked in the city of Strassburg, I do not now recall, but I believe there were many more
good deeds.

Enriched by her experiences there, she went to Paris at the beginning of Winter to continue the relief-work to which America had
contributed so generously.

After the years Eighteen Hundred Seventy and Eighteen Hundred Seventy-one, there grew up a correspondence between Miss
Clara Barton and myself, which has continued to the time of her
summons hence. Many times she returned to Germany, where
her sympathy and appreciation of our public needs made a last-
ing impression. Thus she attended the Congress of the international Red Cross in Karlsruhe in Eighteen Hundred Eighty-
seven, that Congress to which my departed mother, that ever
bright example to all spheres of welfare, vouchsafed her presence.
At that Congress, which also the Emperor of Brazil and other
high dignitaries attended, Japan joined the Red Cross.

Miss Clara Barton, though one of the many American representatives, at that time moved for the legal protection of the Red Cross.

In later years, on the occasion of the Armenian uprising, she went there with her companions to direct relief-work, which is said to have been exceedingly successful.

Her ability for organization in America was wonderfully broad and valuable. For many years she remained President of the Red Cross Society, until changing conditions and increasing age and illness permitted her to seek more rest. Still again and again, she personally undertook, with renewed strength, to give aid during floods and other catastrophes. True to the theory that a great military organization should be permanent, ready to give a helping hand wherever assistance is needed she established the " National First Aid."

Miss Clara Barton had unbounded respect for my parents. She has often mentioned that one of her proudest recollections was the occasion when I was permitted to present her to Emperor William and the Empress Augusta and they spoke words of recognition and gratitude to her.

Emperor William pointed to the Prussian War Cross of Merit, bestowed upon her by him, which she wore next to the Baden Medal of Remembrance. His words ever remained precious to her. She died on the Twelfth of April, Nineteen Hundred Twelve, just past ninety years of age, frail indeed in body, but in spirit unfailing in her deep religious convictions, which her life so beautifully expressed in her work for others.

I have the most profound reverence for her, and she will have my gratitude always.

Louise, Grand Duchess of Baden,
Princess of Prussia.

Porfirio Diaz

F the newspapers have not deceived us, there have been doings down in Mexico.

Revolution and revolt are often temperamental conditions. And as there are individuals who are always in revolt against any and every condition, and at war with their environment, so there are nations that are, like a volcano, in a state of intermittent eruption.

❦ The most telling commentary on Mexico that can be made is the historic fact that in the fifty-nine years previous to the year Eighteen Hundred Seventy-six, Mexico had fifty-two dictators. If any one should ask what it is that the people in Mexico want, the only truthful answer is, they want a change.

No matter what the political condition is in Mexico, it soon becomes irksome.

From November Twenty-fourth, Eighteen Hundred Seventy-six, when Porfirio Diaz made his triumphal entry into the City of Mexico, until his "recall" in Nineteen Hundred Ten, Mexico enjoyed a degree of prosperity never before realized.

Well has it been said that the ideal government is the one under the rule of an absolute monarch—where the monarch is wise and virtuous.

Results seem to prove that Diaz supplied Mexico as nearly the kind of government her needs require, as could be supplied.

Diaz was born in the year Eighteen Hundred Thirty. His father was an innkeeper and farmer. This father died when the boy Porfirio was three years old, so the lad never had any recollection of him.

There was a family of seven children. The boy Porfirio grew up practically as the protector and provider of his brothers and sisters. That is a wonderful schooling.

Poverty and responsibility are great teachers.

The boy had Indian blood in his veins. The question is continually up whether the North American Indian is the rudimentary survivor of a great race, dead and turned to dust, or is he a coming man. The latest idea of biologists seems to be that the Indian is a disappearing race, and not an advancing one. In the Indian are traits suggesting great nobility, great strength, great reserve power ❦ ❦

Porfirio Diaz was essentially the avatar of a great ruler. His mother's ambition was that he should be a priest in the Catholic Church. And accordingly, he was placed in a monastic school from the time he was twelve until he was sixteen.

He then threw off the authority of the Church. His religion was essentially pantheistic, as a good Indian's should be. His love of country manifested itself, fused with the desire of adventure that is in the heart of every boy. Hearing that Mexico was at war with the United States, he walked two hundred fifty miles to enlist. But when he arrived at Guadalupe he was informed that Texas had been ceded to the United States and that the war was over ❦ ❦

He shed a few unnecessary tears and straightway walked back to his native town.

He had had the walk in any event, and no one can walk off two hundred fifty miles and back without being the gainer. Walking is for the walker, and everybody who hikes makes a little journey into his own ego.

Having discarded the Church, and the Church likewise having discarded him, the law seemed to afford an output for his ambition ❦ ❦

Meantime, he farmed and, like Patrick Henry, tended bar. In order to live, also, he taught school and tutored law-students and practised law. The way to learn law is to practise it; and to teach is to learn, Diaz continued in his native town until Eighteen Hundred Fifty-four. Santa Ana was dictator of Mexico.

Alvarez was leading the revolutionists, and Diaz sided with the revolutionists. Orders were given for his arrest. Seizing a rifle and mounting a convenient horse that was placed by Providence near the courthouse, he placed himself at the head of a few revolting neighbors and defied the insidious capias.

The revolution grew. The troops under Diaz increased in numbers. ❡ Promotion followed. Victory came trooping after victory. The privations were great, difficulties supreme, but not insurmountable. Porfirio Diaz became Captain, Lieutenant-Colonel, Colonel, Brigadier-General and then General of Division.

Emperor Maximilian went to his death; and Diaz was given the task of paying the arrears due to the soldiers, without any money in the exchequer, and of building up a bankrupt government. ❡ The first thing he did was to proclaim death as the penalty for plunder and theft. Any soldier insulting a civilian, or interfering with his wife or family, was taken out and filled with cold lead. Here was a brand new proposition that the Mexicans were not used to. The Mexican soldiers thought that "to the victor belong the spoils." Diaz did not see it that way.

He became Provisional President of Mexico in Eighteen Hundred Seventy-six, quickly followed by the full presidency.

His term of office at once marked a change in the history of Mexico. From that date he fixed a practical, financial and political reform in the tide of events. He scrupulously made satisfactory settlement of national debts. He welded together the people and the hundred or so Indian tribes. He established railroads and telegraphs, encouraged manufacturing, and placed a premium on enterprise of any sort.

Mexico has great natural advantages. She has the four great sources of wealth in a degree practically as yet untapped. These are the forest, the farm, the mine, the sea. Practically, it was Diaz who put Mexico on the map. He lifted her out of the realm of barbarism and made of her a great power. It is easy to criticize the powerful man, but when we make an estimate of his character, in justice we should set down on one side of the account a list of the worthy things that he has brought about and accomplished; then strike your balance.

Diaz was overcome and banished by the forces of Francisco Madero ✒ ✒

The reforms that Madero promised were not brought about. In degree, Madero was a Utopian, and the wealth that he had inherited and that his father had accumulated came through the safety that Diaz had provided. Madero did n't know that, for the man who has not known poverty is not apt to become an economist ✒ ✒

With Diaz gone, Mexico was in a swirl and a whirl of discontent. They had more freedom than they could fletcherize. The victors turned highwaymen, with a swiftness that would have done credit to a vaudeville artist. In fact, Madero fought his fight with the help of the criminal classes. The difference between the criminal and the reformer is like the lines of latitude and longitude—purely imaginary. Safety for the people at large was not what the reformers had at heart. What they wanted was excitement to prevent introspection. They revolted against the puling arts of peace ✒ ✒

And so behold Diaz, the grand old man, deposed, and Madero discovering that the arts of peace are much more difficult than the arts of war. It is easier to set men to fighting than to set them to work. It is easier to stir up discontent than to evolve temperance, peace, prosperity and plenty.

Madero could not bring about co-operation. His soldiers were continually asking, " Where do we come in? " And when he was forced to explain to them that peace was the great achievement, they straightway said, " Not for us! " and took to the road. Then Madero had to fight the people who had helped him to fight Diaz. The result was a toss up.

And behold, into the seething unrest is injected the nephew of
Porfirio Diaz—Felix Diaz. About the only thing that recommends
Felix Diaz is his name. He is big and strong and does justice to
a spangled uniform. But the man lacks brain. He can not make
decisions, much less hold to them.

And the forces of Madero captured Felix Diaz. They were going
to shoot him, but better counsel prevailed and he was imprisoned.
Madero is the man who spared his life.

Then behold a split in the forces of Madero, and cries of " Vive
Diaz!"; and Diaz is released from prison by the revolting followers
of Madero and a battle occurs in the streets of the City of Mexico,
between the forces of Felix Diaz and those of Francisco Madero.
Three thousand people or more are killed in the streets. The
gutters run with human blood. Madero finds the fight pretty
nearly a draw, but telegraphs to Washington saying that all is
well and that it is only a question of a few hours before he will
capture Diaz and peace will be restored.

But alas and alack, Madero had not counted on the disloyalty
of the people in his own household!

General Huerta, Chief of Staff under Madero, arranges a classic
coup d'etat, all this in the interests of peace.

Perhaps it was the best thing to do. Who knows? And certainly,
the writer of this is not sitting in judgment on Huerta. I am not
arguing the case. I am only stating the facts.

Madero invites General Huerta to lunch, possibly on the suggestion of Huerta. And when they have given their orders and
the waiter has gone out to fill them, Huerta presses the button, and
instead of the waiter coming back, and saying, " In a minute;
coming up!" there enters a file of soldiers and the guest reaches
over to the host and says, " You are my prisoner! "

So Madero was arrested by his best friend. Not being able to
vanquish Felix Diaz, General Huerta double-crosses his chief,
and gets himself declared Provisional President.

Huerta is Provisional Governor, and he and his erstwhile enemy, Felix Diaz, issue a joint proclamation to the people. Also, they send a telegram to President Taft stating that peace has been declared, the rule of the mob been put down, and prosperity and plenty are at hand.

This telegram when read at a Cabinet meeting, created a merry smile, which burst into an undignified ha-ha.

Huerta is a strong, able, influential man. He has fought on both sides and all sides. He has fought with the Government, and against the Government. He is a part of the great seething temperamental unrest.

Gustavo Madero, brother of the recalled President, was given the sweet privilege of " the fugitive law," which is a refinement of the Indian scheme of allowing the prisoner to run the gauntlet.

❡ The fugitive law has this to its credit, that it stops all post-mortem argument. To take a man out and back him up to the wall and tell the firing squad to do their duty, is one thing; but when the man runs away everybody knows that his captors have the perfect right to kill him. Even a New York policeman exercises this sweet privilege, on occasion. Gustavo got a run for his money, and his body was filled with cold lead. That disposed of a portion of the Madero family, and taught the rest a lesson.

It will never do to suppose that peace in Mexico is assured. There will be one dictator a year for the next fifty years, unless the Powers provide a government that has the iron hand; or a man of the caliber of Porfirio Diaz arises.

It would be a miraculous thing for another Diaz to appear upon the scene.

Ben Greet

NCE upon a day the Ben Greet Players came to East Aurora and gave *Twelfth Night* for The Roycrofters. The play was given in the woods, the audience of perhaps a thousand people being scattered over a natural amphitheatre. The stage was simply a cleared piece of green sward, surrounded by trees and shrubbery, fifty feet wide, and defined by calcium lights trained so to cover the spot. There was no artificial scenery of any kind, only the towering trees, and the gentle moonlight, soft and ghostly, shimmering through the trees. The costumes of the players were complete and costly, but even these so " belonged " that the audience did not think to admire them ❧ ❧

Just two things about the Bengreeters upon which I desire to throw my literary lime-light, that is to say, my tallow dip. One thing is the ability to work a great, beautiful and artistic illusion without a costly constructed environment, and the other is the personnel of the players.

In giving a play out-of-doors, or without complex scenic effects, Ben Greet has made a discovery. The game is his, it is his idea, let those cheapen it or take it away from him who can. Merry villagers, fat moral bilge, obtuse persons drunk on what the world calls success, may say, " Oh, it is naught—it is naught! His advertising manager may remark, " It is I who hath made him and not he himself."

The fact remains that Ben Greet has done something never done since William Shakespeare and necessity demanded it. He cuts the Gordian Knot of conventional stage-craft and just gives the play—we do the rest. All great literature compliments the reader. I once heard Ellen Terry say of Doctor Joseph Parker, " I never knew a man who had such confidence in his auditors."

All sublime oratory is founded on faith in the hearer, as Ellen Terry, being a really great woman, knows. But if the orator does not first have faith in himself, he can have no faith in the hearer, and moreover, the hearer will at once distrust the speaker. When this occurs, all is lost but the door receipts.

Ben Greet allows the audience to supply the scenery; and so does he stir the imagination of even the orthodox unco gude, who stand outside the ropes, too conservative to pay for seats, that they forget to go, and stand breathless, silent or moved to bursts of bucolic mirth. Ben Greet allows us to construct palaces, such as no stage carpenter can boast.

Mind is the only material, and mind under proper treatment is plastic. He alone is great who can make men change their minds. These woodland players are psychologists. How they do it, they probably do not know; but that they do it I know. They capture young, old, innocent, intelligent, cynical, blase, even the dull and tired, in the silken spider thread of their art and bind them hand and foot.

Now about Ben Greet himself. He is an Englishman, and I believe his people are all English born—probably, however, not from choice. They are not titled, nor are they costers and cockneys. The Bengreeters are not stage Englishmen. They do not stand on the railway platform and call in a loud Bow Bells voice of wrath and distress, " Aw now me deah bhoy, where is me bloomin' luggage, you know—this is really most distressing, you know. I 'ave lost me bloomin' brasses and the insolent guard refuses, you know, to give up even me 'at box, you know. A thing like this could n't 'ave 'appened in Lunnon, you know. I 'll report it to the *Pall Mall Gazette,* you know—that 's what I 'll do! "

None of that.

You could neither pick the Bengreeters on a railroad train as players or beef-eaters. They are quiet, kindly, intelligent, well bred, considerate men and women. They do not quarrel with hack drivers nor scrap with the conductor. No one ever insults their women. There is no peroxide in the bunch.

You no more see them on the street than you see a quail in a stubble field, and yet a quail is a most beautiful bird.

Ben Greet personally selected these players—his spirit plays through them. He is sort of father to his family They look out for him, and he looks out for them.

"Good—good!" I heard him say to one of his players, in a whisper. "Splendid—you did that better than ever!" Players are all like women—even the women players. You can get a good woman to do anything for you if you go about it rightly. Go about it the wrongly, and your cake is not only dough, but it is burnt on the bottom and sticks to the pan. Don't talk back to me, I know what I am saying!

Ben Greet is friendly without being familiar. Again I say, to get the work out of a woman or a player you must exercise respect, reverence and regard. Wise men and good neither crawl to women nor use them to bat up flies.

A great man has recently written his epitaph, thus: " Here sleeps a man clever enough to surround himself with people more clever than himself." Ben Greet is a great actor, but he often plays minor parts. And like all great actors, he knows the whole play, not only his particular part in it. And all of his people know all of the plays which they produce. Like a McCormack reaper, the parts are interchangeable—you order by number. Ben Greet's talent is even, that is to say it is all good. He lets big people take a little part and make it a big one.

As for the man off the stage, Ben Greet is the slowest, stupidest, most exasperating dullard you ever saw. He cracks no jokes nor will he laugh at yours—just a suggestion of a twinkle out of his big, bright, blue eyes, that are usually half closed—that is all. Seemingly he is without nerves—never elated, never cast down— nothing matters—who cares!

But all this stupidity is only seeming—he conserves for his business. When he acts he is the impersonation of animation and life. When he plays clowns' parts, he is the clown, and the cap, bells and bauble are his by divine right. Off the stage his voice is slow and drawling—in the play you can hear him talk half a mile, so clear, crystalline and vibrant is his accent.

" He also acts, I believe? " said a woman to Whistler of an all-round genius—and Whistler replied: " Madam, he does nothing else."

People who act off the stage do not do much on the boards. You must not get drunk if you are going to play the drunkard on the stage

Acting is supreme self-consciousness. Conservation of energy and wise reserve are its secrets. I myself, once had the histrionic itch. I 'm a mime by nature—I have worked at the business just enough to know its difficulties, and get scared out. Yes, I know the mummer's art, and I say that Ben Greet is not only a gentleman and a business man, with a fine head for method and organization, but he is a very great actor, and all his players are Bengreeters.

Brann

IT 'S a grave subject: Brann is dead. Brann was a Fool. The Fools were the wisest men at Court; and Shakespeare who dearly loved a Fool placed his wisest sayings into the mouths of men who wore the motley. When he adorned a man with cap and bells it was as though he had given bonds for both that man's humanity and intelligence.

Neither Shakespeare nor any other writer of books ever dared to depart so violently from truth as to picture a Fool whose heart was filled with perfidy.

The Fool is not malicious. Stupid people may think he is, because his language is charged with the lightning's flash; but they are the people who do not know the difference between an incubator and an egg plant.

Touchstone, with unfailing loyalty, follows his master with quip and quirk, into exile. When all, even his daughters, had forsaken King Lear, the Fool bares himself to the storm and covers the shaking old man with his own cloak. And when in our own day we meet the avatars of Trinculo, Costard, Mercutio and Jacques, we find they are men of tender susceptibilities, generous hearts and intellects keen as a rapier's point. Brann was a Fool.

Brann shook his cap, flourished his bauble, gave a toss to that fine head, and with tongue in cheek, asked questions and propounded conundrums that stupid Hypocrisy could not answer. So they killed Brann.

Brann was born in obscurity. Very early he was cast upon the rocks and nourished at the she-wolf's teat.

He graduated at the University of Hard Knocks and during his short life took several post-graduate courses. He had been wage-earner, printer's-devil, printer, pressman, editor.

He knew the world of men: the struggling, sorrowing, hoping, laughing, fallible world of men. And to those whom God had tempted beyond what they could bear, his heart went out. He read books with profit, and got great panoramic views out into the world of art and poetry; dreaming dreams and sending his swaying filament of thought out and out, hoping it would somewhere catch and he would be in communication with Another World 🙠 🙠

Discreet and cautious little men are known by the company they keep. The Fool was not particular about his associates: children, sick people, insane folks, rich or poor—it made no difference to him. He sometimes even sat at meat with publicans and sinners. He was a Mystic and lived in the ideal. This deeply religious quality in his nature led him into theology, and he became a clergyman—a Baptist clergyman.

But no church is large enough to hold such a man as this: the fool quality in his nature outcrops, and the jingle of bells makes sleep to the Chief Pew-Holder impossible.

So the Fool had to go.

Then he founded that unique periodical which in three years attained a circulation of sixty thousand copies. This paper was not used for pantry shelves, lamp lighters, or other base utilitarian purposes. It cost ten times as much as a common newspaper, and the people who bought it read it until it was worn out. All the things in this paper were not truth: mixed up amid a world of wit were often extravagance and much bad taste. It was only a Fool's newspaper! In this periodical the Fool railed and jeered and stated facts about smirking Complacency, facts so terrible that folks said they were indecent. He flung his jibes at Stupidity and Stupidity sought to answer criticism by assassination.

Texas has a libel law patterned after the libel law of the State of New York. If a man takes from you your good name you can put him behind prison bars and place shutters over the windows of his place of business.

The people who had thought Brann had injured them did not invoke the law. They invoked Judge Lynch.

A mob seized the Fool, and placing a rope about his neck led him naked through the October night, out to the Theological Seminary, which they declared he had traduced.

There they smote him with the flat of their hands and spat upon him. It was their intention to hang the Fool, but better counsel prevailed, and on his signing, *in terrorem,* a document they placed before him, they gave him warning to depart to another state. And on his promising to do so they let him go.

But the next day he refused to leave; and his flashing wit still filled the air, now embittered, through the outrages visited upon him ♠ ♠

His enemies held prayer meetings, invoking Divine aid for the Fool's conversion—or extinction. One man quoted David's prayer concerning Shimei: "Bring Thou down his hoar head to the grave in blood!" And others still, prayed, "Let his children be fatherless and his wife a widow."

But still the Fool flourished his bauble.

Then they shot him.

That hand which wrote the most Carlylean phrase of any in America is cold and stiff. That teeming brain which held a larger vocabulary than that of any living man in America is only clay that might stop a hole to keep the wind away. That soul through which surged thoughts too great for speech has gone a-journeying. Brann is dead.

No more shall we see that lean, clean, homely face, with its melancholy smile. No more shall we hear the Fool eloquently, and oh! so foolishly, plead the cause of the weak, the unfortunate, the vicious. No more shall we behold the tears of pity glisten in those sad eyes as his heart was wrung by the tale of suffering and woe. His children are fatherless, his wife a widow. Brann the Fool is dead ♠ ♠

Wilbur Wright

HE death of Wilbur Wright is an event worthy of more than passing notice.

It was a bit of fateful irony that the man who defied the laws of gravitation more than three hundred times should have slowly died of fever in his bed.

This man's name will surely live in history.

Wilbur Wright was the first man to solve the principles of aerial navigation ❧ ❧

To be sure, others did the thing in Europe at about the same time. But these men were debtors to the Wright Brothers.

What the Wright Brothers were doing in America was known to the world. They animated and inspired others to similar tasks. It will not do to say that the death of this man was an irreparable loss. That phrase, " irreparable loss," is the copyright possession of the literary sophomores. No loss is irreparable. The Law of Compensation never rests. Every great man does his work and does it the best he can. He carries the flag to the front as far as he is able, and when his tired steps falter, others seize the staff and carry it on.

Wilbur Wright was the son of a clergyman, born in the country, educated at the public schools, worked his way through college, became a schoolteacher, and naturally rode a bicycle. He rode a wheel so well that the bicycle interested him more than books. So he became a bicycle-maker; and while tinkering bicycles he thought out a machine that would take no man's dust.

And he succeeded in making it, and in using it.

In England, Wilbur Wright was sought out by Edward the Seventh, each man a king, and their pictures were taken together. In France, men of intellect and worth vied with one another to do him honor.

In Spain, Alphonso tackled the air with Wilbur as pilot. But the attention Wilbur Wright received did not turn his head. He was always gentle, always modest, and the things that he had done never seemed to him much, on account of the things he had in mind that he intended to do.

He was a simple and very noble type of man. In him there was no alloy ᴐᴐ ᴐᴐ

A reference to *Who's Who* will show that forty-seven Wrights are given space in this most valuable " peerage." The space occupied by Wilbur Wright is very small indeed, the reason apparently being that he was the only one who did n't have anything to do with the preparation of his own biography. *Who's Who* simply states where the man was born, gives the names of his parents, and adds a few other matter-of-fact details, probably all that were available.

In speaking of his achievements, Wilbur Wright never told of the things that he himself had done. It was always the Wright Brothers, or " We."

There is no romance, save the romance of mechanics, in the lives of the Wright Brothers. Neither ever married. They were devoted to their parents, their sister, and their own immediate family.

❡ The money that was supplied them, about the years Nineteen Hundred Three and Nineteen Hundred Four, when they made their first flight of twenty miles, carrying a weight of seven hundred pounds, was furnished by their sister, who had saved up her dollars as a teacher and a trained nurse. Every dollar, beyond the barest necessities, this young woman, with unfaltering faith in her brothers, turned over to them.

However, it is pleasant to know that Wilbur Wright was able to repay the loan. A French syndicate paid him fifty thousand dollars for control of the French patents on his inventions. Various prizes awarded him in Europe for exhibitions amounted to more than one hundred thousand dollars.

The United States Government turned him over one check of
thirty thousand dollars for the first aeroplane purchased for
army purposes. The Hudson-Fulton Celebration Commission
paid him fifteen thousand dollars. As a money-making proposition
aerial navigation is not recommended. However, Wilbur Wright
left a very comfortable estate; and best of all, he left a great and
unsullied name. Simple, honest, unaffected, truthful, devoted to
his art, he lived and worked as becomes a man. No matter what
the future may hold in store in way of aerial navigation, and
despite the flight of time, the name and fame of Wilbur Wright
will live with those of Watt, Stephenson, Arkwright, Fulton and
Edison ෨ ෨

White Hyacinths

A COMMON question is this one, "Would you care to live your life over again?"

Not only is it a common question, but a foolish one, since we were sent into life without our permission, and are being sent out of it against our will, and the option of a return-ticket is not ours. But if urged to reply I would say with Benjamin Franklin, "Yes, provided, of course, that you allow me the author's privilege of correcting the second edition." If, however, this is denied, I will still say, "Yes," and say it so quickly it will give you vertigo.

In reading the *Journal of John Wesley* the other day, I ran across this item written in the author's eighty-fifth year, "In all of my life I have never had a period of depression nor unhappiness that lasted more than half an hour." I can truthfully say the same. One thing even Omnipotence can not do, and that is to make that which once occurred never to have been. The past is mine ❧ ❧

What does life mean to me? Everything! Because I have everything with which to enjoy life. I own a beautiful home, well furnished, and this home is not decorated with a mortgage. I have youth—I am only fifty—and as in degree the public is willing to lend me its large furry ear, I have prospects. I have a library of five thousand volumes to read; and besides, I have a little case of a hundred books to love, bound in full levant, hand-tooled.

I have four paid-up Life-Insurance Policies in standard companies; a little balance in the Savings-Bank; I owe no man, and my income is ample for all my wants.

Then besides I have a saddle-horse with a pedigree like unto that of a Daughter of the Revolution; a Howard watch, and a fur·

ALICE HUBBARD

lined overcoat. So there now, why should n't I enjoy Life?
I anticipate your answer, which is, that a man may have all
of these things enumerated and also have indigestion and
chronic Bright's Disease, so that the digger in the ditch, than
he, is happier far. Your point is well taken, and so I will gently
explain that if I have any aches or pains I am not aware of them.
I have never used tobacco, nor spirituous liquors, nor have I
contracted the chloral, cocaine, bromide or morphine habit,
never having invested a dollar in medicine, patented, proprietary
nor prescribed.

In fact, I have never had occasion to consult a physician. I
have good eyesight, sound teeth, a perfect digestion, and God
grants to me His great gift of sleep.

And again you say, " Very well, but you yourself have said,
' Expression is necessary to life,' and that the man who has
everything is to be pitied, since he has nothing to work for, and
that to have everything is to lose all, for life lies in the struggle."
All the points are well made. But I have work to do—compelling
work—that I can not delegate to others.

This prevents incipient smugosity and introspection. For more
than twelve years I have written the copy for two monthly
magazines. During that time no issue of either magazine has
been skipped. The combined paid-in-advance circulation of these
periodicals is more than two hundred thousand copies each
issue, giving me an audience, counting at the conservative rate
of three readers to a magazine, of more than a half-million souls.
Here is a responsibility that may well sober any man, and which
would subdue him, actually, if he stopped to contemplate it.
The success of Blondin in crossing the Niagara Gorge on a wire,
with a man on his back, hinged on his not stopping to think it
over ა ა

When I write I never consider what will be done with the matter,
how it will be liked, and who will read it.

I just write for myself. And the most captious, relentless critic
I have is myself. When I write well, as I occasionally do, I am
filled with a rapturous intoxicating joy. No pleasure in life
compares with the joy of creation—catching in the Cadmean mesh
a new thought—putting salt on the tail of an idea. And a certain
critic has said that I can catch more ideas with less salt than any
other man in America.

I am not sure whether the man was speaking ironically or in
compliment, but since the remark has been bruited abroad, it has
struck me as being fairly good, and so I here repeat it, for I am
making no special attempt to conceal the fact that I am still on
earth ᴥ ᴥ

One book I wrote has attained a sale of more than a hundred
thousand copies, although selling at the unpopular price of two
dollars a volume. And one article I wrote and published in one of
the magazines has been translated into eleven languages and
reprinted more than twenty-four million times, attaining a wider
circulation, I believe, than any other article or book has ever
attained in the same length of time.

In saying these things I fully realize that no man is ever in such
danger of being elected an honorary member of the Ananias
Club as he who states the simple truth.

In order to write well you require respite and rest in change.
Ideas come to one on the mountains, while tramping the fields,
at the woodpile. When you are in the best condition is the time
to do nothing, for at such a time, if ever, the divine current
surges through you.

If we could only find the cosmic switchboard when we want to
think, how delightful it would be to simply turn on the current!
But no, all we can do is to walk, ride horseback, dig in the garden,
placing ourselves in receptive mood, and from the Unknown the
ideas come. Then to use them is a matter of the workroom. And
so to keep my think-apparatus in good working order I dilute

the day with much manual work—which is only another word for play.

Big mental work is done in heats. Between these heats are intervals of delightful stupidity.

To cultivate his dull moments is the mark of wisdom for almost every thought-juggler who aspires to keep three balls in the air at one time. In the course of each year I give about a hundred lectures *so* *so*

Public speaking, if carried on with moderation, is a valuable form of mental excitation.

Ill-health comes from too much excitement, or not enough. Platform work keeps your mental pores open and tends to correct faulty elimination of mental dross.

To stand before an audience of a thousand people for two hours with no manuscript, and only your tongue and brain to save you from the ruin that may engulf you any instant, and which many in your audience hope will engulf you, requires a goodly modicum of concentration.

I have seen the giving way of a collar-button in an impassioned moment cross-buttock a Baptist preacher. I am always prepared for accidents in oratory, such, say, as a harmless necessary cat coming on the stage without her cue. In public speaking one shakes the brush-piles of thought and starts a deal more game than he runs down at the time, and this game which he follows up at his leisure, and the stimulus of success in having stayed the limit, make for mental growth.

But besides writing and public speaking, I have something to do with a semi-communistic corporation called The Roycrofters, employing upwards of five hundred people.

The work of The Roycrofters is divided into departments as follows: a farm, bank, hotel, printing-plant, bookbindery, furniture-factory and blacksmith shop.

The workers in these various departments are mostly people

of moderate experience, and therefore more or less superinten-
dence is demanded. Eternal vigilance is not only the price of
liberty but of success in business, and knowing this I keep in
touch with all departments of the work. So far, we have always
been able to meet our payroll. All of the top-notchers in the
Roycroft Shops have been evolved there, so it will be seen that
we aim to make something besides books. In fact, we have a
brass band, an art-gallery, a reading-room, a library, and we
have lectures, classes or concerts every night in the week. Some
of these classes I teach, and usually I speak in the Roycroft
Chapel twice a week on current topics.

These things are here explained to make clear the point that I
have no time for ennuil or brooding over troubles past or those
to come. Even what I say here is written on by-product time, on
board a railroad-train, going to meet a lecture engagement,
seated with a strange fat man who talks to me, as I write, about
the weather, news from nowhere, and his most wonderful collection of steins. All of which, I hear you say, is very interesting,
but somewhat irrelevant and inconsequential, since one may have
all of the things just named, and also hold the just balance
between activity and rest, concentration and relaxation, which
we call health, and yet his life be faulty, incomplete, a failure
for lack of one thing—Love.

Your point is well made. When Charles Kingsley was asked to
name the secret of his success he replied, " I had a friend."

If asked the same question I would give the same answer. I
might also explain that my friend is a woman.

This woman is my wife, legally and otherwise. She is also my
comrade, my companion, my chum, my business partner.

There has long been a suspicion that when God said, " I will
make a helpmeet for man," the remark was a subtle bit of
sarcasm. However, the woman of whom I am speaking proves
what God can do when He concentrates on His work.

My wife is my helpmeet, and I am hers. I do not support her; rather, she supports me. All I have is hers—not only do I trust her with my heart, but with my pocketbook. And what I here write is not a tombstone testimonial, weighted with a granitic sense of loss, but a simple tribute of truth to a woman who is yet on earth in full possession of her powers, her star still in the ascendent ❧ ❧

I know the great women of history. I know the qualities that go to make up, not only the superior person but the one sublimely great. Humanity is the raw stock with which I work.

I know how Sappho loved and sung, and Aspasia inspired Pericles to think and act, and Cleopatra was wooed by two Emperors of Rome, and how Theodora suggested the Justinian Code and had the last word in its compilation. I know Madame De Stael, Sarah Wedgwood, George Eliot, Susanna Wesley, Elizabeth Barrett. I know them all, for I can read, and I have lived, and I have imagination.

And knowing the great women of the world, and having analyzed their characters and characteristics, I still believe that Alice Hubbard, in way of mental reach, sanity, sympathy and all-round ability, outclasses any woman of history, ancient or modern, mentally, morally and spiritually.

To make a better woman than Alice Hubbard one would have to take the talents and graces of many great women and omit their faults. If she is a departure in some minor respects from a perfect standard, it is in all probability because she lives in a faulty world, with a faulty man, and deals with faulty folks, a few of whom, doubtless, will peruse this book.

Right here, of course, I hear you say: " But love is blind, or at least myopic, and every man who ever loved says what you are saying now."

The nature of love is exaggeration, and to take a woman and clothe her with ideality, this is love. And you speak wisely.

But let me here explain that while the saltness of time in my ego has not entirely dissolved, I have reached a time of life when feminine society is not an actual necessity.

I am at an age when libertines turn saints, and rogues become religious. However, I have never gone the pace, and so I am neither saint nor ascetic, and the Eternal Feminine is not now, and never was, to me a consuming lure. And while the flush of impetuous youth, with its unreasoning genius of the genus, is not mine, I am not a victim of *amor senilis*, and never can be, since world problems, not sensations, fill my dreams and flood my hours.

The youth loves his doxy in the mass; I analyze, formulate and reduce character to its constituent parts.

And yet, I have never fully analyzed the mind of the woman I love, for there is always and forever an undissolved residuum of wit, reason, logic, invention and comparison bubbling forth that makes association with her a continual delight. I have no more sounded the depths of her soul than I have my own.

What she will say and what she will do are delightful problems; only this, that what she says and what she does will be regal, right, gracious, kindly—tempered with a lenity that has come from suffering, and charged with a sanity that has enjoyed, and which knows because through it plays unvexed the Divine Intelligence that rules the world and carries the planets in safety on their accustomed way—this I know.

Perhaps the principal reason my wife and I get along so well together is because we have similar ideas as to what constitutes wit. She laughs at all of my jokes, and I do as much for her.

All of our quarrels are papier-mache, made, played and performed for the gallery of our psychic selves. Having such a wife as this, I do not chase the ghosts of dead hopes through the graveyard of my dreams.

I have succeeded beyond the wildest ambitions of my youth,

but I am glad to find that my desires outstrip my performances, and as fast as I climb one hill I see a summit beyond. So I am not satisfied, nor do I ever declare, " Here will I build three tabernacles," but forever do I hear a voice which says, " Arise and get thee hence, for this is not thy rest."

Who can deny that the mother-heart of a natural and free woman makes the controlling impulse of her life a prayer to bless and benefit, to minister and serve?

Such is Alice Hubbard—a free woman who has gained freedom by giving it. But her charity is never maudlin.

She has the courage of her lack of convictions, and decision enough to withhold the dollar when the cause is not hers, and when to bestow merely means escape from importunity. To give people that which they do not earn is to make them think less of themselves—and of you. The only way to help people is to give them a chance to help themselves.

She is the only woman I ever knew who realizes as a vital truth that the basic elements for all human betterments are economic, not mental or spiritual. She knows that the benefits of preaching are problematic, and that the good the churches do is conjectural, but that good roads are the first and chiefest factor in civilization.

She knows and advocates what no college president in America dare advocate: that the money we expend for churches if invested in scientific forestry and good roads would make this world a paradise enow. She does not trouble herself much about Adam's fall, but she does thoroughly respect Macadam.

If she ever sings, " Oh, for the wings of a dove," it is not because she desires them to adorn her hat, nor as a means to fly away and be at rest.

As a schoolteacher, woman was not deemed capable or acceptable until about Eighteen Hundred Sixty-eight. Woman's entrance into the business world is a very modern innovation.

It all dates since the Civil War, and was really not accepted as a fact until Eighteen Hundred Seventy-six, the year the typewriter appeared.

Even yet the average man keeps his wife in total ignorance of his financial affairs, thinking that she has n't the ability to comprehend the intricacies of trade.

The world was discovered in Fourteen Hundred Ninety-two; but man was not discovered until Seventeen Hundred Seventy-six. Before then man was only a worm of the dust, and the tradition still lingers, fostered by the sects that believe in the ministry of fear.

Woman was not discovered until Eighteen Hundred Seventy-six. Her existence before then was not even suspected, and the few men that did have their suspicions were considered unsafe, erratic, strange and peculiar.

In youth, when she was pink and twenty she was a plaything; when she grew old and wrinkled she was a scullion and a drudge. All laws were made by men, and in most States a woman has only yet a secondary claim on her child. If she is a married woman, all the money she earns belongs to her husband. Woman's right to have her political preferences recorded is still denied. Orthodox churches will not listen to her speak, and the logic of William Penn, " The Voice may come to a woman exactly as to a man," is smiled at indulgently by priests and preachers. In English common law she is always a minor.

It does not require much reasoning to see that as long as a woman is treated as a child the tendency is that she shall be one.

The success of the Bon Marche at Paris, not to mention Mary Elizabeth, Her Candy, proves what woman can do when her head is not in a compress, and her hands tied.

Man's boldness and woman's caution make an admirable business combination.

And in spite of that malicious generalization, pictured in print and fable, about woman's enterprise being limited to exploiting the trousers of peacefully sleeping man, I believe that women are more honorable in money matters than the male of the genus *homo*. Women cashiers do not play the races, hearken to the seductive ticker, nor cultivate the poker face. Alice Hubbard is an economist by nature, and her skill as a financier is founded on absolute honesty and flawless integrity. She has the savings-bank habit, and next to paying her debts, gets a fine tang out of life by wise and safe investments. She knows that a savings-bank account is an anchor win'ard, and that to sail fast and far your craft must be close-hauled to weather squalls ॐ ॐ

In manufacturing she studies cost, knowing better far than most businessmen that deterioration of property and overhead charges must be carefully considered, if the Referee in Bankruptcy would be kept at a safe distance. She is a methodizer of time and effort, and knows the value of system, realizing the absurdity of a thirty-dollar-a-week man doing the work of a five-dollar-a-week boy. She knows the proportion of truth to artistic jealousy in the melodious discord of the anvil chorus; and the foreman who opposes all reforms which he himself does not conjure forth from his chickadee brain is to her familiar.

The employee who is a knocker by nature, who constantly shows a tendency to get on the greased slide that leads to limbo, has her pity, and she in many gentle and diplomatic ways tries to show him the danger of his position.

With John Ruskin she says: " It 's nothing to give pension and cottage to the widow who has lost her son; it is nothing to give food and medicine to the workman who has broken his arm, or the decrepit woman wasting in sickness. But it is something to use your time and strength to war with the waywardness and thoughtlessness of mankind; to keep an erring workman in your service till you have made him an unerring one, and to direct your fellow-merchant to the opportunity which his judgment would otherwise have lost."

In my wife's mind I see my thoughts enlarged and reflected, just as in a telescope we behold the stars. She is the magic mirror in which I see the divine. Her mind acts on mine, and mine reacts upon hers. Most certainly I am aware that no one else can see the same in her which I behold, because no one else can call forth her qualities, any more than any other woman can call forth mine. Our minds, separate and apart, act together as one, forming a complete binocular, making plain that which to one alone is invisible ❧ ❧

Now there be those, wise in this world's affairs, who may say that this man is evidently a victim of the gumwillies. Love, like all other things, has its limit. A month of close contact usually wears off the new, and captivity reduces the butterfly to a grub. Don't tell us—we know! The very intensity of a passion betokens its transient quality. Henry Finck in his great book, *Passionate Love and Personal Beauty,* recounts the great loves of history, and then says, " The limit of the Grand Passion is about two years." ❧ ❧

Hence I here make the explanation that I have known this woman for twenty years. I have written her more than three thousand letters, and she has written as many to me.

Every worthy theme and sentiment I have expressed to the public has been first expressed to her, or, more likely, borrowed from her. I have seen her in almost every possible exigency of life: in health, success, and high hope; in poverty, and what the world calls disgrace and defeat. But here I should explain that disgrace is for those who accept disgrace, and defeat consists in acknowledging it.

I have seen her face the robustious fury of an attorney weighing three hundred pounds, and reduce him to pork cracklings by her poise, quiet persistence, and the righteousness of her cause.

She is at home with children, the old, the decrepit, the sick,
the lonely, the unfortunate, the vicious, the stupid, the insane.
She puts people at their ease; she is one with them, but not
necessarily of them.

She recognizes the divinity in all of God's creatures, even the
lowliest, and those who wear prison-stripes are to her akin—all
this without condoning the offense. She respects the sinner, but
not the sin.

Wherever she goes her spirit carries with it the message, " Peace
be still! " With the noble, the titled, the famous, she is equally
at home.

I have seen her before an audience of highly critical, intellectual
and aristocratic people, stating her cause with that same gentle,
considerate courtesy and clearness that is so becoming to her.
The strongest feature of her nature is her humanitarianism, and
this springs from her unselfish heart and her wide-reaching
imagination. And imagination is only sympathy illumined by
love and ballasted with brains.

She knows and has performed every item of toil in the ceaseless
round of woman's drudgery on the farm; she realizes the stress
and strain of overworked and tired mothers; the responsibility
of caring for sick and peevish children; the cooking, sewing,
scrubbing, washing, care of vegetables and milk; the old black
dress that does duty on Sunday with the bonnet that carries a
faded flower in Summer and its frayed ostrich-feather in Winter;
the life of men who breakfast by lamplight and go to work in
winter woods ere dawn appears, coming home at dark, with
chores yet to be done, ere supper and bed are earned; the children
who follow frozen country roads to school, and eat at noon their
luncheon of corn bread and molasses and salt pork and count it
good, being filled with eager joy to slide downhill ere the bell
rings for the study of McGuffey's Reader; the slim, slender girl,
mayhap with stocking down, who herds turkeys on the upland

farm in the cool October dew, that she may get money to go to the distant High School or the coveted "Normal," and who finally receives the longed-for teacher's certificate and earns money to help satisfy the hungry mortgage on the farm; the young women who work in box-factories under the menacing eye of the boss; the tired, frayed-out, heedless clerks; the smartly dressed cashiers; the men who drive horses or work with pick, adz, maul and ax; the pilots who creep their crafts through fog along rocky coasts, or in mid-ocean take the temperature of the water, locating icebergs; the woman who flees the world in order to be "good;" the businessman mousing over his accounts, fearing to compare assets and liabilities, hoping for a turn in the tide; the flush of the orator, the joy of the author, the deep, silent pleasure of the scientist who finds a new species; the serene confidence of the railroad president who knows his departments are all well manned; the moment of nightmare and doubt when the general manager holds his breath and listens for the rumble of his "Limited," speeding with precious treasure through the all-enfolding night; the fever of unrest that comes to the captain of the man-of-war the night before the battle; the soldiers in the trenches, blissfully ignorant, needlessly brutal in their attempts to be brave as they peer at the enemy's camp-fires on the distant hills; the joyless, yellow-eyed children who toil in the mills and forget how to play; boys home from school; girls in cap and gown graduating at Wellesley or Vassar; city children from the slums in the country for the first time, begging permission to pick dandelions and daisies; women discarded by society and relatives for faults—or virtues; wives whose hearts are stamped upon by drunken husbands; men who are crazed through the vanity of wives who walk the borderland of folly; the hesitating, doubting, fearing, sick, through lack of incentive—work; to all these is she sister, and still the joy in work well done, the calm of honesty, the sense of power through facing unpleasant tasks, the sweet taste of food earned by honest effort, the absolution that comes through following one's highest ideals, the self-sufficient purpose and firm resolve to do still better work tomorrow through having done good work today—all these are hers ✒ ✒

She is patient under censure, just or unjust; and unresentful toward hypocrisy, pretense and stupidity. Of course, she recognizes that certain people are not hers, and these she neither avoids nor seeks to please or placate. Some indeed there be who have called to her in insulting tones upon the public streets; and to sundry and various of these she has given work and taught them with a love and a patience almost past belief. She has the sublime ability to forget the wrongs that have been visited upon her, the faults of her friends, and the good deeds she has done.

She knows history from its glimmering dawn in Egypt down to the present time. The reformers, thinkers, martyrs, who have stood forth and spoken what they thought was truth, and died that we might live, are to her familiar friends.

She knows, too, the poets, writers, sculptors, musicians, painters, inventors, architects, engineers of all time. And those who can build a bridge or make good roads are to her more worthy of recognition than those who preach.

She believes in the rights of dumb animals, of children, and especially women. She knows that woman can never be free until she owns herself, and is economically free. To this end she believes that a woman should be allowed to do anything which she can do well, and that when she does a man's work she should receive a man's wage.

To those who disagree with her she is ever tolerant; in her opinions she is not dogmatic, realizing that truth is only a point of view, and even at the last, people should have the right to be wrong, so long as they give this right to others. She does not mix in quarrels, has none of her own, nor is she quick to take sides in argument and wordy warfare.

She keeps out of cliques, invites no secrets and has none herself, respects the mood of those she is with, and when she does not know what to say, says nothing, and in times of doubt minds her own business.

Her seeming indifference, however, does not spring from a lack of sympathy, for nothing that is human is alien to her. On a railroad-train at night she always thinks of two persons—the engineer, with one hand on the throttle and the other on the air-brake, looking out down two glittering streaks of steel that stretch away into the blackness of the night, and the other man is the one a hundred miles or so away, with shade over his eyes, crouching over a telegraph-key.

At the hotels she thinks of those who wash dishes, and scrub and clean windows, and toward all servants she is gentle in her demands and grateful for service.

She wins by abnegation and yet never renounces anything. She has the faith that gives all, and therefore receives all.

She has proved herself an ideal mother, not only in every physical function, but in that all-brooding tenderness and loving service which is contained in the word Mother. She, of all mothers, realizes that the mother is the true teacher: that all good teachers are really spiritual mothers. She knows that not only does the mother teach by precept, but by every action, thought and attribute of her character. Scolding mothers have impatient babies and educated parents have educated children.

That supreme tragedy of motherhood, that the best mothers are constantly training their children to live without them, is fully appreciated and understood by Alice Hubbard.

To be a good teacher requires something besides knowledge. Character counts more than a memory for facts, and as the great physician benefits his patients more through his presence than by his medicines, so does the superior teacher leave her impress upon her pupils more through her moral qualities than by her precepts.

Franz Liszt did not teach at all: rather, he filled his pupils with a great, welling ambition to do, and be, and become. I believe it was Goethe who said that great teachers really do not teach us anything—in their presence we simply become different people. Those who are admitted into the close presence of Alice Hubbard are transformed into different people. This is especially true of budding youth—boys and girls from fourteen to eighteen. For them she has a peculiar and potent charm—Her vivacity, her animation, her sympathy, her knowledge of flowers, plants, trees, birds and animals delights them.

Then she knows the heroes of history, and all of the literature of story and romance is to her familiar. If her pupils wish to talk, she lets them—for to her listening is a fine art. Her mental attitude brings out the best in each, so in her presence the boor becomes gentle, and the loud and coarse moderate their voices and are on their good behavior.

She carries with her an aura in which vulgarity can not thrive nor pretense flourish. She has a gentle and gracious dignity that contains not a trace of affectation, prudery, pedantry or priggishness. She has the happy faculty of putting people at their ease and making them pleased with themselves; so with her they are wise beyond their wont and gracious beyond their accustomed habit.

In a room full of people she is not likely to be seen, nor even to speak; but if she chooses, she keys the conversation, dictates the theme, arouses genial animation, and by her presence and the gentle, finely modulated quality of her voice, the indifferent and the mediocre subside and fade away. Alice Hubbard has the bodily qualities of grace, lightness, ease and manual skill, and the crown of her head obeys the laws of levitation.

She imparts joy, never heaviness or weariness. Her raiment is always neat and becoming, not expressed in fancy nor of a kind or quality to beckon or bid for attention. In fact, very few people seem ever to remember the exact color of her attire; all that they can recall is that she was sweetly gracious, kind, considerate and dignified in all of her words and manner.

She wins without trying to win, and if she pleases, as she always does, it is without apparent effort.

In moral qualities she has a steadfastness in the right; a sharp distinction as to *meum et tuum*; a persistence in completing the task begun; the habit of being on time and keeping her word, especially with servants and children and those who can not enforce their claims; an absence of all exaggeration, with no vestige of boasting as to what she has done or intends to do—all of which sets her apart as one superior, refined and unselfish beyond the actual as we find it, except in the ideals of the masters in imaginative literature.

In mental qualities she appreciates the work of the great statesmen, creators, inventors, reformers, scientists, and all those who live again in minds made better.

Dozens of times I have heard her refer to the unresentful qualities of Charles Darwin, and tell of how he, as a scientist, was ashamed of himself in once jumping to a conclusion by saying, " It must be this, for if it is not, what is it? "

Herbert Spencer's monograph on *Education* is to her a textbook. Max Muller's *Memories* is her favorite love-story, and Emerson's *Essays* are always to her a sweet solace and rest. She admires Browning, but neither dotes nor feeds on any poet—life is her great theme, and to live rightly and well, without shame, regrets, compromises, explanations, apologies or complaints, is to her the finest of fine arts.

So these, then, are the qualities that mark Alice Hubbard as the teacher with very few peers and no superiors.

She holds all ties lightly, never clutching even friendship—growing rich by giving. She is an economist and a financier, making a dollar go further, without squeezing it, than any man or woman I have ever seen. She buys what she needs, and has the strength not to buy what she does not need. She never spends money until she gets it, and avoids debt as she would disease. She is a model housekeeper, and her ability to manage people and serve the public is shown in the fact that the Roycroft Inn, of which she is sole manager, made a profit of the past year of a little more than a thousand dollars. To direct and train the "help" (at times a somewhat ironical term) does not even supply her a topic for conversation. She never complains of the stupidity of others, knowing that such complaint is in itself a form of concrete stupidity.

However, the management of the hotel is to her only incidental, for she is Vice-President of the Roycroft Corporation, and General Superintendent of all the work. She hires all employees and has the exclusive power to discharge, fixing all salaries, and passing on all expenditures. She also teaches, gives lectures, and writes at least one book every year.

Assuming that one hundred is the perfect standard, a judicial rating would place Alice Hubbard somewhere between ninety and ninety-nine in the following: As a mother, housekeeper, economist, methodizer, diplomat, financier, orator, writer, reformer, inventor, humanitarian, teacher, philosopher.

Tammas the Techy said, "We must be patient with the fools." But he never was. She is. And I myself have ever prayed, "For this, Good Lord, make us duly thankful." She has an abiding faith in Nemesis, and never for an instant considers it her duty to transform herself into a section of the Day of Judgment. She believes that people are punished by their sins—not for them. In her nature there is a singular absence of jealousy, whim and prejudice. She can hear her enemies praised without resentment, and for those in competition with her, if such there be, she has good-will at the best and indifference at the worst. These things are possible only in a very self-centered character, one tenoned and mortised in granite, with an abiding faith in the justice and righteousness of the Eternal Intelligence in which we are bathed. She has the hospitable mind and the receptive heart. She is alert for new truth and new views of life, and is ever ready to throw away a good idea for a better one.

She realizes the necessity of moderation in eating, of regular sleep, of fresh air, and regular daily exercise in the open. And not only does she realize their necessity, but she has the will to live her philosophy, not being content to merely think and preach it. Physically she is strong as a rope of silk; she can outride and outwalk most athletic men, although her form is slender and slight. Those who regard bulk and beauty as synonymous, never turn and look at her in the public streets. In countenance she is as plain as was Julius Cæsar, and to his busts she bears a striking resemblance in the features of nose, mouth, chin and eyes.

In the moral qualities of patience, poise and persistence she is certainly Cæsarian, and in these she outranks any woman I have been able to resurrect from the dusty tomes of days gone by. This, then, is my one close companion, my confidante, my friend, my wife; and my relation with her will be my sole passport to Paradise, if there is one beyond this life.

I married a rich woman—one rich in love, loyalty, gentleness, insight, gratitude, appreciation—one who caused me, at thirty-three years of age, to be born again.

To this woman I owe all I am—and to her the world owes its gratitude for any and all, be it much or little, that I have given it. My religion is all in my wife's name.

And I am not bankrupt, for all she has is mine, if I can use it, and in degree I have used it.

And why I prize life, and desire to live, is that I may give the world more of the treasures of her heart and mind, realizing with perfect faith that the supply coming from Infinity can never be lessened nor decreased.

SO HERE ENDETH " THE ELECT," THE SAME BEING VOLUME FIVE OF THE SELECTED WRITINGS OF ELBERT HUBBARD, GATHERED TOGETHER, PRINTED AND BOUND AS A MEMORIAL TO THEIR BELOVED FOUNDER BY THE ROYCROFTERS AT THEIR SHOPS, WHICH ARE IN EAST AURORA, NEW YORK. MCMXXII